Journal of Research

of the
American Federation
of Astrologers

2018

ISBN-13: 978-0-86690-671-5

Cover Design: Jack Cipolla

Published by:
American Federation of Astrologers, Inc.
6535 S. Rural Road
Tempe, AZ 85283

www.astrologers.com

Contents

From the Editor

The Journal of Research of the American Federation of Astrologers is made possible through the generosity of the Catharine and Ernest Grant Trust. This 2018 issue includes submissions from a wide array of astrologers practicing in the United Kingdom, Finland, Spain, Romania, Canada, Israel, Portugal, Australia, India, and the United States. Astrologers around the world are working with dedication to further the body of astrological knowledge by many different kinds of research investigations.

As part of the AFA's educational mission, the AFA presented a workshop entitled Research Approaches for Astrology Projects at the United Astrology Conference in May 2018 held in Chicago. This is designed as an introductory presentation to the various kinds of research questions and the appropriate methods and resources that can help the novice research astrologer develop a plan to investigate his or her inquiry.

The advent of faster and smarter computers and programs are facilitating the scope and precision of quantitative statistical research methods for investigating and testing astrological premises.

We are pleased to open this journal with a paper by Nick Kollerstrom, PhD, a science historian and eminent research astrologer from the UK. He discusses his new studies into the Gauquelin Character Traits where he confirms the 'character-traits hypothesis' that the planets are much more strongly linked to traits of character, than they are to professions.

Kyösti Tarvainen, a retired mathematics researcher and systems analyst from Finland, has now turned his expertise to an ongoing study and statistical testing of the Gauquelin data. In this paper he investigates how well the Part of Fortune interpretations of Schulman (1978) hold true on the Gauquelin data of twelve professional groups.

Alphee Lavoie's paper, An Astrological Research Study about People Who Have Had Three or More Marriages, examines the astrological correlations in the natal chart of people who have had multiple marriages. He utilizes Air Software's Fast Research Program, a program which he designed and created for model-building and statistical testing.

Changing pace, the next paper by Barcelona academic Jose Luis Belmonte is Enki, the Sumerian God of Aquarius which demonstrates the methodology of careful scholarly research into cross cultural mythologies. Reaching back into Sumerian, Babylonian, Hittite, and Greek myth, Belmonte presents the similarities between the attributes, characteristics, and images of Sumerian god Enki and those of the Greek Ouranus, after whom the modern planet Uranus is named. Likewise, the Babylonian constellation GU.LA, "the waterman" becomes the precursor for the zodiacal sign Aquarius.

Advances are also being made in the qualitative research methods that utilize questionnaires and interviews as part of a process to delve into the beliefs, motivation and behavior patterns of individuals, a natural fit for psychological astrology.

Cornelia Hansen, MA, with a long professional career in child education and therapy, has distilled her experiential knowledge in a forthcoming book Kidwheels: Understanding the Child in the Chart (Wessex, 2018). Her paper, Identifying Astrological Signatures of Modern Temperamental components for Use in Working with Children's Charts, is an excerpt of some of this material where she lays out her procedure and method for defining a child's temperamental type based on modern concepts in the field of child development and correlating it with the elements and qualities in the chart.

Ancuta Catrinoiu from Romania in her paper Monomoira, a lost essential dignity delves into ancient Hellenistic astrology to explore a little know but powerful technique where each single degree of the zodiac (monomoira) has interpretive meaning associated with the Chaldean order of the planets. She utilizes a qualitative approach to analyze the charts of ten sets of twins, using the monomoira associated with the quickly changing degrees of Ascendant, Midheaven, and Fortune to account for the differences and nuances of different personalities with almost identical charts.

Michael Munkasey is an American giant in astrological research with a background in Information Technology and data analysis. His paper Degree Symbolism also looks into the individual degree interpretations made by many different modern authors and questions as to whether they have interpretive meaning. Using a quantitative approach to analyzing several thousand charts, he discovered that there was not an even distribution of the planets by degree, but rather the distribution was random, bordering on chaos. I would be most interested in a discussion between Munkasey and Catrinoiu that could expand our understanding of single degree symbolism.

The next set of papers all investigate mundane situations such as disasters, mass shooting, earthquakes, space launches, social movements searching for the astrological factors that play a role in collective events that impact large groups of people.

Alan Annand, a Canadian astrologer who is well versed in both Western and Vedic astrology as well author crime novels featuring as astrologer- detective. His paper, Mercury Retrograde in Disasters uses a mathematical index of significance to tabulate the frequency of Mercury as well as other classical planetary aspects in natural, maritime, railway and aviation accidents resulting in the loss of many lives. His results are surprising.

Glenn E. Mitchell II, Ph.D. is a research professor with a specialty in applied, statistical research methods with more than 30 years of experience as an astrologer. In The Astrology of Mass Shooting he studies the statistical relationship between 86 mass shooting events between 1982 and 2017 in the United States and astrological factors. Using JigSaw from Esoteric Technologies to construct random data for the control group and Air Software's Fast Research for data analysis, his findings highlight the importance of the Trans-Neptunian planets in identifying warning behaviors and red flags that can be used to predict and prevent violent crimes.

Pamela Rowe, LPMAFA, FMFAA, an esteemed Australian astrologer specializes in Cosmobiology. In her paper, America's True Horoscope: The Las Vegas Shooting Tragedy, she applies her expertise to argue for the accuracy of the USA Gemini rising chart by comparing it to the astrological patterns in the event chart of this deadly mass shooting.

Marilyn Muir, LPMAFA a professional astrologer from Central Florida investigates the space probes of Voyager I and II, twin missions that occurred 16 days apart in 1977. Their objective was to study the outer planets and beyond; and they are still operative now. Using the charts for the launch times and the technique of diurnals, she studies the fly-bys and other main events in their timelines to account for the similarities and differences in their journeys.

Jagdish Maheshri is a chemical engineer with over forty years of practice as a professional astrologer. His paper Earthquake Prediction Model III-A continues his ongoing research analyzing and investigating correlations between astronomical data and the significant earthquakes of magnitude seven and higher. His latest research inquiry focuses upon improving the Model III by including a selection of planetary angle pairs as independent variables employed in linear regression.

John Halloran, creator of Halloran software, shares part of a larger research project in his paper, Declination

Aspects, where he seeks to discover the meaning of each declination parallel and contraparallel aspect. Compiling birth data from the Gauquelin data and Lois Rodden's Astrodatabank and using the Astro/Deluxe Platinum which he designed, he sorted the frequency of these close declinations aspects with 22 different occupational categories and determined which aspects appear most often in association with the various professions.

Steve DeLapp's interest lies in forecasting severe weather patterns and his research focuses upon the role of planetary phenomena that influence geomagnetic atmospheric disturbances. In his paper "Was John Nelson an Astrologer? A Geocentric Review of RCA's John H. Nelson's Work: "Planetary Position Effect on Short-Wave Signal Quality," he critically reviews John Nelson's research and proposes that the moon's lunations and eclipses played a far greater role than was revealed.

Rui Miguel Fernandes from Portugal has an educational background in physics, mathematics and astronomy. In his paper, the Moon's Mathematical Nodes, he demonstates how in the absense of an ephemeris, one can easily compute an approximate value of the ascending lunar node. Recognizing that the mechanical foundations of astrology are mathematical, this article is a preview of additional algorithms he is developing to calculate the astronomical data of other celestial bodies and points used by astrologers.

Our issue concludes with a paper A Study of Leukemia through Medical Astrology by Abdol-Hussein Heidari from Iran who has a mechanical engineering degree from Persian Gulf University and is trained in Classical Vedic astrology. In this first of a three-part study, he investigates the significators of blood cancer using a Western Tropical approach in the charts of 15 AA rated charts of persons diagnosed with leukemia. Forthcoming articles will use two different Vedic Sidereal methods of evaluation for comparison.

The American Federation of Astrologers extends its appreciation to these contributors for their hard work and dedication in furthering the body of astrological knowledge.

Demetra George
Director of Research for the American Federation of Astrologers

The Gauquelin Character Traits: New Studies

By Nick Kollerstrom

The relationship between planet and character-trait could be observed without any need to take account of the professions.—Michel Gauquelin, 1983[1]

Each time statistically significant results showed up, they were maximal in those so-called "cadent houses." Present day traditionalists are shocked by these statistical results in Cadent instead of Angular houses.—Francoise Gauquelin, 1992[2]

ABSTRACT: The Gauquelins published lists of character-traits, with lists of famous people who came under them. No digital record of this exists and so I have been preparing this over the last couple of years: with help from the UK Astrological Association's library, which has been scanning-in the hard-to-find data volumes. Where I am so far is posted at www.correlationjournal.com/research.php. I am majorly confirming the "character-traits hypothesis" as the Gauquelins called it, which is that the planets are much more strongly linked to traits of character, than they are to professions. With modern computer programs we can see what is going on much more clearly than they could, some decades earlier. Perhaps the most surprising finding is the strongly fourfold nature of the phenomenon, in the cadent houses. I also show how Venus appears (as no one was ever able to earlier) by separating the Morning and Evening Star. These two appear as having opposite characters.

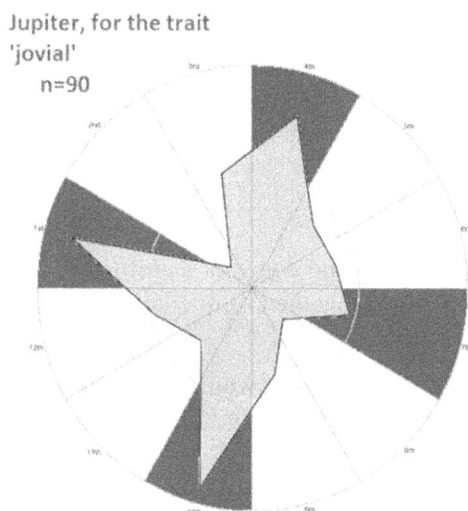

Jupiter, for the trait 'jovial'
n=90

Here is surely the simplest astrological effect we've ever seen: it's the trait "jovial," plotted by the Jupiter day. There were various professional groups, for which the two Gauquelins extracted such trait-terms from their biographies.

Their published data volumes, which are quite hard to get hold of, by the way (These have been scanned by the UK Astrological Association's librarian and will hopefully soon go up online. I managed to obtain one of the four volumes from a French bookshop: *The Mars Temperament and Sports Champions*, Paris 1973. They don't come up on Amazon.) give lists of names underneath each trait. Other volumes of theirs gave the birth data for those names, and these have all been posted on the CURA website[3], which is a great help.

Figure 1, left: Jupiter positions in the diurnal circle for 90 persons with the traits joviale and joyeux in their biographies.

I've logged in all of the birth data published by the Gauquelins for some 35 character-traits, and put it on a Gauquelin research page.[4] So you can check everything I'm writing here from that database, if you have a suitable program. Those character-traits were selected as allegedly belonging to the several planets, in the view of the Gauquelins.[5]

A Fourfold Effect

Four times each day, Jupiter arrives in one of the key sectors, the "cadent" houses in the Placidus system. During those times, people were *twice as likely to be born* who would later be described in their biographies as "jovial." Actually I here combined the two French words *joyeux* and *joviale*. This is good news and it *cheers us up*: Jupiter is jovial! Here is the same data, but using an 18-fold division of the circle, of Jupiter's day.

I was inspired to do this work partly because I knew John Addey, the "harmonics" theorist of the last century (1920-1982); let's have a couple of quotes from him. On the subject of Mars, John, the great Pythagoean theorist, author of the classic *Harmonics in Astrology*—wrote that what he called "the pure 4th harmonic qualities (active, energetic etc gave a distribution where

> . . . there is no longer any tendency for there to be stronger peaks after the rise and upper culmination; all four angles are more or less equal in strength.[6]

That is so crucial and no one else on the great 20th century debates on the subject ever realized this: it's a fourfold effect. Then, concerning the trait "energetic," he wrote:

> The word ENERGETIC was attributed to 187 different people (94 champions, 34 scientists, 42 actors, 17 writers).[7]

He is here alluding to the several professions for which the Gauquelins scored traits, and has added them up.[8] I confirmed these numbers, and that did much to reassure me that I was on the right track.

I think of the Jupiter traits *pride and joy*. Five of the top-scoring ones are *jovial, proud, authority, director, and energetic*—and together they show overall a 78 percent excess. By that we mean, that the four cadent houses had Jupiter in them (for 584 lots of birth data, that is all the people who had these traits)—78 percent more than did the eight other houses.

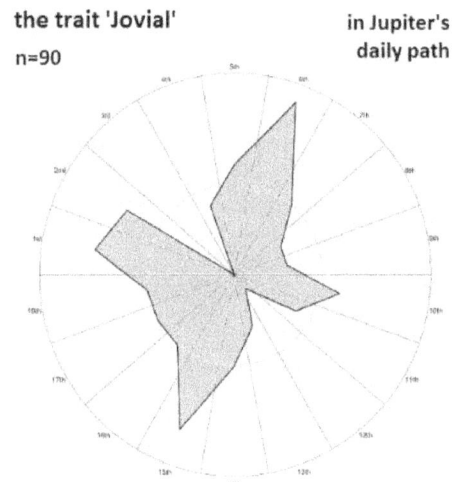

the trait 'Jovial'
n=90

in Jupiter's daily path

Figure 2

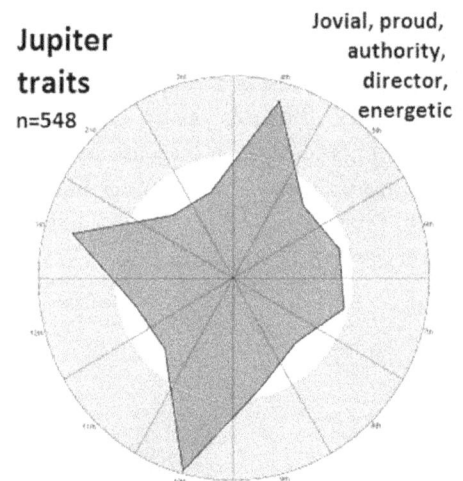

Jupiter traits
n=548

Jovial, proud, authority, director, energetic

Figure 3

Readers familiar with the Gauquelin work will understand that two things here look very different. First, the effect is symmetrically fourfold and does not merely peak in the two "Gauquelin sectors"; and second, it is *several times larger* than any effect that the Gauquelins ever reported for professional groups.

By top-scoring traits we here allude to the group of 35 traits that I have evaluated. It would be possible to log in a couple of hundred of them from the data books. It's hard work and it all has to be carefully cross-checked, but let's hope somebody does it.

When I initally asked various people about these traits, they would doubt whether "authority" was really a jovian trait, and suspect it was saturnine. I guess the idea of being authoritative did not go with their image of

Jupiter as Mr. Nice Guy? But this trait scores negative for Saturn at -26 percent, i.e. it's in deficit: Saturn in the cadent houses at birth *impedes its appearance* in future biographies. As to why Jupiter should be authoritative, we could here quote Michel:

Zeus no preside-t-il pas aux autres dieux, du haut de son Olympe?[9]

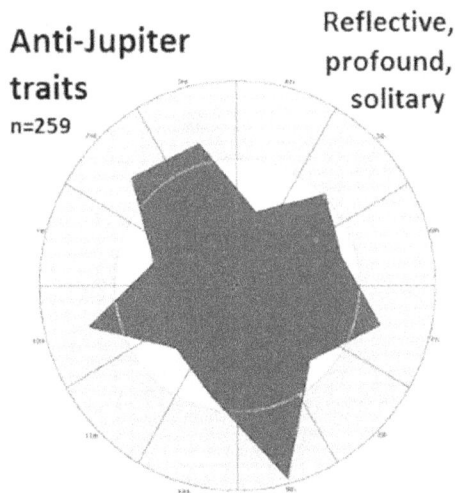

Anti-Jupiter traits
n=259

Reflective, profound, solitary

Figure 4

The three lowest-scoring Jupiter traits (see Figure 4, left) turned out to be *reflective, profound* and *solitary*. One notes the extravert character of Jupiter here, that these introvert traits were scoring lowest (a 25 percent deficit of the four sectors, compared to the other eight). The evident working here of anti-Jupiter traits strongly indicates that the Gauquelins were not cheating—in case anyone were to suspect such a thing.

Concerning the graph here shown, John Addey would have said that this is still a four-fold effect, just as significantly as for the positive traits, but rotated around and so peaking at a different part of the diurnal circle. If perchance some new harmonic science should come to exist in the future, then maybe this would be important.

Moving on to Saturn, here are some top-scoring traits. Let's give per trait its number of citations in the professional biographies, then the number of times Saturn scored in one of the cadent house at the time of birth, and then the percentage excess that implies. The *six top-scoring traits* come out as:

Top Scoring Saturn Character Traits

Silent	46, 21,	+68%
Cold	64, 29,	+65%
Severe	65, 28,	+51%
Noble	79, 33,	+43%
Solitary	106, 42,	+31%
Profound	77, 30,	+27%

(If SA scored 21 in cadent, then scores 46-21 = 25 in all the others, that's 12.5 on average for angular and succedent. So the cadent houes have 21/12.5 = 68% excess.)

All your life you've read of planetary traits that authors have dreamed up or imagined or copied from others, but here is something which has not (I suggest) happened before: a list of planetary traits emerges objectively from a data set without anyone selecting them. We feel Old Father Time in this wonderful (and scary) list of traits, and the Grim Reaper, but also maybe the Wise Counsellor?

And likewise for the Moon, remembering that the Gauquelins found imaginative writers and dreamy poets to be influenced by Selene's Sphere[10], the top five lunar traits, with numbers as before, are:

Top Lunar Traits

Tranquil	58, 31,	+129%
Pure	45, 24,	+128%
Imaginative	85, 40,	+77%
Dreamer	71, 31,	+55%
Fantasy	78, 34,	+54%

These are beautiful traits for Selene's sphere. "Reflective" turned out not to be a lunar trait, contrary to what I'd initially surmised. Yes, physically the Moon is reflective, but this does not come through as a character-trait!

We're looking at a traditionally feminine planet here, while the biographies here used are mainly male.

The fire energy of Mars is direct and unsubtle—its three top-scoring traits (with numbers as before) are:

Top Mars Traits

Combative	110, 56,	+107%
Vitality	63, 32,	+106%
Energetic	185, 92,	+97%

What we might call anti-Mars traits (Figure 5) are those that scored most negatively in the Mars sectors. Here are eight of the lowest-scoring grouped together, and together they display a 25 percent *deficit* in the four sectors. *Minima* appear here in the four cadent houses, using these gentle and dreamy traits, which appear somewhat lunar, do they not? The Red Planet in its daily sojourn has tended to inhibit these traits from appearing many years later in biographies.

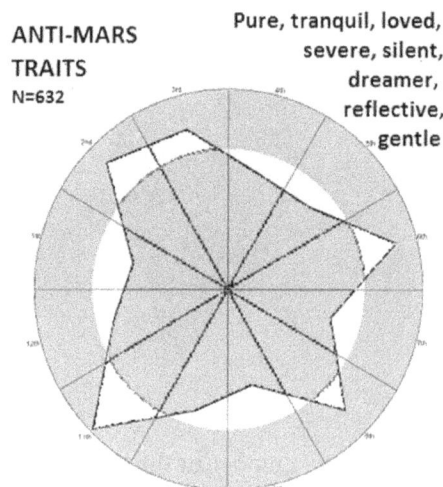

ANTI-MARS TRAITS
N=632

Pure, tranquil, loved, severe, silent, dreamer, reflective, gentle

Figure 5

"Silent" and "severe" were negative Mars, but positive for Saturn, while "pure," "tranquil," and "dreamer" were also negative Mars, but Moon positive. Traits are responding to more than one of the heavenly spheres.

Morning and Evening Star

For half a century on two continents the great debate seethed concerning the Gauquelin research—and we're here talking about the greatest astro-research program ever undertaken—but it never found a thing for Venus. Venus just refused to show up. Could it be that it was too near the Sun, people surmised? The key, it dawned on me one day, was to separate the two sides of Venus, as Morning and Evening Star. These had two different names in antiquity, *Lucifer* and *Hesperus*.

They can usually be separated by subtracting the zodiacal longitudes of Sun and Venus: if {Sun – Venus} is negative, it's the Evening Star. That doesn't work however if 0 Aries is in between them. The two spheres are always less than forty degrees apart. Suppose the Sun is in Pisces and Venus is in Aries; then, subtracting the two will give around 300 degrees, as a positive value, while clearly Venus is the Evening Star, so it's the other way round.

That may sound complicated, but it's very simple if you look at a chart. Click your program so that only the Sun and Venus come up, and you will at once see by inspection what is happening.

A modern computer program will produce solar and Venus longitudes for the several thousand lines of birth data, plus it will also generate house positions for any planet, which is how the tables here were made. Thereby, all of the data was split into two, according to whether Venus was Oriental or Occidental.

We should add here, that normally a diurnal Venus distribution will be very asymmetric, showing a large bulge in the bottom left corner, i.e. the first and second houses, because natural births peak before dawn and Venus is generally close to the Sun.[11]

Traits here plotted around the Evening-Star Venus-day, with citation-counts are: charming (108), passionate (95), enthusiastic (73), elegant (48), noble (35), dreamer (34), gracious (33) fantasy (33) and silent (24), totalling 488. Venus as the Evening Star expresses traditional qualities, as shown for these nine traits (n=488), here depicted with both 12- and 36-fold divisions of the circle. It's fun looking at a 36-fold division of the circle, but one might not wish to do numerical or statistical analysis using it. These are credible Venus traits, and this is the first time ever they have shown up in the diurnal circle. The net excess here in the four houses is 60 percent.

Evening star
n=488

Traits: charming, dreamer, elegant, enthusiastic, fantasy, gracious, noble, silent, passionate

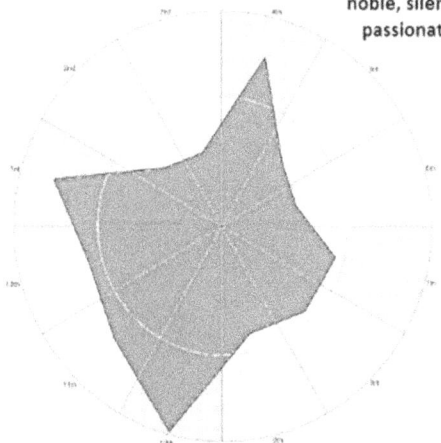

Figure 6

EVENING STAR

N=488

36 - fold division

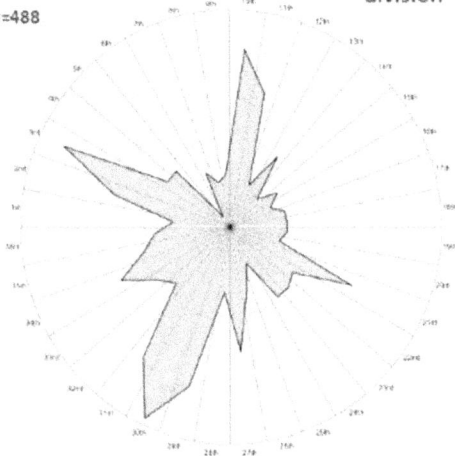

Figure 7

Here for comparison are the *10 top traits* for the Morning Star, with numbers as before. Do they seem different from the earlier Evening Star traits?

Top-scoring Venusian Traits as Morning Star

Loved	70, 32	+68%
Vitality	31, 14,	+64%
Severe	36, 15,	+42%
Profound	30, 12,	+33%
Proud	34, 13,	+23%
Pure	27, 10,	+17%
Authority	66, 24,	+14%
Director	45 16,	+10%
Fantasy	45 16	+10%
Tranquil	31 11	+10%

I combined two French trait-words *amoureux* and *aimé* into the one English word—loved—here seen as top of the list! The numbers are of course smaller, as we've split the data in half, so one cannot go too much by individual trait percentages. We sense an inverse-correlation with the more traditional Evening-star traits: *charming, passionate, friendly, ardent, seductive, enthusiastic, gracious, gentle, dreamer*—these are all *in deficit*, meaning they have been *inhibited by* the Morning Star.

Is the Morning Star bossy? Could there be a contrast between the stern and dominant Morning Star (think: Meryl Streep in *The Devil wears Prada*) and a sweet and gentle Evening Star? Is there a missing archetype here, an antithesis to the Aphrodite-image we may have of the Evening Star? At her bold appearance in the morning sky before dawn, she would put the stars to flight (then the whole mythos of *Lucifer* vanished, turning into the Christian archfiend, but let's not go into that . . .). For the Mayans of central America who had a Venus-based calendar, the appearance of the Morning Star was the time for blood-letting rituals and going to war. Is the Morning Star more strident and connected to decisive action?

Do astrologers need to start using these two opposite polarities of Venus? To help answer that, let us contrast the scores for some traits, Morning versus Evening Star, giving the excess or deficit only to the nearest 10 percent as the numbers per trait are rather small.

	Evening	Morning		Evening	Morning
Graceful, (grace de la)	+90%	-30%	Silent	+70%	-50%
Dreamer	+60%	-40%	Elegant	+40%	-20%
Deep, profound	-20%	+30%	Director	-30%	+10%
Passionate	+20%	-10%	Proud	-10%	+20%

The Evening Star is *graceful, silent, dreamy* and *elegant*, while the Morning Star is none of these things—quite the opposite! She's got work to do. . .

(Other traits that have not been used, together with their numbers of citations in the four volumes, which might throw some more light on this interesting question, are: self-willed 207, lively 163, faithful 146, gay 136, verve 135, always smiling 125, great-hearted 100, lyrical 83, funny, fantasist (fantastique + fantasist) 75, violent 74, laughing 67, poetic 63, naïve 62, moral courage 60, picturesque 50, romantic 45, young 39, exuberant 30, scandalous 27, beauty 26, enjoys life 26 and happy 25.)

Correlations

Let's plot the same figures we've here been using, i.e. percentage excesses and deficits per each trait in the four key sectors, but now using all 35 traits. For example, in the top left-hand corner there is the trait "vitality," which scores around 200% as a Mars trait but is quite low, only 86%, for Jupiter. Overall we see a positive correlation between Mars and Jupiter. In other words, over all the trait-citations they co-vary. Why should that be? Presumably, they are both extravert and outgoing, while Jupiter and Saturn traits in contrast correlate negatively.

If we sort the list by Mars strength per trait, then plot that for the Moon, there appears a strong *inverse correlation*. Does this show the Mars trait of *aggression*, with the more pushy, aggressive and fiery Martial traits scoring negative with the gentle, dreamy Moon? Astral philosophers may want to mull over this question.

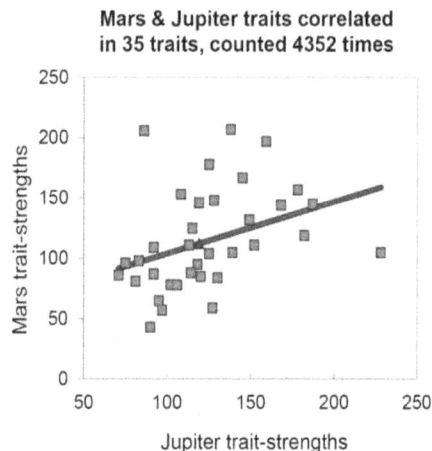

Mars & Jupiter traits correlated in 35 traits, counted 4352 times

Figure 8

Introvert versus Extravert

In 1974 Gauquelin met Hans Eysenck, Britain's best-known psychologist, and suggested that his questionnaire for measuring introversion-extraversion could be relevant to the personality-trait work that he, Michel, was doing. A few years later, pro-astrology results were reported in academic psychology journals, based on the concept of introversion-extraversion:

> Gauquelin, M& F. and Eysenck, S. B. G. (1979) 'Personality and position of the planets at birth: An empirical study *British Journal of Social and Clinical Psychology*, Vol:18: pp.71-75.

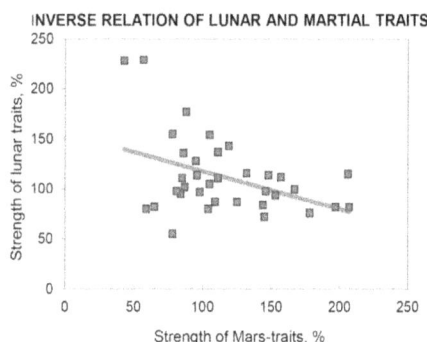

INVERSE RELATION OF LUNAR AND MARTIAL TRAITS

Figure 9

> Gauquelin, M& F. and Eysenck, S. B. G. (1981) 'Eysenck's personality analysis and position of the planets at birth: A replication on American subjects' *Personality and Individual Differences,* Vol 2(4) pp.346-350.

In the 1979 paper the Gauquelin character-traits were used, and one person (Sybil Eysenck, wife of Hans) rated them as being either introvert or extravert. In the present study, four people, me and three others, graded traits on a five-point scale, such that +2 was definitely extravert and -2 was definitely introvert, and the zero score meant the trait was neither introvert or extravert. A score of 1 meant, maybe or perhaps extravert and likewise "-1" maybe introvert. Here are scores for the first few traits, with the average value taken:

Average Trait Scores for Introversion-Extraversion, from Four Estimates

Active	1, 1, 1, 2	=> 1.25
Ardent	0, 0, 2, 0	=> 0.5
Authority	0, 0, 1, 2	=> 0.75
Charming	2, 1, 0, 1	=> 1
Cold	-2,-1,-2,-2	=> -1.75
Combative	0, 2, 2, 2	=> 1.5

Mars in Character-traits & introvert - extravert score

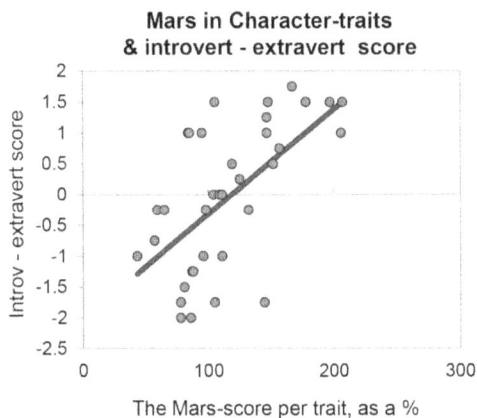

Figure 10

We see much disagreement here between the several judges, and yet one may have some confidence in the averaged-out values. As a quantitative measure, it is inevitably going to be a fuzzy concept. But this procedure may be preferable to that used in the published papers by Sybil Eysenck and the Gauquelins, where just one person made a summary yes/no judgement.[12]

Let's take Mars strengths for all the character-traits. We saw that the top three scoring Mars traits were *combative* at 207 percent, *vitality* 206 percent and *energetic* 197 percent (Earlier, we described that value of 207 percent as a 107 percent excess. I hope that isn't confusing.), while the bottom three-scoring (anti-Mars traits) are *loved* at only 59 percent, *tranquil* at 57 percent and *pure* at 43 percent. These figures indicate how often Mars was in cadent houses, at time of birth, compared to the other houses, as a percentage, and does so for the group of people who had this trait in their biographies. OK so far?

We now plot one against the other:

Thus, we can here see those three top-scoring Mars traits in the graph, on the top, right-hand side, around the 200% mark. Clearly, the strong Mars traits are highly extravert while weak Mars-traits score as introvert. This is the strongest and clearest astrology-effect I have ever seen. As regards its statistical significance—which matters here because there are a lot more traits in the Gauquelin volumes, so the effect can be replicated—the correlation coefficient gives a significance level of one in 20,000. (The correlation coefficient is 0.61, and an online p-value calculator was used, for sample size of 35, a one-tailed test.)

Jupiter in Character-traits & introvert - extravert score

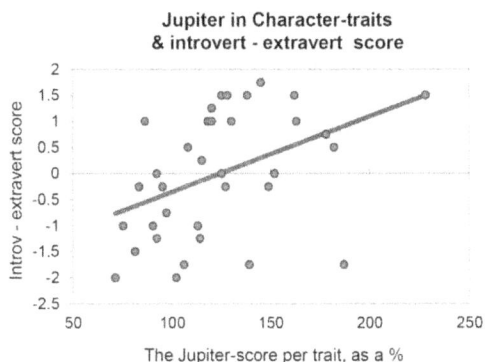

Figure 11

Saturn in Character-traits & introvert - extravert score

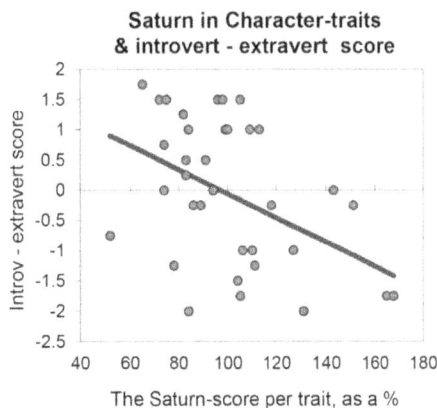

Figure 12

The Eysenck-Gauquelin paper found Mars and Jupiter to be extravert and Saturn to be introvert. Those are totally traditional results, but the point here is that these results have emerged from the data; no-one has selected them.

Looking at the Saturn graph, its line is going in the other direction because it shows an *introvert* character. Thus for example, we can see the two strongest traits scoring around 160, which are *silent* 168% and *cold* 165%, and they score way down on the vertical scale, around -2, i.e. very introvert. Turning to the Jupiter-graph, the top-scoring trait we see is *jovial* at 228%. That's where we started off. . . .

Conclusion

We have seen how, from the work of the Gauquelins, a new vocabulary can emerge for describing the eternal, divine archetypes that are so to speak behind astrology. I've here tried to show how, from their work we get a vindication of the *qualitative being* of the planets. A strongly fourfold effect appears, one which highlights the "cadent" houses. The effects are large, in contrast with the Gauquelin professional-group effects of the last century that were only around ten percent magnitude. From them we begin to sense an active cosmos—or *Kosmos* to use the Greek word—which is deeply affecting the human psyche, in a rhythmical manner. In the words of Mr Ray Grasse, "I would argue that the ground-breaking research of French statistician Michel Gauquelin provides us with compelling evidence for the existence of meaning in our world.[13]

It is a very new thing, that the relevant data-sets are becoming available for home computer programs to inspect in this 21st century: in the great debates that went on in earlier decades, the protagonists did not in general have this ability.

Let us look forward to the day when psychology students start to demand modules whereby they can inspect and check over these results. Academics may try to resist this because they well realise, there is nothing else in modern psychology so interesting as these effects! Much remains to be done to ascertain how these very "elitist" results—which seem only to show up for very eminent people, for whom biographies were written—relate to ordinary folk.

Acknowledgement: Thanks to Sven Raphael for helpful discussion and assistance at every stage of this work, especially with the computer programs and data-checking.

Endnotes

[1]Gauquelin. *The Truth About Astrology*, 1983, p. 63.

[2]Gauquelin, Francoise. Astra-Psychological Problems, September 1992, p.21.

[3]http://cura.free.fr/gauq/17archg.html.

[4]http://newalchemypress.com/gauquelin/research11.php. Click on opening of second paragraph to download Excel file.

[5]See, e.g., Francoise Gauquelin, *Psychology of the Planets*, ACS 1982.

[6]Addey, John. *A New Study of Astrology*, 1996, Ch8 (Addey died in 1982).

[7]Ibid, p. 118

[8]For traits they took from actors, see http://newalchemypress.com/gauquelin/research6.php, section "Character-trait data Volumes."

[9]M.G., Les Hammes et les Astres, 1955, p.225: "Zeus, does he not preside over others from the top of his Mount Olympus?"

[10]See http://newalchemypress.fom/gau~lin/research8.php

[11]See http://newalchemypress.com/gauquelin/research2.php

[12]For the traits that were here selected, see Michel Gauquelin, *The Truth about Astrology*, 1983, p. 77.

[13]Ray Grasse. *The Waking Dream, Unlocking the Symbolic Language of our Lives*, 1996, p. 266.

A Study of the Part of Fortune on the Gauquelin Data

By Kyösti Tarvainen, Ph.D

ABSTRACT: The working of the Part (or Lot) of Fortune (PF) was studied by considering how well the PF interpretations of Schulman (1978) hold true on the Gauquelin data of twelve professional groups. Based on this book, 16 hypotheses could be set up for the PF's locations in houses and signs. They obtained statistical support with p = 0.08. Schulman's descriptions for the PF's aspects are very short, and no hypotheses could be set up based on these descriptions. But the importance of the PF's aspects gained statistical support in that the total amount of Ptolemaic aspects of ten planets to the PF had an excess of 0.9 % with p = 0.02. Also, the following three observations were made. The single formula for determining the PF worked better than the use of different formulas for the day and night births. The Koch house system, used in the study, performed better than the Placidus, Equal and Whole Sign Houses. The aspect orbs recommended by the Faculty of Astrological Studies were used. It could be estimated that, in this data, these were indeed working orbs, except that the additional orb for the Sun and Moon was 1°, instead of 2°.

The Notion of the Part of Fortune (PF)

In Antiquity, astrologers noticed that when one moves in an anti-clockwise direction from the Ascendant the same distance forward, as the Moon is from the Sun, one arrives at a sensitive point, called Part (or Lot) of Fortune (PF). That is, mathematically in the longitudes, PF = Ascendant + Moon - Sun.

Nowadays we can theoretically consider the PF by using the concept of midpoints. Adding the longitude of the Sun to both sides of the above equation and dividing both sides by 2, we obtain the following equation: (PF + Sun) /2 = (Ascendant + Moon)/2.

On the left, we have the longitude of the midpoint of the PF and Sun; on the right, the midpoint of the Ascendant and Moon. That is, the PF is such a point that the midpoint of it and the Sun conjuncts the midpoint of the Ascendant and Moon. Let us consider the astrological interpretation of, for example, the case where Mercury conjuncts the PF. Then the midpoint of Mercury and the Sun conjoins the midpoint of the Ascendant and the Moon, which can be interpreting in the following way.

The functions of Mercury and the Sun co-operate at their midpoint (Hand, 1981): this midpoint relates to, for example, the individual's will (Sun) to express his thoughts (Mercury). When both the Ascendant and Moon transmit interaction between the individual and other people, the midpoint between them is a strong interaction point. Therefore, when the midpoint of Mercury and the Sun hits this midpoint, the individual's will to express his thoughts to other people has a good outlet. Meyer (1974, p. 245) says more generally that Mercury contacting the PF refers to an "intellectual" personality.

Likewise, we can generally consider that when there is a planet at the PF, the Sun gives energy to it and then the midpoint of the Ascendant and the Moon may transmit the activated planet's energy to the surroundings. Even if there is no planet at the PF, we can theoretically think that if the PF's house or sign are active in the individual's life, this activity can be similarly stimulated.

This theoretical analysis is in line with the statements of modern astrologers. Meyer (1974, p. 245) states: "The Part of Fortune is the point of most natural externalization of personality." Sheldon (2017) says: "The Part of Fortune tells us what types of work and activity will make us most fulfilled and therefore, will also attract wealth, happiness, and good fortune to our lives." Rudhyar (1967) considers the PF in terms of the lunar cycle and characterizes the PF as a point which "can give information concerning the personality of the individual and the best ways in which he can operate in society, seek happiness and release his vital energies."

The above theoretical analysis and the characterizations of the PF in modern astrology indicate that the word "fortune" in the term "the Part of Fortune" is misleading. As Rudhyar (1967) states: "The Part of Fortune may refer to the individual's wealth [a common old interpretation for the PF] and "good fortune," but this is not its most significant meaning, certainly not its primary."

The problem with the theoretical considerations of the PF is the question as to how strong the final effect is: we have here the conjunction of two midpoints, which evidently generally is not as strong as the conjunction of two planets. On the other hand, the three most influential chart factors are involved here; the midpoint study of Tarvainen (2016) gave statistical support for Hand's statement (1981, p. 167) that midpoints including the Sun, Ascendant, MC or Moon are the strongest ones. The motivation for this study was to study how strong a factor the PF is.

Ptolemy used the above formula to determine the PF, but most astrologers in Antiquity used a different formula (PF = Ascendant + Sun - Moon) for the night births. The use of the PF and some other Parts in the Hellenistic astrology is treated by Brennan (2017); a historical account of the use of Parts in different times is included in the book by Zoller (1989). Also today two ways of determining the PF are used. For example, Rudhyar (1967) and Schulman (1978) have used the single formula, whereas, for example, Hand (1996) uses different formulas for the day and night births. In this study, we could compare these two methods.

The Considered Data

The Part of Fortune was considered in the following twelve professional groups collected by the Gauquelins, available on http://cura.free.fr: actors (n = 1,407), military leaders (n = 3,608), aviation pioneers (n = 392), freedom fighters (n = 616), journalists (n = 673), musicians (n = 1,248), painters (n = 1,472), physicians (n = 2,552), politicians (n = 1,002), scientists (n = 1,094), sports champions (n = 2,144), and writers (n = 1,352). The Gauquelin groups of mental patients, murderers and alcoholics were not taken into account in this study since there were no references to these groups in PF interpretations.

Research Hypotheses

The primary source for the research hypotheses was the book by Schulman (1978), which is the most comprehensive presentation of this subject. Though Schulman refers to a specific profession only a couple of times, we can infer the following expectations based on his text:

1. Schulman states that when the PF is located in the fifth house, the individual feels his greatest joy when engaged in the act of creation. He makes specific references to art and drama. Thus, one can expect that the writers, painters, musicians and actors may have the PF in the fifth house more often than expected.

2. In the case of the PF in the third house, Schulman says that communication will bring the greatest fulfillment and that language and the use of words are very important to the individual. Groups, where these issues are central, are journalists, writers and actors.

3. Schulman relates the PF in the sixth house to an active person who is happy at work, attends to details, is always serving and accomplishing and can be genuinely compassionate. Schulman doesn't give any example profession, but some astrologers have explicitly stated that, due to these kinds of traits, the PF in the sixth house may be appropriate for a health professional. Therefore, we anticipate that physicians have the PF in the sixth house more often than expected.

4. Schulman states that the placement of the PF in the tenth house can draw positions of trust and authority

to an individual. We could thus assume that military leaders and politicians have this PF placement more often than expected.

5. Schulman says that the PF in the ninth house allows an individual to experience his greatest joy through the discovery of truth. So scientists may have this placement more often than expected.

6. Schulman connects the PF in the first house with a highly competitive nature. Sports champions are very competitive.

7. For the PF's sign positions, Schulman's descriptions are still more psychological, and it is more difficult to connect them to specific professions. But two direct connections outlined here and in the next point can be made. Schulman mentions that an individual with the PF in Aries experiences the need and energy for activity. As the freedom fighters are very energetic and active individuals, we may expect that at least they have this placement more often.

8. Schulman relates the PF in Gemini to communication, much in the same way as the PF in the third house. Therefore, we expect that, as in the above second point, journalists, writers and actors have this placement. But for the other sign placements, there is no similar straightforward relationship between the house and sign placements.

In all, we have here 16 expectations, research hypothesis. We have obtained at least one hypothesis for all twelve groups, except for the particular group of the aviation pioneers.

Results for the House and Sign Placements of the Part of Fortune

The house placements of the PF were determined using Koch's house system and the single formula for the PF. It was first identified how many times the above research hypotheses hold true in the twelve groups.

Then, for each professional group, a control group was generated by the *shuffling* method (the dates, years, birth hours and places were taken randomly and independently without replacement; cf. Ruis, 2007/2008; Tarvainen, 2012). In the same manner as for the data, it was determined how many times the research hypotheses holds true in these twelve control groups.

This generation of controls for the twelve groups was repeated 1,000 times, and it was observed that 75 times the total number of fulfilled hypotheses was as high as or higher than that in the data. Thus we obtain as an estimate of the p-value: $75/1000 = 0.075 \approx 0.08$ (for p-value estimations, cf. Tarvainen, 2012; Ruis, 2007/2008). The p-value of 0.08 gives some statistical support for the importance of the house and sign placement of the PF.

Possible Additional Hypotheses

When setting up the 16 hypotheses above, we considered the most straightforward and evident interpretations of Schulman's text. The above results ending up with $p = 0.08$ are the main results concerning the PF houses and signs.

But it is also possible to set up hypotheses that are not as directly based on Schulman's text. In particular, we can consider the third house and Gemini in this and future studies with famous people. The individuals in the Gauquelin data are prominent. Therefore, they tend to have good mental capabilities. We may thus expect that the PF is in the third house or Gemini more often in the following groups, where communication is essential: politicians, liberation fighters, scientists, military leaders. If we add these hypotheses, the p-value decreases to 0.05.

Furthermore, we know from ability tests that verbal and motor skills correlate. Therefore, we might expect that the PF is more often in the third house or Gemini in the following groups where the motor skills and dexterity are important: musicians, painters, aviation pioneers and sports champions. If we still add these hypotheses, the p-value decreases to 0.03.

Results for the Aspects of the Part of Fortune

Schulman regards aspects to the PF as important but gives such short and general interpretations for them that no specific expectations as above can be set up.

Therefore, aspects to the PF were considered as a whole by determining how many Ptolemaic aspects the ten usual planets SO, MO, ME, . . . , PL make with the PF. The aspect orbs recommended by the Faculty of Astrological Studies (4° for sextiles, 8° for other Ptolemaic aspects, plus 2° for aspects involving the Sun or Moon) were used.

It turned out that there is an excess of 0. 9 % of these aspects in the twelve groups compared with the controls. The corresponding p = 0.02, which gives statistically significant support for the importance of the PF for prominence.

Table 1 presents the aspect excess for each planet in descending order. We see that Jupiter's excess is biggest. Meyer (1974, p. 246) says of the Jupiter's contacts with the PF: "Characterizes an optimistic personality that functions well within the social sphere." After Jupiter, comes Mercury (mental faculties), Uranus (originality), and Saturn (sense of duty). For example, the number of Jupiter's Ptolemaic aspects with the Part of Fortune in the twelve groups of prominent persons is 2.8 percent greater than that in the controls.

Table 1. Planet-wise Excess of Aspects with the Part of Fortune

Planet	Excess of Ptolemaic Aspects to the Part of Fortune in Twelve Groups
Jupiter	2.8% (p = 0.02)
Mercury	2.1 % (p = 0.08)
Uranus	2.0 % (p = 0.08)
Saturn	1.8 % (p = 0.11)
Sun	0.9 % (p = 0.23)
Neptune	0.9 % (p = 0.28)
Pluto	0.3 % (p = 0.42)
Mars	-0.3 % (p = 0.59)
Venus	-0.5 % (p = 0.63)
Moon	-0.6 % (p = 0.69)

In Table 2, different Ptolemaic aspect types are considered. Here, we only take into account the aspects of Jupiter, Mercury, Uranus and Saturn which, according to Table 1, make relatively more aspects to the PF than other planets.

These more specific numbers of Table 2 may include significant inaccuracies since, in the Gauquelin data, many birth hours are rounded to the full or half hour, causing inexactitudes especially to the position of the Ascendant. Therefore, the differences in the excess percentages in Table 2 may not be significant, but the main indication is that all Ptolemaic aspects seem to work with the PF. For example, Jupiter, Mercury, Uranus and Saturn have with the Part of Fortune 1.1 % more conjunctions than the controls.

Table 2. Excess of Different Aspect Types

Aspect	Excess of Jupiter, Mercury, Uranus and Saturn Aspects with the Part of Fortune in 12 Groups
Conjunction	1.1 % (p = 0.30)
Sextile	2.1 % (p = 0.19)
Square	2.9 % (p = 0.03)
Trine	1.4 % (p = 0.19)
Opposition	3.5 % (p = 0.06)

Comparison of House Systems

Above, the p-value of 0.08 was obtained for the PF house and sign positions when Koch's house system is used. When we repeat the calculations applying the three other most used house systems, the resulting p-values are higher: Placidus 0.21, Whole Sign Houses 0.36, Equal Houses 0.35. This indicates that Koch works here best for the PF among the four house systems.

Estimation of the Working Orbs

Above, the p-value of 0.02 was obtained for the aspects. To study the working orbs, we repeat the calculations using different orbs for sextiles, other Ptolemaic aspects and the additional orb for the Sun and Moon. We obtain the lowest p-value, 0.01, when the orbs are the same as recommended by the Faculty of Astrological Studies, but 1° is used for the additional Sun and Moon orb, instead of 2°. As explained by, for example, Tarvainen (2013), these orbs at the minimum p-value are estimates for the working orbs in this data.

Study of the Use of Different Formulas for the Day and Night Births

Above, the single formula for determining the PF was used, ending up with the p-value 0.08 for the PF house and sign positions. When the calculations are repeated using different formulas for the day and night births, the p-value increases to 0.16. Concerning the PF aspects, the single formula yielded p = 0.02 above; if two formulas are used, the p-value increases to 0.33. These two cases are an indication that the single formula works better.

Discussion

The name "the Part of Fortune" is somewhat misleading and may have confused and hampered the use of this point. The midpoint analysis in the text and the experience of modern astrologers point to the fact that "fortune" is not the primary signification of this astrological factor, but citing, for example, Meyer (1974): "the Part of Fortune is the point of most natural externalization of personality."

This means that the Part of Fortune has some similarity to the chart Ruler (the Ruler of the Ascendant sign), whose house and sign placements and aspects also can support the individual to fulfil himself or herself.

More specifically, Zoller (1989, p. 151) relates the Part of Fortune to the inner motivation of the individual, which is in line with the above midpoint analysis including the midpoint of the Sun (inner motivation) and the Part of Fortune. And, on the other hand, Zoller relates the chart Ruler to the external motivation.

This study gives statistical support for the Part of Fortune. Based on the obtained p-values, it seems not to be as important as the chart Ruler since, in the study by Tarvainen (2017), the p-value related to the chart Ruler's house is smaller (0.005) than the p-values in this study.

Today, it is not as easy to include the Part of Fortune into an astrological analysis as it was in the Antiquity since, due to the modern planets, we already have much more aspects to take into account, whereby additional aspects to the Part of Fortune are difficult to handle. Possibly the easiest and most central thing to take into account regarding the Part of Fortune is its house location since this is related to the important factor of the lunar phase, as Rudhyar (1967) points out.

Acknowledgements

Many thanks to Dr. Patrice Guinard for the Gauquelins' data on the website http://cura.free.fr and astrologer Robert Currey for comments.

Bibliography

Brennan, C. *Hellenistic Astrology, The Study of Fate and Fortune*, Denver, Colorado: Amor Fati Publications, 2017.

Hand, R. *Horoscope Symbols*, Rockport, Massachusetts: Para Research, 1981.

Hand, R. *The Lot or Part of Fortune*, http://www.astro.com/astrology/in_fortune_e.htm, 1996.

Meyer, M. R. *A Handbook for the Humanistic Astrologer*, Garden City, New York: Anchor Press/Double Day, 1974.

Rudhyar, D. *The Lunation Cycle: A Key to the Understanding of Personality*, Santa Fe, N.M.:   Aurora Press, http://www.mindfire.ca/The%20Lunation%20Cycle/Contents.htm,1967.

Ruis, J. Statistical analysis of the birth charts of serial killers, *Correlation*, 25(2), 7–44, 2007/2008.

Schulman, M. *Karmic Astrology, Volume III, Joy and the Part of Fortune*, York Beach, ME: Samuel Weiser, 1978.

Sheldon, P. *Align Your Life with your Part of Fortune*, http://consciousshiftcommunity.com/align-your-life-with-your-part-of-fortune/, 2017.

Tarvainen, K. Henning's synthesis method shows validity of astrology in the Gauquelins' data, *Correlation*, 28(1), 25–43, 2012.

Tarvainen, K. Favorable Astrological Factors for Mathematicians,*Correlation*29(1): 39-51, 2013.

Tarvainen, K. Chart Rulers work on the Gauquelins' data, to appear in *Correlation*, 2017.

Tarvainen, K. A study of midpoints in theologians' charts, to appear in *Correlation*, 2016.

Zoller, R. *The Arabic Parts in Astrology: A Lost Key to Prediction*, Rochester, Vermont: Inner Traditions International, 1989.

An Astrological Research Study About People Who Had Three or More Marriages

By Alphee Lavoie

ABSTRACT: The goal of this research study is to determine if there is any astrological correlation in the natal charts of people who have been married numerous times, in this case three or more times. Additionally, we will focus on which planets and houses have the most to do with marriage.

Introduction

This research project will attempt to determine if there are any astrological correlations in natal chart for people who have been married three or more times. This will be compared with the control group of those who have been married for 15 years or more. I only analyzed the natal chart; not the day they married. I wanted to see if this kind of action is embedded in the date, time, and place of birth.

Methodology

In this research I used more than 1,500 timed charts for people who have been married three or more times. I calculated the charts in the tropical zodiac, and used the five Ptolemaic aspects with a 7° orb. I also used the modern house rulers and Placidus house system. I analyzed signs, houses, aspects, house rulers, planets in houses, phases of planets, out-of-bounds planets and more.

Air Software's Fast Research Program was used to do the research. Anything in the sky that moves can be included in the research model. Using these astrological models, the chi-square and the probability for each criterion in the models was tested against a control group. This methodology is based on scientific research techniques. If it has a high probability found as **often,** it means that this astrological criteria in the sample group happens with a high chi-square and probability in comparison to the control group. If the criteria is found as **seldom** it means that this criteria **seldomly** occurred in the sample group in comparison to the control group. In other words the control group has a close or higher amount of these criteria in comparison with the sample group. This is why when conducting research having a control group, chi-square and probability is so important. Let's say you do a research with a sample of people born between 1939 and 1956. As you calculate planets in sign you would find that Pluto has the highest occurrence in the sign of Leo. If this sample had been calculated with software program that utilizes a chi-square and probability against the control group, it would result as **not important** because everyone in the control and sample groups would have Pluto in Leo.

Aries rising	Chi-square 7.0 probability 99.2%	Often
Mars conjunct the Descendant	Chi-square 6.4 probability 98.9%	Often
Moon in the seventh house	Chi-square 6.9 probability 98.2%	Often
Venus in Aries	Chi-square 6.1 Probability 98.6%	Often
Venus in the tenth house	Chi-square 5.8 probability 98.4%	Often
Mercury in Pisces	Chi-square 5.5 probability 98.1%	Often
Moon and Capricorn	Chi-square 4.2 probability 95.9%	Often
Mars conjunction the Ascendant	Chi-square and probability 5.8%	Often
Mars in the first house	Chi-square 3.3 probability 93.1%	Often
Mars in Capricorn	Chi-square 3.0 probability 91.5%	Often
Ascendant in air sign	Chi-square 2.9 probability 91.1%	Often
Saturn in the fourth house	Chi-square 2.3 probability 87.8%	Often
Venus in the first house	Chi-square 2.1 probability 84.8%	Often
Saturn in the first house	Chi-square 2.1 probability 84.8%	Often
Mars conjunction the Descendant	Chi-square 5.2 probability 97.7%	Often
Mercury trine the Descendant	Chi-square 4.5 probability 96.6%	Often
Saturn trine the Ascendant	Chi-square 4.2 probability 95.9%	Often
Moon conjunction the Ascendant	Chi-square 3.49 probability 93.5%	Often
Saturn square the IC	Chi-square 3.3 probability 93.0 %	Often
Mars square Jupiter	Chi-square 3.0 probability 91.6%	Often
Mars opposition Saturn	Chi-square 2.8 probability 90.8%	Often
Mars sextile Uranus	Chi-square 2.7 probability 89.8%	Often
Venus square Saturn	Chi-square 2.6 probability 89.1%	Often
Mercury sextile Saturn	Chi-square 2.3 probability 87.4%	Often
Jupiter conjunction South Node	Chi-square 2.4 probability 87.9	Often
Mercury square Uranus	Chi-square 2.2 probability 85.9%	Often
Moon conjunction the IC	Chi-square 2.2 probability 85.9%	Often
Sun trine the Moon	Chi-square 2.1 probability 85.5%	Often
Sun conjunction Jupiter	Chi-square 2.1 probability 84.9%	Often
Seventh house ruler conjunction South Node	Chi-square 7.2 probability 99.3%	Often
Moon's last aspect to Venus	Chi-square 6.0 probability 98.6%	Often
Seventh house ruler conjunction Mercury	Chi-square 5.5 probability 98.1%	Often
Saturn rises before the Moon	Chi-square 3.9 probability 95.3%	Often
Ascendant ruler square North Node	Chi-square 3.7 probability 94.6%	Often
Venus rises before the Sun	Chi-square 3.5 probability 94.1%	Often
Ascendant ruler opposition Jupiter	Chi-square 3.2 probability 92.5%	Often
Descendant ruler opposition Saturn	Chi-square 3.1 probability 92.1%	Often
Descendant ruler conjunction Saturn	Chi-square 2.8 probability 90.9%	Often
Ascendant ruler square Mars	Chi-square 2.5 probability 88.8%	Often
Ascendant ruler square Saturn	Chi-square 2.4 probability 87.8%	Often
Sun in the seventh house	Chi-square 7.5 probability 99.4%	Seldom
Venus in Cancer	Chi-square 5.7 probability 98.3%	Seldom
Ascendant in Earth signs	Chi-square 3.7 probability 94.6%	Seldom

Alphee Lavoie | Research Stidy About People Who Had Three or More Marriages

Pluto in the first house	Chi-square 3.5 probability 93.5%	Seldom
Uranus in the tenth house	Chi-square 3.4 probability 93.4%	Seldom
Venus in the seventh house	Chi-square 3.3 probability 93.1%	Seldom
Sun in Sagittarius	Chi-square 3.3 probability 93.0%	Seldom
Mars in Scorpio	Chi-square 3.2 probability 92.5%	Seldom
Venus in the seventh house	Chi-square 3.2 probability 92.4%	Seldom
Sun in Leo	Chi-square 2.5 probability 88.8%	Seldom
Moon in the fifth house	Chi-square 3.0 probability 91.7%	Seldom
Venus in the fifth house	Chi-square 2.8 probability 90.5%	Seldom
Venus in Libra	Chi-square 2.2 probability 86.3%	Seldom
Mercury in the fifth house	Chi-square 2.2 probability 86.3%	Seldom
Ascendant in mutable sign	Chi-square 2.1 probability 85.4%	Seldom
Venus trine the Ascendant	Chi-square 10.2 probability 99.9%	Seldom
Moon sextile Jupiter	Chi-square 7.3 probability 99.3%	Seldom
Mars conjunction the IC	Chi-square 7.0 probability 99.2%	Seldom
Moon conjunction Venus	Chi-square 5.8 probability 98.4%	Seldom
Saturn conjunction the IC	Chi-square 5.6 probability 98.2%	Seldom
Moon square Uranus	Chi-square 5.5 probability 98.1%	Seldom
Sun conjunction the Descendant	Chi-square 5.0 probability 97.5%	Seldom
Pluto square the IC	Chi-square 4.1 probability 95.6%	Seldom
Saturn conjunction Uranus	Chi-square 3.4 probability 93.4%	Seldom
Sun opposition Saturn	Chi-square 3.2 probability 92.6%	Seldom
Uranus conjunction the Ascendant	Chi-square 3.2 probability 92.4%	Seldom
Venus sextile Mars	Chi-square 3.1 probability 91.9%	Seldom
Venus opposition Pluto	Chi-square 2.6 probability 89.5%	Seldom
Sun trine Uranus	Chi-square 2.6 probability 89.5%	Seldom
Sun square the IC	Chi-square 2.4 probability 87.6%	Seldom
Mercury in the seventh house	Chi-square 2.2 probability 86.6%	Seldom
Jupiter sextile the Ascendant	Chi-square 2.0 probability 84.4%	Seldom
Venus rising before the Moon	Chi-square 9.6 probability 99.8%	Seldom
Descendant ruler opposition Uranus	Chi-square 4.8 probability 97.1%	Seldom
Ruler of the Descendant trine Uranus	Chi-square 4.8 probability 97.1%	Seldom
Venus out of bounds	Chi-square 4.8 probability 97.1%	Seldom
Ruler of the Descendant square the Sun	Chi-square 4.1 probability 95.7%	Seldom
Ruler of the Ascendant square Mercury	Chi-square 3.3 probability 93.0%	Seldom
Mercury out of bounds	Chi-square 2.9 probability 91.3%	Seldom
Uranus rising before the Moon	Chi-square 2.7 probability 90.0%	Seldom
Ruler of the Ascendant square Venus	Chi-square 2.4 probability 88.2%	Seldom
Disseminating Moon	Chi-square 2.1 probability 85.4%	Seldom
Mars intercepted	Chi-square 2.1 probability 85.0%	Seldom

Neptune played a big part in this research.

Mercury sextile the Descendant	Chi-square 4.1 probability 95.6%	Often
Moon opposition Neptune	Chi-square 3.5 probability 93.8%	Often

Moon sextile Neptune	Chi-square 2.3 probability 86.7%	Often
Mars trine Neptune	Chi-square 2.2 probability 86.6%	Often
Mercury conjunction Neptune	Chi-square 9.6 probability 98.8%	Seldom
Venus square Neptune	Chi-square 5.1 probability 97.6%	Seldom
Moon square Neptune	Chi-square 4.3 probability 96.2%	Seldom
Venus sextile Neptune	Chi-square 3.5 probability 94.0%	Seldom
Mercury trine Neptune	Chi-square 3.4 probability 93.3%	Seldom
Mercury square Neptune	Chi-square 2.6 probability 89.5%	Seldom
Saturn opposition Neptune	Chi-square 2.1 probability 84.9%	Seldom
Neptune conjunction the Midheaven	Chi-square 2.0 probability 84.4%	Seldom

Conclusion

I also researched planets in the natal first house and planets in the natal seventh house aspects to planets with a chart file of people who were married more than 15 years (not shown here). The study came out with 28 criteria with a high chi-square and probability. Twenty-two of these criteria were trines, sextiles, and positive conjunctions to these points and 6 of them had squares and oppositions. That proves that you need more positive aspects to the ascendant and the seventh house for longevity in the marriage.

I also found that Neptune and Uranus are very important in analyzing marriages, and that Aries, Mars and the first and seventh houses are quite active in multiple marriages.

The astrological research group that I founded in 2002 is the Astro investigators, or "Gators" for short. The group has grown to include an international membership that works with me doing scientific astrological research. Check all the research that the Gators have done at www.AstroInvestigators.com

Enki: The Sumerian God of Aquarius

By Jose Luis Belmonte

ABSTRACT: This paper first examines the attributes, characteristics, and images of the Sumerian god *Enki* (the Akkadian god *Ea*) to find similitudes with the attributes of Uranus. Then the paper explores the constellations that Babylonians associated with *Enki* to see if they have anything to do with Aquarius. Finally, the paper explores the origins of the Greek god Uranus and the possible transmission of *Enki* to Greece via Syria or via Phoenicia.

Introduction

During the Bronze age, Sumerians of the south of Mesopotamia (modern Irak) used irrigation channels and new tools to improve the efficiency of barley and wheat crops, and as a result, cities and civilization expanded; and linked to those new technologies was *Enki*, the wise and clever Sumerian god known as *Ea* in Akkadian.

On the other hand, modern astrology associates Uranus with rebellion, freedom, liberation, reform, revolution, the unexpected break up of structures; and with insight, intellectual brilliance, invention, creativity, originality, and individualism. Richard Tarnas refers to Uranus as the "cosmic trickster" because not only Uranus is responsible of sudden breakthroughs and liberating events but also it is linked to unpredictable and disruptive changes.[1]

Despite that technology in Sumer may appear to us today as primitive, the goal of this paper is to analyze who was the god *Enki*, focusing on its characteristics, images, and the constellations to which it was associated. Then the next goal is to compare *Enki* with the characteristics of Uranus, and to explore first whether Uranus had Near Eastern origins, and second if Uranus has attributes, images, and constellations in common with *Enki*.

The Sumerian God Enki

The Sumerian word *Enki* means "Lord Earth." The Sumerian word KI stands for "below," as the underground world. The earliest documents of the Old Sumerian period associated *Enki* with underground sweet waters, known in Sumerian as *Apsû*.[2] Thordkild Jacobsen translates *Enki* as "Lord of the soil," "Owner of the river," and "Owner of the *Apsû*," and argues that the power in water to fecundate the earth was considered akin with the engendering power of human semen; besides, since Sumerian used the same word for both semen and water, Jacobsen concludes that *Enki* was the power to fecundate.[3]

Enki's association with water does not facilitate the task of finding a Greek counterpart. A Babylonian myth known as *Athra-hasis* seems to provide a possible match. Before man had been created, the gods had had to work themselves, dig canals, and shoulder all the other hard tasks of irrigation agriculture. The three highest gods, *Anu*, *Enlil*, and *Enki* had divided the universe between them by lot. *Anu* got the heavens, *Enlil* (the warrior and their counselor) got the earth, and *Enki* received the underground waters and the sea.[4]

Such division into three reminds of Zeus, Neptune, and Hades dividing the world among themselves. Since *Enki* was a subterranean god of water, both Neptune, the god of the sea, and Hades, the lord of the Underworld, could be matches for *Enki*. Nevertheless, the character and the attributes associated with *Enki* rule out both Neptune and Hades.

On the other hand, Assyriologists associate *Ea* (*Enki*) with wisdom. According to Simo Parpola, one-third of all the extant epithets of *Ea* associated him with wisdom, while a further quarter of the epithets defined *Ea* either as creator god, or as lord of the *Apsû* or of the waters of life; finally, the rest of epithets emphasized on the greatness of the god.[5] Gwendolyn Leick describes *Enki as a god of wisdom, crafts and arts, intellectual faculties, and as the most approachable among the great gods; and notes that one of the literary epithets of Enki* was *nudimmud*, which meant 'who creates.[6] Those epithets of *Enki* somehow resemble the modern attributes of Uranus. *Enki* was a god of the Bronze age in which the new technologies were irrigation channels and new tools to improve the efficiency of barley crops in an area where the salty waters of the sea mixed with the sweet waters of the Tigris and the Euphrates. *Enki* seemed to be the wise and clever god associated with those new technologies. Thus, without hesitation, *Enki* could be considered the Uranus of Sumer.

In addition to that, *Enki* was depicted holding an eaglelike bird, a thunderbird called *Imdugud*. According to Jacobsen, the thunderbird signified the clouds rising from the waters, and its feet resting on an ibex was an emblem of sweet underground springs: the *Apsû*.[7] Another kind of depiction usually showed two streams flowing out either of *Enki*'s shoulders or from a vase he held. The image of those streams usually showed fish swimming. Those two streams most likely represented the Tigris and the Euphrates.[8] The symbol of *Enki* pouring water from a vase (or from his shoulders) seems to be a predecessor of the symbol of the water-pourer.

Water courses, such as rivers or streams, were depicted in Babylonian art as a pair of wavy lines; to current scholars those lines represented the banks of a river. In Cuneiform writing, the "a" sign not only shared the same image (a pair of wavy lines), but also signified water; Gavin White argues that the basic form of this sign evolved into the zigzag symbol currently used as a symbol for Aquarius.[9] *Enki* and Aquarius share the depiction motive of water being poured down; in the case of Aquarius water is poured down from a jar. Therefore, *Enki* matches Aquarius not only as water-pourer, but as a pair of wavy lines indicating the banks of a river which later became the zigzag symbol of Aquarius.

Babylonian Constellations Identified with *Enki*

The three highest Sumerian gods, according to many of the extant lists of the Mesopotamian pantheon, were *An*, *Enlil*, and *Enki*. The three cuneiform tablets of the mul.APIN, a compilation astronomical Babylonian knowledge up to 700 BCE, attested that the constellation of Aquarius was known to Babylonians as GU.LA.[10] Douglas Kidd argues that GU.LA ('waterman') belonged to an area of the sky known to Babylonians as "sea," and that the water-pourer might have been associated with the rainy season from the time it contained the winter solstice (ca. 4000-2000 BCE); Aratus of Soli (ca. 310 BCE-240 BCE) referred to that area of the sky as "water."[11] In Babylonian astrology the constellation of Aquarius was known as the "Great star."[12] According to Edith Porada, H. Gundel translated GU.LA as "The Great Constellation" or as the "Constellation of the Giant," and Walker and Hunger added a commentary on GU.LA which read "Lord of the Springs, EA."[13]

According to Porada, the history of Aquarius can be traced to a figure called *lahmu* or 'nude hero', which appeared in artwork during the third millennium BCE. It was in the Agade period (around 2340-2150 BCE) that the nude hero became allied with the water-god. In Syria and Anatolia, during the early centuries of the second millennium BCE, the iconography of the nude hero played an important role and even seemed to have taken over the role of the water-god himself. Porada surmises that the old Syrian figure was the prototype for the western Aquarius who originally poured out water from two vessels.[14] During the second millennium BCE, some wintertime constellations embodying aquatic symbolism became increasingly associated with

Enki.[15] Surprisingly, the origins of Aquarius might not be in Assyria or in Babylon, but in Syria and Anatolia (Turkey).

The second tablet of the mul.APIN divided the year into four astronomical seasons, each one containing three months: from XII to II the sun was in the path of *Anu* (wind and storm); from III to V the sun was in the path of *Enlil* (harvest and heat); from VI to VIII the sun was again in the path of *Anu* (wind and storm); and from IX to XI the sun was in the path of *Ea* (cold).[16] Thus, the path of the sun was a circle divided into four equal parts by the zones of *Anu*, *Enlil* and *Ea*. The zone of *Ea* was in the south, the zone of *Enlil* in the north, and the two zones of *Anu* were near the equator.[17] *Enki* was associated to an area which later would comprise Capricorn, Aquarius and Pisces.

Another section of Tablet II of the mul.APIN listed the dates of morning rising of stars and constellations. During the months related to *Ea* (from IX to X, from X to XI, and from XI to XII), PA.BIL.SAG (Sagitarius) rose in month IX; SHIM.MAH and *shi-nu-nu-tum* rose in month X, GU.LA (Aquarius), IKU (Perseus), and *Anunītu* (north east of Pisces) in month XI.[18]

In Babylonian astrology the constellation of Capricorn was known as the "Goat-Fish,"[19] a goat figure with a fish tail. According to Jeremy Black and John Greene, the Goatfish was identified not only with the *suhur-mashu* (Babylonian Capricorn) but also associated with the god *Ea* (*Enki*) which is suspected from the frequent iconographic juxtaposition with the ram-headed staff; Black and Green also suspect that the goat-fish could also be a magically protective type often coupled with the pictorial representation of the merman.[20] According to Kidd, the fish tail is justified by association of the goat-fish with the rainy season; the connection of Capricorn with water was reinforced by Aratus who included Capricorn in the "water" area of the sky.[21]

An extant Babylonian omen concerning the constellation of the Goatfish (Capricorn) read:

> If Mars rides the Goatfish: devastation of *Eridu*: its people will be annihilitated.[22]

Babylonian astrologers referred to the Goatfish as 'the Star of Ea', and deemed Mars as the "enemy star" and associated the planet to the god *Nergal*. Death, war, destruction, devastation, and plague were common attributes of *Nergal*.[23] Mars transiting through the Goatfish meant destruction to *Eridu*, a Mesopotamian city whose patron god was *Enki*. Since Mars, according to its nature, inflicts destruction, then *Eridu* was somehow linked to the Goatfish. In conclusion, the omen showed a connection between the constellation of the Goatfish and the god *Enki*.

The Greek God Uranus

Hesiod's *Theogony* has a significant description on the begetting of the Greek god Uranus:

> Verily at the first Chaos came to be, but next wide-blossomed Earth, the ever-sure foundation of all […] And Earth first bare starry Heaven (*Ouranos*) equal to herself, to cover her on every side, and to be an ever-sure abiding place for the blessed gods.[24]

Hesiod lists all the children begotten by *Gea* and *Uranus*. First came the Titans: *Ocean, Coeus, Crius, Hyperion, Iapetos, Theia, Rhea, Themis, Mnemosyne, Phoebe, Tethys*, and *Cronos* (Saturn) as the youngest of the group. Then came the *Cyclopes*: *Brontes* (Thunder), *Steropes* (Lightning), and *Arges* (Bright).[25] Finally came *Cottus, Briareus* and *Gyges*, who were immense, presumptuous, strong, and distinguished by the hundred arms which sprang forth from their shoulders.[26]

On the characteristics of Uranus, a great deal can be deduced out of his progeny. All sort of creations arose from him: titans, cyclops, or even terrible big children. All these render Uranus prolific in begetting new creations, and that is somehow in tune with the role of inventor and creator of disruptive new things (technologies) assigned by modern astrologers to Uranus.

Uranus hated all of his sons with *Gea* and hid them within the Earth (*Gea*) without letting them out. Next, *Gea* planned to castrate Uranus to liberate herself, her sons, and the world from Uranus' oppressive sexual embrace. Finally, Cronos (Saturn) carried out the castration using a sickle. Out Uranus' blood spilled on earth, the Erinyes and the Giants were born.[27]

> And when at first he had cut off the genitals with the adamant and thrown them from the land into the strongly surging sea, they were borne along the water for a long time, and a white foam rose up around them from the immortal flesh; and inside this grew a maiden.[28]

From Ouranos severed genitals came the foam goddess Aphrodite, whom Hesiod named 'genial' because she came forth from the genitals.[29] Uranus is still today associated with geniality, and it is not straightforward to find where that geniality came from. Hesiod associated geniality to an offspring of Uranus, Aphrodite, even though such geniality was related to the castration of Uranus.

On the other hand, Hesiod named Aphrodite 'Cyhterea' because she arrived at *Cythera* (an island between Crete and mainland Greece), and 'Cyprogenes' because she was born in Cyprus.[30] Hence Hesiod attested that Aphrodite came from Cyprus. The city of Kition (modern Larnaca) in Cyprus hosted from some time an important Phoenician colony. Besides, Aphrodite not only corresponded with her title *Ourania* to the Phoenician *Astarte* (Queen of Heaven), but also her relationship with Ouranos as bodily daughter matched that of the Babylonian *Ishtar* to *Anu* (Heaven).[31]

Furthermore, in Hesiod's *Theogony Iapetos* fathered *Atlas*, *Menoitios*, *Prometheus* (Forethought), and *Epimetheus* (Afterthought).[32] According to West, the name *Iapetos* was non-Greek and reminiscent of the biblical Japeth.[33] *Atlas* has been compared with the giant *Ubelluri* mentioned in 'Song of Ullikummi' from the Hurro-Hittite mythology.[34] *Prometheus* was, along with *Enki*, a great benefactor of mankind. West writes not only that Prometheus helped mankind to gain advantages and avoid hardships against Zeus' will, but notes that the role of Prometheus in Hesiod´s Theogony was "analogous to that of the crafty *Ea* (Sumerian *Enki*) in the Babylonian Flood narrative."[35] West adds that in the fifth century, when there is a Greek Flood myth, Prometheus appears to have had a similar part in it, and to have been assimilated to *Ea* in other ways.[36] In addition to that, Tarnas insists that the myths associated with Prometheus are more appropriate to describe the attributes of Aquarius than the myths associated with Uranus.[37]

The discovery of the first texts from Ugarit in 1929 and the publication of the "Kumarbi cycle" in 1936, incited many scholars to consider that perhaps Hesiod draw his *Theogony* from sources coming from the Near East. Additionally, scholars began to take seriously the assertion of Philo of Byblos that the Phoenician history of the gods was written by the time of the Trojan war, therefore antedating Hesiod.

The Phoenician Theogony: Philo of Byblos

Philo of Byblos, writing during the first to second century CE, composed a work called *Phoenician History* which unfortunately has not come down to us. However, Eusebius of Caesarea (260-340 CE), the church historian, preserved in his *Praeparatio Evangelica* significant quotes from Philo's *Phoenician History*.[38] Apparently, *Phoenician History* contained a Phoenician theogony disguised as a historical document. Philon translated the work of another author whom he called *Sanchouniathon* and who supposedly lived shortly before the Trojan war; *Sanchouniathon*, in turn, knew his Phoenician version form *Taautos*, the inventor of writing.[39] Following is an excerpt of the Phoenician theogony according to Philo of Byblos:

> (18) And so Kronos waged war against Ouranos and drove him from power, succeeding him in his kingship [...].

> (20) Time had passed when Ouranos, who was in exile, sent his maiden daughter Astarte, along with two of her sisters, Rhea and Dione, to kill Kronos through trickery, But Kronos captured them and made them, who were sisters, his lawful wives.

> (23) [...] Kronos has seven daughters with Astarte, the Titanids or Artemis. [...]

> (29) In the thirty-second year of his dominion and reign, Elos, that is, Kronos, trapped his father Ouranos in an inland location and, having him in his power, castrated himm in the vicinity of some

springs and rivers. This is where Ouranos was deified and his spirit was finished. The blood of his genitals dripped into the springs and the waters of the rivers. [...] [40]

The similitude of the *Theogony* of Hesiod with the fragments of theogony of Philo of Byblos is significant. Besides, in his cosmogony Philo presented a human figure named *Chousor* who, along with his brothers, were the inventors of iron-working and other crafts. On the other hand, the Ugaritic epics taught that *Chousor* was the Ugaritic craftsman god known as *ktr whss*. Philo´s figure and the god of the Ugaritic epics are identical in function except that the Ugaritic god does not perform magical acts in the epics. Several Ugaritic texts identify corresponding Ugaritic and Akkadian gods; in one of these *ktr whss* is equated with *Ea* (*Enki*).[41] This provides evidence of how *Ea* was transmitted to Ugarit where he was considered an inventor god, and how the Phoenicians turned him into a human.

The Hurro-Hittite Theogony

Some Hittite poems involved motifs of fights between different generations of gods, and the establishment of a new order in heaven. Those poems, based largely on Hurrian texts dating to the end of the Late Bronze Age (1200 BCE), have all in common the presence of a god called Kumarbi and, therefore, they are known as the "Song of Kumarbi" or as the "Kumarbi cycle."[42] Within the "Song of Kumarbi," there is a story called "Kingship in Heaven" in which a god called *Alahu* was defeated and banished to dark earth by *Anu* (the Babylonian Sky-god); *Anu*, in turn, was confronted and defeated by *Kumarbi* who bit off *Anus'* genitals and swallowed them. By swallowing the genitals, Kumarbi implanted inside of him three fearful gods, one of which was to become the king of Heaven.[43] In the "Song of Kumarbi," the succession of an Sky-god and the castration motive are very close to those in Hesiod's *Theogony*.

Conclusion

Enki was a god of wisdom, crafts and arts, intellectual faculties, and the most approachable among the great gods; one his literary epithets was *nudimmud*, which meant "who creates." Besides, *Enki* seemed to be the wise and clever god behind the new technologies associated with irrigation and with new tools for agriculture which propitiated the growth of cities and of civilization in Sumer. Without hesitation, *Enki* could be considered the Uranus of Sumer.

The symbol of *Enki* pouring water from a vase or from his shoulders seems to be a predecessor of the symbol of the water-pourer. Water courses, such as rivers or streams, were depicted in Babylonian art as a pair of wavy lines. Therefore, *Enki* matches Aquarius not only as water-pourer, but as a pair of wavy lines indicating the banks of a river which later became the zigzag symbol of Aquarius.

The constellation of Aquarius was known to Babylonians as GU.LA ("waterman") and belonged to an area of the sky known to Babylonians as "sea"; moreover, the Babylonians associated the constellation of GU.LA to the lord *Ea* (*Enki*).

Furthermore, it is very likely that Hesiod draw parts of his Theogony from sources of the Near East. In the Hurro-Hittite "Song of Kumarbi," the succession myth and the castration motive of an Sky-god are very close to those in Hesiod's *Theogony*. In addition to that, the similitude of the *Theogony* of Hesiod with the fragments of theogony of Philo of Byblos is significant. Therefore, it is very likely that some of the characteristics of Ouranos were imported from the Near East. In conclusion, the original figure behind the Greek Uranos might have been the Sumerian god *Enki*.

Endnotes

[1]Richard Tarnas, *Prometheus the Awakener: An Essay on the Archetypal Meaning of the Planet Uranus* (Woodstock: Spring Publications, 1995), pp. 11-2.
[2]Gwendolyn Leick, *A Dictionary of Ancient Near Eastern Mythology* (London: Routlegde, 1991), p.40.
[3]Thorkild Jacobsen, *The Treasures of Darkness: A History of Mesopotamian Religion* (New Haven: Yale University Press, 1976), p. 111.

[4]Jacobsen, *The Treasures of Darkness*, p. 117.

[5]Simo Parpola, "The Assyrian Tree of Life: Tracing the Origins of Jewish Monotheism and Greek Philosophy," *Journal of Near Eastern Studies*, Vol. 52, No. 3 (Jul., 1993), p. 177.

[6]Leick, *A Dictionary of Ancient Near Eastern Mythology*, p.40.

[7]Jacobsen, *The Treasures of Darkness*, p. 111.

[8]Jacobsen, *The Treasures of Darkness*, p. 111.

[9]Gavin White, *Babylonian Star-Lore: An Illustrated Guide to the Star-Lore and Constellations of Ancient Babylonia* (London: Solaria Publications, 2014), p. 157.

[10]B. L. van der Waerden, *Science Awakening II: The Birth of Astronomy* (Leyden: Noordhoff, 1974), p. 70.

[11]Aratus, trans. by Douglas Kidd, *Phaenomena: Cambridge Classical Texts and Commentaries vol. 34* (Cambridge: Cambridge University, 1997), p. 288.

[12]Ulla Koch-Westenholz, *Mesopotamian Astrology: An Introduction to Babylonian and Assyrian Celestial Divination* (Copenhagen: Museum Tusculanum Press, 1995), p. 207.

[13]Edith Porada, "On the Origins of Aquarius," in *Language, Literature and History: Philological and Historical Studies presented to Erika Reiner* (New Haven: American Oriental Society, 1987), p. 281.

[14]Porada, "On the Origins of Aquarius," pp. 284-9.

[15]White, *Babylonian Star-Lore*, p. 159.

[16]van der Waerden, *Science Awakening II*, p. 80.

[17]van der Waerden, *Science Awakening II*, p. 83.

[18]van der Waerden, *Science Awakening II*, p. 75.

[19]Koch-Westenholz, *Mesopotamian Astrology*, p. 207.

[20]Jeremy Black and Amthiny Green, *Gods, Demons and Symbols of Ancient Mesopotamia* (London: British Museum Press, 1998 [1992]), p. 93.

[21]Aratus, *Phaenomena*, p. 288.

[22]Hermann Hunger, *Astrological Reports to Assyrian Kings, State Archives of Assyria vol. VIII* (Helsinki: Helsinki University Press, 1992), [hereafter Hunger, *SAA 8*], report 104, lines r 5 ff.

[23]Koch-Westenholz, *Mesopotamian Astrology*, p. 191.

[24]Hesiod, *Theogony*, translated by Hugh E. Evelyn-White (Cambridge: Harvard University Press, 1974 [1914]), pp. 7-9.

[25]Hesiod, *Theogony*, 139, p. 15.

[26]Hesiod, *Theogony*, 147, p. 15.

[27]Hesiod, *Theogony*, 160-85, pp. 17-9.

[28]Hesiod, *Theogony*, 187-90, p. 19.

[29]Hesiod, *Theogony*, 195-200, p. 19.

[30]Hesiod, *Theogony*, 195-200, p. 19.

[31]Martin L. West, *The East Face of Helicon: West Asiatic Elements in Greek Poetry and Myth* (Oxford: Clarendon Press, 1999 [1997]), hereafter *The East Face of Helicon*, pp. 291-2.

[32]Hesiod, *Theogony*, 507-11, pp. 43-5.

[33]West, *The East Face of Helicon*, p. 289.

[34]West, *The East Face of Helicon*, pp. 295-6.

[35]West, *The East Face of Helicon*, p. 295.

[36]West, *The East Face of Helicon*, p. 295.

[37]Tarnas, *Prometheus the Awakener*, p. 13.

[38]Albert I. Baumgarten, *The Phoenician History of Philo of Byblos: A Commentary* (Leiden: Brill, 1981), p. 36.

[39]Carolina Lopez-Ruiz, *When the Gods Were Born: Greek Cosmogonies and the Near East* (Cambridge: Harvard University Press, 2010), pp. 94-5.

[40]Lopez-Ruiz, *When the Gods Were Born*, pp. 95-7.

[41]Baumgarten, *The Phoenician History of Philo of Byblos*, pp. 140, 166.

[42]Lopez-Ruiz, *When the Gods Were Born*, p. 91.

[43]Lopez-Ruiz, *When the Gods Were Born*, pp. 91-2.

Bibliography

Aratus, trans. by Douglas Kidd, *Phaenomena: Cambridge Classical Texts and Commentaries vol. 34* (Cambridge: Cambridge University Press, 1997).

Black, J., and A. Green, *Gods, Demons and Symbols of Ancient Mesopotamia* (London: British Museum Press, 1998 [1992]).

Baumgarten, Albert I., *The Phoenician History of Philo of Byblos: A Commentary* (Leiden: Brill, 1981).

Hesiod, *Theogony*, translated by Hugh E. Evelyn-White (Cambridge: Harvard University Press, 1974 [1914]).

Hunger, Hermann, *Astrological Reports to Assyrian Kings, State Archives of Assyria vol. VIII* (Helsinki: Helsinki University Press, 1992).

Jacobsen, Thorkild, *The Treasures of Darkness: A History of Mesopotamian Religion* (New Haven: Yale University Press, 1976).

Koch-Westenholz, Ulla, *Mesopotamian Astrology: An Introduction to Babylonian and Assyrian Celestial Divination* (Copenhagen: Museum Tusculanum Press, 1995).

Leick, Gwendolyn, *A Dictionary of Ancient Near Eastern Mythology* (London: Routlegde, 1991).

Lopez-Ruiz, Carolina, *When the Gods Were Born: Greek Cosmogonies and the Near East* (Cambridge: Harvard University Press, 2010).

Parpola, Simo. "The Assyrian Tree of Life: Tracing the Origins of Jewish Monotheism and Greek Philosophy," *Journal of Near Eastern Studies*, Vol. 52, No. 3 (Jul., 1993), pp. 161-208.

Porada, Edith, "On the Origins of Aquarius," in *Language, Literature and History: Philological and Historical Studies presented to Erika Reiner* (New Haven: American Oriental Society, 1987), pp. 279-291.

Tarnas, Richard, *Prometheus the Awakener: An Essay on the Archetypal Meaning of the Planet Uranus* (Woodstock: Spring Publications, 1995).

van der Waerden, B. L., *Science Awakening II: The birth of astronomy* (Leyden: Noordhoff, 1974).

West, M. L., *The East Face of Helicon: West Asiatic Elements in Greek Poetry and Myth* (Oxford: Clarendon Press, 1999 [1997]).

White, Gavin, *Babylonian Star-Lore: An Illustrated Guide to the Star-Lore and Constellations of Ancient Babylonia* (London: Solaria Publications, 2014).

Identifying Astrological Signatures of Modern Temperamental Components for Use in Working with Children's Charts

By Cornelia Hansen

ABSTRACT: How does analyzing a child's chart differ from an adult's? How does the astrologer consult with parents about their child? This article provides an overview of the author's forthcoming book, *Kidwheels: Understanding the Child in the Chart*. The purpose of the book was to answer these questions by providing a method for defining a child's temperamental type based on modern concepts in the field of child development and correlating it with the elements and qualities in the chart.

To accomplish this task, a sample of 43 children, aged two to four years, were used for observation. Each child was rated as low, medium or high on the eight components of temperament. Parent questionnaires were collected which detailed the child's behavior in infancy. Individual horoscopes were created from data on the birth certificates. Group charts of children rated either low, medium or high on a particular component, were examined for common astrological signatures.

It was found that each component had a distinctive astrological signature. From the components, patterns emerged which defined a temperamental "type." Each type has a behavioral style requiring special parenting strategies.

How can astrologers provide helpful insights to parents without delving too deep into predictive language that might cause undue concern? Temperament provides a safe terrain to assist parents in better understanding their child's specific needs and behavioral style. These insights can help ensure a positive course for the child's development.

Introduction

Children differ from each other at birth because of their temperaments. These differences affect parent responses during the course of development. The children also make contributions to their physical and social environments. Modern understanding of the course of the child's development transcends the conflict between "nature versus nurture" by viewing the process as a double-directed, interactive one. As such, in order for the developmental process to progress in a positive direction, parents need to understand the primary importance of their ability to adjust their parenting strategies to fit the temperamental needs of each child.

This paper presents a method for astrologers to use to meet this need. The key to this method is the use of the child's chart to determine the individual's temperamental "type" so that parents can be advised as to best parenting strategies which will fit the child's behavioral style and emotional needs. We begin with the historical background of ancient concepts of temperament and then explore the modern theories of temperament in child development and child psychiatry. We review the components of temperament and how they correlate with the elements and qualities of the natal chart to produce definite astrological "signatures". From a combination of the components, temperamental "types" emerge. Methods used in this study are reviewed as well as a list of available astrological literature addressing the topic of development.

The Nature of Temperament

Historical Background: One of the first systems to develop the concept of temperament was astrology using the 12 signs of the zodiac symbolized by the elements fire, earth, air and water along with the qualities of cardinal, fixed and mutable. The Greco-Roman physicians Hippocrates and Galen used bodily humors in relation to an individual's health and temperament as to whether they were balanced, in excess, or suffered a deficiency. They described the melancholic as negative and prone to sadness; the choleric individual as explosive and anger-prone; the sanguine person as positive and outgoing; and the phlegmatic person as slow to react.

Research on individual differences has persisted to the present day. One of the earliest modern studies of temperament was the New York Longitudinal Study (NYLS) conducted in the 1950s by Thomas, Chess and Birch (1968) who followed a group of infants up to young adulthood. In analyzing their data, they defined nine components of temperament: Activity Level; Rhythmicity; Approach versus Withdrawal; Adaptability; Emotional Intensity; Quality of Mood; Distractibility; Attention Span/Persistence; and Threshold of Response. They found that these components tended to cluster and form specific temperamental "types," such as the "Easy Child"; the "Slow-to-warm-up Child"; and the "Difficult Child." They also posited that the interaction of the child with his/her social and cultural environment was of primary influence on the course of development. They termed this process the "Goodness of Fit" model which had great influence on later research. Temperament has also been determined to be relatively stable over time, although it can be heightened or diminished or otherwise modified during the course of development. Temperament is also biologically based, probably inherited.

Definitiion of Temperament: Thomas, Chess, and Birch defined temperament as: "Thus, temperament is the *behavioral style* of the individual child—the *how* rather than the *what* (abilities and content) or *why* (motivations) of behavior. Temperament is a phenomenologic term used to describe the characteristic tempo, rhythmicity, adaptability, energy expenditure, mood, and focus of attention of a child, independently of the content of any specific behavior." (1968, p.4)

Simply put, as is used in this paper, temperament is an individual's behavioral style and characteristic way of emotionally responding.

Components of Temperament: The descriptions of each component come from Thomas, Chess, and Birch (1968, p.20-24).

1. Activity level describes the motor component; the level, tempo, and frequency with which a motor component is present in a child's functioning.

2. Rhythmicity describes the degree of regularity of repetitive biological functions such as sleeping, eating and bowel functions.

3. Approach or withdrawal describes the child's *initial response* to any new stimulus such as food, people, places and toys.

4. Adaptability describes the ease or difficulty with which the initial pattern of response can be modified.

5. Intensity of Reaction describes the energy content of the emotional response regardless of the direction, either positive or negative. For instance, some children are screamers while others whimper.

6. Threshold of Response refers to the level of a stimulus required to evoke a response. For instance, some children wake at the slightest sound while others can sleep through anything.

7. Quality of Mood describes the amount of pleasant, joyful, friendly behavior as contrasted with unpleasant, crying, unfriendly behavior.

8. Distractibility refers to the ability of environmental stimuli to alter the direction of ongoing behavior. For instance, a child engaged in an activity turns away from the activity when a person enters the room.

9. Attention Span/Persistence are related to each other. Attention span is the length of time a particular activity is pursued. Persistence describes the child's ability to maintain an activity in the face of obstacles in the environment.

Review of the Literature

Astrologers have written about child development and temperament in a variety of ways. Bruno and Louise Huber (1980) describe development from the perspective of the "age point" as it progresses through the houses at the rate of six years per house, each phase being influenced by the crosses and elements it experiences. Tamise Van Pelt (1985) combines concepts of Jung, Horney, and Freud along with Maslow, Perls and Sartre while writing about personality assessment. She uses birth chart patterns related to the four basic human needs of Growth, Security, Stimulus and Love. Liz Greene and Howard Sasportas (1987) approach development from an astrological-psychological perspective based largely on the work of Jung. The book deals with childhood development and the structure of the personality using archetypes to illustrate the process.

Bruce Scofield (2001) presents an astrological developmental model based on the planetary cycles and the imprints they make on the developing child. Dorian Giesler Greenbaum's book (2005) is the one book based on temperament alone. She studied 35 children in the fifth through eighth grades using the four temperamental types from Classical Greece (choleric, melancholic, sanguine and phlegmatic) and their various combinations. Stephanie Jean Clement (2007) uses astrological cycles of each planet to define the developmental process of the individual from birth to old age. (Note: There may be others missing from this list but these were the only ones studied for the purpose of this paper.)

Research Question

To combine astrology with modern thinking on temperament as established by the research in the fields of child development and child psychiatry, it was necessary to formulate a research question which could be answered by a study of preschool children. The questions were: Can the eight components of temperament be found in the horoscope by correlating them with the elements and qualities? Could patterns of these components describe a temperamental type?

Research Methods

The research study was carried out in a Los Angeles Unified School District's Early Childhood Education Center. Permission to do the study was granted by the Early Childhood Division. Fortunately, the birth data was available from the birth certificates which were on file at the Center.

Sample Group: The initial group of children to be observed was 43, ages two through four. The group included a variety of children who were white, black, Hispanic, Indian and Asian. The majority of families at the Center came from a low socioeconomic class since the purpose of the Center was to provide inexpensive child care for poor, working mothers. Since temperament is rooted in biology and is universal, this was not considered a problem in the sample.

Parent Survey: To gain permission for their child to be included in the study group, parents were given a detailed survey which covered general information about the family, including the health history of the child, form of discipline used in the home, habits, fears, birth order and questions related to temperament. Following the example of the NYLS, parents were asked to rate their child as low, medium or high on all the temperamental characteristics from infancy on. Sample questions included, for example:

How much did your baby move around? (check one)

_____Very active (constant motion, wiggled a lot, hard to dress, hard to keep covers on).

_____Low activity (quiet, stayed where placed, easy to change and dress).

_____Average (activity level varies).

How did your child react to new situations? For example, did it take him/her a long time to adjust to a bath, a new food, or a new person?

_____Adjusted quickly

_____Took a long time.

_____Average

All of them filled out the questionnaire and turned them in so the study could proceed.

Children's Natal Charts: The next step was to construct a natal chart for each child based on the data from the birth certificates and the parent surveys. All the surveys and charts were set aside for examination at a later time.

Observations: To gather data, observation sheets were developed to be used by myself and the staff which included another teacher and three teacher aides. (The one component of "Rhythmicity" was not included in this study because it was not considered significant unless it fell in the category of the "difficult child.") It should be noted that all of the staff were already well trained in making and recording observations of children since we were required by the District to fill out extensive reports on each child's developmental progress twice a year. These reports also contributed valuable information to the study.

Each staff member was familiarized with the concepts of each temperamental component and how they should be rated. The observation sheets each had a class list along with descriptions of the various ratings to be used in making their observations, the date observed, and any comments on what they had observed. For example, on the Activity Level sheet, high activity is described as "Spends majority of time running, climbing, bike riding, ball play, active games." Average was described as "Divides times between active play and quiet activities such as painting, puzzles, and manipulatives." Low activity was described as "Prefers quiet activities like coloring, puzzles, housekeeping corner, and table games.

The classroom was divided into several learning centers and each staff member was assigned to an area for a week. The same was true for the outside area. Over time, this procedure gave all of us an opportunity to observe multiple children during the various activities of the day. Observations also extended to small and large group activities, mealtimes, and entering and exiting the classroom. Each staff member met with their small group of eight to 10 children on a daily basis for small group learning and meals. This allowed them to develop a close relationship to and knowledge of the children in their group. Since we saw the mothers (or fathers) every day and had frequent conferences with them, knowledge of the parent/child interaction was gathered. Staff meetings allowed us to discuss their daily observations.

The collection of data continued over time until each child had been observed and rated on each temperamental characteristic.

Analzying the Data: Once all the data had been collected, examination of the natal charts of the children were examined for astrological connections to the observations along with the parent ratings. The procedure entailed selecting a temperamental trait, such as activity level, and grouping the children's charts by categories of low, medium or high. Examining the charts of a group, such as high activity level, was used to find the astrological signatures they had in common, giving numerical weights to each according to the frequency they occurred. To give one example, the High Activity Level includes the astrological factors (in descending order of frequency) Mars aspects to the Ascendant (30 pts,); Mars in Aries. Gemini or Sagittarius (25 pts.); Mars aspects to Sun,

Jupiter, Uranus (20 pts.); Sun aspects to Jupiter (10 pts.). Low Activity Level includes the astrological factors (in descending order) Mars in Leo, Scorpio, Taurus, Cancer, Pisces (30 pts,); Neptune aspects to the Ascendant (25 pts.); Saturn aspects to the Ascendant (20 pts.); Mars aspects to Neptune, Saturn (15 pts.); Bowl pattern (10 pts.). The same procedure was followed for every rated temperamental component.

Results

The data answered the research questions in a positive way. Each temperamental component was positively related to an astrological signature of five to six factors. The one exception was the component of Threshold of Response. This component was defined using the work of Marc Edmond Jones (1974) and Bob Makransky (2001) on "mental chemistry." This model proposes that perception and the response to it can fall into four categories based on the speed of the Moon and whether Mercury precedes or follows the Sun in the chart. The categories included two which are considered balanced: Type I is the *alert,certain* child who is quick to react but restrains his impulses; Type II is the *eager/deliberate* child who is slow to react but is flexible and adaptable. The two categories considered imbalanced are: Type III is the *alert, eager child* who is impulsive and impatient, more apt to make mistakes that later need correcting; Type IV is the *deliberate, certain* child is perverse and contrary and their responses tend to be too little, too late.

In order to organize the findings into a useful, numerical system, six worksheets were developed. The first worksheet presents a method for determining the astrological type (as opposed to the temperamental type), by adding the elements and qualities and examining other factors such as a lack or overemphasis of an element or quality, and compatible or incompatible combinations [(based on the work of Stephen Arroyo, (1975)]. Using the numerical weights given in each astrological signature, a child could be rated on each component. Combinations of components formed characteristic patterns which defined the temperamental type of the child, therefore answering the second research question in a positive way. For example, the Slow-to-warm-up Child would have the following characteristics: Low to moderate activity level; initial withdrawal responses to anything new; slow adaptability; negative mood; may or may not be distractible or persistent. The Difficult Child has these characteristics: Irregular body functions; negative responses to anything new; slow to adapt to new things; intense reactions; can be high or low in persistence.

A numerical scale was also developed for the purpose of rating the child on each component as very low, low, balanced, high or very high according to the level of points given. An example is the chart of Hayden (birth data from the birth certificate) who is a Cardinal/Water type and has the following ratings on the components: Quality of Mood negative; Approach/Withdrawal high with 65 Points; Adaptability low with 30 points; Intensity of Reaction mild with 35 points; Threshold of Response Type IV the deliberate/certain type; Low distractibility 25 points; High Persistence 70 points; Low Activity Level. Hayden's pattern of components fits with the Slow-to-warm-up Child.

Study of preschool children continued for many years, observing their behavior and examining their charts for astrological signatures. Charts from family, friends and clients were added. The total number of charts used for the book was 125. This system was found to be accurate and valuable when consulting parents about their child.

General Conclusions

A child's temperament is present at birth and stays relatively stable over time. Whether or not the child develops in a positive way is dependent on the interaction with the parents. Research has shown that when parents are made aware of the child's individual temperamental characteristics and needs, they can adapt their parenting strategies to provide as good a "fit" as possible while refraining from making value judgments on these differences. When the astrologer-counselor is facing parents to tell them about their child, temperament presents a safe terrain in which to discuss the child's individual characteristics and needs as well as presenting parenting strategies that will soothe, control and stimulate the child. Today, there are many books, articles and web sites that offer the astrologer much information on temperament, temperamental types and their characteristics, and the best strategies for parents to use in connection to them which can be passed on to the parents or by directing them to places where they can find this information.

The main purpose for which this system was developed was to assist the astrologer in helping parents raise happy, healthy children.

Bibliography

Arroyo, Stephen. *Astrology, Psychology & the Four Elements*, CRCS Publications, 1975.

Clement, Stephanie J. *The Astrology of Development*, American Federation of Astrologers, 2007.

Greenbaum, Dorian G. *Temperament: Astrology's Forgotten Key*, Wessex Astrologer, 2005.

Greene, Liz & Sasportas, Howard. *The Development of the Personality*, Samuel Weiser, 1987.

Huber, Bruno & Louise. *Life Clock*, Samuel Weiser, 1980.

Jones, Marc E. *Essentials of Astrological Analysis*, Trefoil Publications, 1960.

Makransky, Bob. "Mental Chemistry in the Birth Chart," *The Mountain Astrologer*, Issue #98, Aug/Sept, 2001:73-79.

Scofield, Bruce. *The Circuitry of the Self*, One Reed Publications, 2001.

Thomas, A., Chess, Stella, & Birch, Herbert G. *Origins & Evolution of Behavior Disorders*, Brunner/Mazel, 1968.

Van Pelt, Tamise. *Birth Pattern Psychology*, Para Research, 1985.

Degree Symbolism: Expect the Unexpected

By Michael Munkasey

ABSTRACT: About 20 different authors have made interpretations for each of the 360 zodiacal degrees. Quoting a degree interpretation has become, for some people, a way of providing astrological insight. But do individual degree interpretations carry meaning? This was the question I sought to address.

A study method was devised, 2,305 charts with accurate data were cast, and their planets arranged by degree. The expectation was for an even arrangement of bodies by degree. BUT that evenness is NOT what was found. What was found in the planet distribution by degree was randomness bordering on chaos.

Thoughts and insights about the implications of this randomness are provided in the article. As to the validity of individual degree interpretations? Those are left to the beholder.

Preface

According to Australian author Isidore Kozminsky, D. Sc., the twenty-first degree of Aries carries this idea:

"21° to 22° Aries: UNDER THE INFLUENCE OF THE PLANET MARS.

A pilgrim crossing himself in front of an ancient temple, an overdressed official and a soldier mocking at him.

[This] Denotes a devout person who will be subjected to many trials and taunts in life, but who will, by the strength of his faith, overcome them all. He comes from the masses rather than from the classes, and his sympathy will ever be with the struggling people of the nations. From officialdom and materialism he receives scant courtesy. It is a symbol of FAITH."

The Degrees

For more than a century, more than twenty different authors[1] have given their reasoning behind what each individual degree of the Tropical Zodiac means. A degree interpretation usually consists of an author's symbol or a mental image with a commentary of a few or more words explaining that image. Aside from traditional chart interpretation methods, quoting a degree image/interpretation when providing an astrological interpretation has created a following of its own.

"Degree symbolism" is a practice used to enhance traditional astrological insight. In an article or when meeting with a client, is it revealing or naïve to state something like, "The 11th degree of Gemini means … "? Using degree symbolism involves taking commentary by an author who has by psychic impression or other means, by self or with others, alone or explaining another's degree description, provided wording for what a particular zodiac degree means, regardless of any planet placement there.

One typical degree interpretation example, like this one for the sixteenth degree of Aries (15 Aries 00 to 15 Aries 59) from Charubel is: (Image) "A man with a sheaf of corn under one arm, and a sickle under the other. (Text): This denotes a hardworking person, one who will devote his energies to husbandry, and who will prosper by his labor. ..."

A few of these individual degree interpretations or symbols are more commonly cited, like the Sabian Symbols, created by the psychic Elsie Wheeler, and written down by Dr. Marc Edmund Jones in 1925. More than one author, like Dane Rudhyar in 1935, has expanded on these Sabian Symbols, thus adding to their notoriety. Many other degree interpretations are relatively unknown but are still there in astrological literature, asking for equal consideration.

To assume that there is an abrupt boundary separating an image energy description associated with a particular degree is seductive. But however enticing this may be, using individual degree symbols as part of an astrological practice raised questions for me.

Does each zodiacal degree carry its own energy? Have past authors and psychics been able to define and assign meanings that start and stop at degree boundaries? Is there a barrier between (say) 10 Cancer and 11 Cancer that cements an author's degree interpretation without crossing the degree boundary at 10 Cancer and 59 minutes? Is this interpretation fixed forever in time and space, or do the interpretations progress or precess along with the chart positions?

Horoscopic vs. Divinatory Astrology

Horoscopic astrology involves the use and interpretation of planets, signs, houses, aspects, etc., laid out in an astrological chart, and relates to Uranus. If degree interpretations derive from impressions, psychic or otherwise, then I would assign the use of such interpretations or explanations to Neptune and call this practice divinatory astrology.

Both approaches provide a certain usefulness for the astrologer. Horoscopic astrology has a much longer lineage, having been defined through many schools of application, e.g. horary, natal, or mundane. However, this tradition should not detract from using divinatory images. The English Astrologer Geoffrey Cornelius has lectured and written on the use of the chart as a divinatory tool[2], and you can reference his work and ideas if you wish to pursue his ideas.

Practitioners using divinatory astrology feel degree interpretations add meaning. Practitioners of horoscopic astrology rely on chart patterns and planet, sign, etc. interactions. One side feels an author's degree interpretations add counseling insight. The other side generally ignores such auxiliary commentary. These practices do not conflict with or negate the other, they simply offer differing points of approach and style. It is not that one side is right and the other is wrong; they exist as separate ideas and serve different purposes.

Did each of the 20+ degree interpretation authors create individual works or did they copy from each other? For the most part I think their works are individual efforts, except for those who comment on the degree symbolism of others.

Psychic Insight vs. Horoscopic Tradition

I wanted to determine if any one author's interpretation for a degree is more insightful than another author's interpretation for that same degree. With more than 20 different author degree descriptions to choose from, devising an approach to provide an answer, or even provide insight, into whether degree interpretation is a worthy practice seemed daunting.

Here are four author interpretation examples for one degree, the seventh degree of Libra. This degree was chosen at random:

Charubel: *An angel standing in mid-air, with a long scroll in his hand, unfolded. This scroll is covered with writing.*"

E. C Matthews: *SPEECH. Usually loquacious. Given to speculation. Paint, perfume or chemicals may play a part in the vocation. Not a very powerful degree. . . .*

Sepharial: *A naked man in the act of falling from a rock into a lake. It indicates a person of susceptible and weak nature, easily led away, and liable to be drawn to his destruction by the agency of the opposite sex. . .*

Ada Muir: *One who sacrifices self in the furtherance of a cause. Idealistic and romantic.*

Quotes like these from various author's interpretations of a degree's meaning have appeared in many articles and books. This idea of using word images like the above to help with chart interpretation is alluring and maybe it could add insight, but I wanted to know if such degree interpretations had or even added any validity to chart delineation.

Regardless of the author, use of these degree interpretations carries an attraction that seems irresistible. The idea persists that each 360th division of the ecliptic somehow carries an underlying meaning. The notion persists that there could be a precise "on-off" division at each degree boundary. To imagine that a particular degree, say 6 Taurus for example, has a meaning that transcends time somehow attracts the mind in a seductive way. Is there a meaning for 6 Taurus that stops at the degree boundary and then a meaning for 7 Taurus takes over? Are degree considerations valid within either the tropical or the sidereal zodiac?

But any attraction to degree symbolism is probably a Neptunian-type seduction, for reality then asks: "Does the implication of the transit of a planet like Mars through 12 Leo change with the degree interpretation?" Is transiting Mars in 12 Leo now something more than transiting Mars in other degrees? Does transiting Mars in 11 Leo or 13 Leo cast a different Mars from the one in 12 Leo? What happens if the twelfth degree of Leo is in exact aspect to another natal planet or point at, say, 12 Scorpio? How does that Moon placement or transit in 12 Scorpio affect personal reality due to the given degree interpretation for 12 Leo?

More important, which author's interpretation is more descriptive of the potential energies for a degree?

A central question is whether such degree interpretations could help add insight for a working counseling astrologer. A burr in my consciousness asked how could I approach doing this evaluation in a meaningful way?

A Straightforward Approach

There is an accepted scientific approach to systematically solving such problems or answering such questions. Such an approach ignores psychic insight, or perhaps psychic insight occurs first and then a pragmatic agenda to formulate that psychic insight takes over. That is what happened when I chose to address this question of degree interpretation validity. I formed an idea, and then laid out a straightforward approach.

The original question was whether an astrologer should interpret the patterns within a chart using planets, signs, etc., and augment this with individual degree meanings derived by psychic insight? Does the practice of horoscopic astrology deny or enhance a practice of using divinatory astrology?

How should one answer the questions: "Do individual degree interpretations have validity?" "Do the individual degree interpretations help or hinder a counseling astrologer in their work?" I looked to answer such questions in a way that would ease that burr on my consciousness.

Method

Suppose, I asked myself, if I were to cast a large number of charts, enough charts so that I could assume that there would be an average of six Suns per degree, six Moons per degree, six Jupiters per degree, etc. Since there are 360 zodiacal degrees, then I would need to cast at least 6 times 360, or, 2160 charts. Then after casting the charts I would need to sort planet positions by degree. Whew, a lot of work—day after day of chart casting, and then concentrated periods of planet sorting.

I sought accurate chart data and then selected and used 2,305 natal and event charts from mostly AA and A Rodden Ratings, as available from chart data information sources. The AA and A Rodden ratings ensure data accuracy within birth records. In the end, more than 80 percent of the chart data used had AA or A ratings.

I took pains to try and include a variety of occupations and not concentrate on (say) actors and actresses, people in the news, sports figures, etc. I purposely wanted representations from business, legal, military, the arts, etc., professions. With this large number of chart selections I was expecting to see an average of six Suns per degree, six Venus' per degree, etc. What I had as my expectation when I began was seeing order and consistency. I thought that if I found order and consistency then making an analogy to author degree interpretations could be done.

Planets only? No, as long as I was doing this work I also added in the four major Asteroids, Chiron, Moon's North and South Nodes, the chart angles (Ascendant, MC, Equatorial Ascendant, Vertex, etc.), New and Full Moons in a degree, eclipses in a degree, and various other such points or bodies. Sample 1 is provided to show a typical degree compilation, the degree of the natal U.S. Sun. This selection gave me a fairly large set of data to work with. Without a computer to sort and arrange the body of data this would have been a difficult task.

Measuring Deviation from Expectations

The discipline of statistics is considered a science and allows measurement of deviation from expectations. My expectation was to see about six Suns per degree, six Moons per degree, etc. Statistics is a practice that allows users to see if the data being examined has deviations from presumptions that are within or outside of normal expectations.

There are relatively straightforward statistics, like average and deviation from average, and more complicated statistical measures. If my expectations were to see six Suns per degree, then if a degree had two or fewer Suns, or 10 or more Suns, statistics would say that those degrees show statistical deviation.

Finding orderly planet and point consistency by degree placement I could then match author's individual degree interpretations to try and determine whether or not: one, some, many, or all author's descriptions added insight and helped with chart interpretation. I spent a good part of six years collecting, sorting, analyzing and formatting data from the 2,305 charts.

Significant and repetitive deviation of planet placement results in a degree was not something I expected to see. Throughout the many, many months of casting charts and sorting planet positions I was envisioning and expecting order and consistency with the way the planets arranged by degree. In the beginning I could not foresee that a random arrangement of people and event planet positions might occur.

By the end however I did not see expected consistency. I saw deviation bordering on chaos in the way planets arranged themselves by zodiacal degree.

The results of how the planets and chart angles arranged by degree did NOT come out as expected. I had expected to see an average of about six Suns per degree, six Moons per degree, etc. But this is not what happened.

Uranus—The Unexpected

It should have been obvious, and in hindsight it was. But I had to go through years of sorting, correlating, and formatting data before I realized that astrological planet placement by degree results were not Saturn fixed and consistent, but Uranus scattered and uneven. In the end I did not see the expected six planets per degree, as I saw some consistency here and there along with a lot of deviation.

What to make of this?

After arranging the planets, etc., by degree, I saw that some degrees had more Suns than expected and some had fewer Suns than expected. The same distributions happened for the other planets and points. *There was no even or symmetrical distribution by degree for any of the planets or points from these 2305 people and events.* Some degrees had ten or more Suns, while others had only two or less Suns.

If six is the expected number for say a Moon in any one zodiacal degree then having only two or fewer placements represents (for me) a statistical low, while having 10 or more placements represents (for me) a statistical high. Statistical highs and lows could occur at random in life, every now and then, but if they occur too often, too many times in a data sample, then the data is telling us something needs to be investigated and explained.

A Change of Direction

The placing of planets from the 2,305 chart basis by degree results showed there to be an unusual distribution of planet or point positions in virtually every zodiacal degree. So the thrust of investigating degree commentary appropriateness changed to one of investigating planet and point degree count anomalies.

Asking if author degree interpretations provided were helpful in any way was question one. But far more interesting after seeing the results of planet distribution by degree was to address question two, which is why planets and points did not lay out in consistent and expected numerical patterns.

Every degree of the 360 zodiacal degrees but one, 28 Gemini, showed some statistical bias or anomaly for one or the other of the planets or points. Every degree but one, 28 Gemini, has at least one or more low or a high statistical bias for at least one of the planets or points. That is, 359 degrees showed at least one bias, and one showed without any bias. That result in and of itself in a statistical way shouts that something needs to be further investigated. Is 28 Gemini the only "normal" degree? Or, is 28 Gemini the most "deviant" degree?

Here is what a statistical bias looks like for one typical degree, selected at random. Taking the fourteenth degree of Scorpio as typical (13 Sco 00 to 13 Sco 59), the tabulation results show that for the low side where six is the expected number there are only two Sun, two Uranus, and two Chiron placements. On the high side where six placements are the norm, we find 12 Jupiter, 12 Pallas, and 10 North Node placements. For this degree then there are six statistical anomalies. Some degrees show as many as a dozen or more statistical anomalies, and some (a few) have only one. What does this mean?

Why? These 2,305 people or event charts chosen had achieved some notoriety, they had historically available references about their lives and life events available online and in references. Could there be a bias involved by choosing such samples?

Talent vs. Occupation

The question of occupational importance by degree also arose; that is, do certain degrees attract certain occupations? There is *nothing* in the effort I could find to support this idea. Occupations are one thing, but talents and how these are used in life despite occupation are quite another. What I found is that chart patterns show talents and potentials, not occupations. The chart shows the "gifts" you have chosen for yourself for this life. How you choose to use and develop those "gifts" is up to you.

Through study I found that a chart shows both strong and weak energies, and these can be nurtured to develop talents. It is then up to the person having those chart energies to put those stronger energies to the wisest and most comfortable use toward whatever talent, path or occupation in life they chose. Those who are most successful and happy in life are those who discover their strong talents and put them to wise usage. Those who have trouble in life are those who try to take any of the weaker chart energies and work to enhance or augment those.

The Questions Continued

The uneven planet distributions found raised an additional question about whether individual degree interpretations were based on anything other than psychic impressions. Is there something about a particular zodiacal degree that attracts or repels famous or infamous people or event placements? Did any of the degree interpretations account for or anticipate asymmetrical planetary placements?

Why was there an asymmetrical set of distributions? I could expect some distortion for the far outer planets because most of the people and events chosen had births over the past 120 or so years when the 2,305 sets of data were available. The outer planets like Neptune and Pluto would not have made a complete planetary revolution during that time, so their appearance in a zodiacal degree could be influenced by their orbital characteristics. I ignored and did not consider the impact of Neptune and Pluto deviations to achieve more credible and statistically viable results.

Other bodies like the asteroids and Chiron have more elliptical orbits and as such tend to stay in one degree more than in another degree. Still, these considerations could not account for the results obtained, and which are shown in accumulated compilations. Only 2,259 of the charts selected had Lilith or chart angles included, due to various factors like the date of the chart (e.g., before 1,700), potential inaccuracy of the birth data, etc.

What happened as the results were compiled was that my focus shifted from "Do degree symbolisms carry meaningful insights?" to, "Why are there asymmetrical planetary or chart angle distributions within degrees?"

New Questions

I asked: "Do these asymmetrical distributions carry implications for the many people who have a planet in a degree with a low or a high distribution?" For example, the degree of 2 Aquarius shows 12 Moon placements (six expected), a statistical high; while the degree of 23 Aquarius shows one Moon placement (six expected), a statistical low. That person is the actress Glenn Close. People with their Moon at 2 Aquarius include the artist Balthus, actor Steve McQueen, entrepreneur Aldo Gucci, basketball coach Phil Jackson, actress Vicki Carr, author Machiavelli, etc. These people show a wide range of talents and interests.

Based on these results if your natal Moon is in 23 Aquarius does this mean you have a diminished chance at achieving notoriety? Does this imply that a person with a natal Moon at 23 Aquarius has more difficulty relating to their Moon energies? Does a person with their natal Moon at 23 Aquarius have to work harder than normally expected to align with Moon traits like compassion, emotional response, family needs, rhythm, etc.? Or do they tend to the more negative side of the Moon's energies, like increased fickleness, uncertainty, hesitation, etc.?

To help me understand any potentially uneven distribution I compiled a list, by degree, of which planets or points, had statistically low or statistically high placements. By statistically low I took two or less placements; by statistically high I took ten or more placements. These results are quite detailed and lengthy (many pages) and not included here, but can be made available outside of this work.

For instance, in the ninth degree of Gemini, out of 2,305 people and events, there is only one Sun placement—where six Sun placements are expected. That person is Walt Whitman, the poet, whose Sun is at 8 Gemini 55. The first degree of Gemini goes from zero degrees and zero minutes to zero degrees and 59 minutes. The ninth degree of Gemini goes from 8 degrees and zero minutes of Gemini to 8 degrees and 59 minutes of Gemini. In the ninth degree of Gemini there are 15 Uranus placements, where only six would be expected. There are 10 Midheaven placements where only six would be expected. Why is this so? Is there something special about this degree as related to the MC or Uranus? Or is there some bias in the 2305 charts selected? Does the high Uranus bias for this degree affect the person or events with a Sun, or Mercury, etc., placement in this degree

Why out of 2,305 sets of chart data was there only one Sun in the ninth degree of Gemini? The implication from this is that there is some other degree where there are a large number of Suns to offset the one Sun in the ninth degree of Gemini. There are 2,305 Sun positions in this study to be distributed into 360 degrees, which calls for an average of about six Suns per degree—if the distribution of those Suns is even, consistent and normal.

The fourth degree of Libra (three degrees and zero minutes to three degrees and 59 minutes of Libra) for instance, has 14 Sun placements. Is that an offset degree to the ninth degree of Gemini, or is that just a spurious circumstance? Do people whose chart data has been selected and used tend more to three degrees of Libra Sun placements than to eight degrees of Gemini Sun placements? Is this even a valid question to ask?

I did take some pain to try and ensure that the occupations within the 2,305 sets of chart data were not skewed to actors and actresses, sports figures, etc. That is, I deliberately sought out accurate chart data for scientists and business people, etc.—although from the 30,000 or so sets of chart data provided as a pool, there are not as many in those professions as in some others like actors or actresses.

Analysis by Zodiacal Sign

An Excel spreadsheet created for showing the counts of "irregularities" within degrees by zodiacal sign is too large to show in this format. The spreadsheet shows which zodiacal sign, by planet, has a statistical abnormality, high or low, for the 2,305 test cases used. A statistical abnormality is defined as a one standard deviation hit or more from expected. Below is a more readable account by columns of those spreadsheet results.

From this accounting if a sign has a "high" anomaly, then people or events with the planet in that Sign were more likely to be chosen as examples for this study. That is, they had achieved some degree of historical notoriety. For a "low" listing, then people or events with the planet in that sign were less likely to have been chosen for this study. The implications of this are that planet-sign placements in the "high" column are more likely to indicate some degree of notoriety.

Planet	Signs High	Signs Low
Sun	Taurus, Capricorn	Scorpio, Sagittarius
Moon	Aquarius	Aries, Scorpio, Sagittarius
Mercury	Capricorn	Taurus, Cancer, Virgo
Venus	Virgo, Aquarius	Leo, Libra, Capricorn
Mars	Gemini, Leo	Capricorn, Aquarius, Pisces
Jupiter	Scorpio, Sagittarius	Aries, Taurus, Gemini
Saturn	Scorpio	Aries, Cancer
Uranus	Taurus, Gemini, Pisces	Scorpio
Neptune	Leo, Virgo, Libra	None

Pluto, due to its long orbital cycle, did not make for a good example

Planet	Signs High	Signs Low
North Node	Gemini	Capricorn
South Node	Sagittarius	Cancer
Ceres	Aquarius	Cancer, Virgo
Juno	Capricorn, Aquarius, Pisces	Gemini, Cancer, Leo
Pallas	Scorpio, Sagittarius	Taurus, Gemini, Cancer
Vesta	Taurus, Gemini, Cancer	Virgo, Scorpio, Sagittarius
Chiron	Aries, Taurus	Virgo, Libra
Lilith	Gemini, Leo, Virgo	Aquarius, Pisces
Ascendant	Leo, Virgo, Libra, Scorpio	Aries, Pisces
Midheaven	Gemini, Sagittarius	Libra, Scorpio, Pisces
Equatorial Asc.	Cancer, Sagittarius	Aries, Aquarius
Vertex	Virgo, Scorpio	Aries, Aquarius, Pisces
Co-Ascendant	Virgo, Scorpio	Aries, Taurus, Pisces
Polar Asc.	Virgo	Aries, Taurus, Aquarius, Pisces

A final cross-summation shows that Virgo and Libra planet placements tend for "high" inclusions, while Taurus, Aquarius and Pisces planet placements tend for "low" inclusions in this study about historical notoriety.

In one way what these results are saying is that if you have a Sagittarius Sun, then the chance of your chart data being selected for this study is low, but if you have a Capricorn Mercury then the chance of having your chart data selected for this study is higher than average.

Of the 2,305 sets of chart data, there are a statistically low number of Aries, Scorpio, and Sagittarius Moons, and a statistically high number of Aquarius Moons. The natal U.S. chart and this author have an Aquarius Moon. Perhaps this is an author bias in data selection or influence within the U.S. populace for an Aquarius Moon selection. I can't ignore Leo: Leo shines with a Mars placement in Leo, but not a Venus placement in Leo.

Comments and Opinions

I really don't have any specific answers or conclusions. I remain baffled as to why there is such uneven distribution of the placement of planet and point results by sign, but I can provide comments and opinion.

The chart data used implies there is some notoriety associated with the selected person or event. Perhaps more than the degree interpretations there is something within each degree that attracts or repels notoriety. Perhaps this is a part of the universal randomness that happens within life.

The Universe, as represented by an ecliptic divided into 360 equal degree divisions, does *not* appear to be a steady or consistent place. It exists while imposing and generating chaos, upheaval, change and randomness, and that is part of what makes life interesting. There are a complicated but consistent set of cycles to daily life and movement, and historical perspective.

Examples include: Sun spot cycles, Moon phase cycles, financial cycles, production cycles, birth cycles, migration cycles, and war cycles. Perhaps this imposed cyclical factor is a way of proving validity for astrology.

Cycles are a generally accepted scientific phenomenon describing life, while astrology is not so accepted. But here astrology is showing a yet to be understood distribution of planets or angles of a cyclical/random nature. What other discipline is there beside astrology that could take this randomness and begin to ask reasonable questions or offer some explanation?

There is a "Great Year" of about 25,920 years shown by the movement of the Earth's axis through a wobble cycle. This is the time in years it takes for the wobbling Earth's axis to return to its starting position. At this time "science" does not have an answer for this precessional movement. This movement shows that each degree of the zodiac moves backward in about 72 calendar years.

Dividing that 25,920 year cycle by 12, for the 12 signs of the zodiac, you get 2,160 years for one Age, such as the Age of Pisces or the Age of Aquarius. These Ages are referred to in historical texts and move backward through the signs of the zodiac. Each Age lends a distinctive "color" to the 2160 years within that part of the precessional cycle. Investigating authors[3] have noted that an unrecognized binary interaction between our Sun, Sol, and another stellar body, most likely Arcturus, could account for this movement of Ages. Such binary pairings between two sun-like bodies are the norm in our Universe.

The 2,160 year value for an Age is an approximation. There is no definition for either the length of an Age or when an Age starts or ends. Ages may overlap, and as the energy for one Age is waning the energy for another could be building. During time periods when Age boundaries approach there may be energies associated for both the old and the new Age.

Taking the 2,160 year value for an Age, and subtracting one year, to get 2,159 years yields a number, as David Wilcock[4] describes in his book, *The Synchronicity Key*, which is evenly psychology and finance as showing important psychological and developmental divisions of life. As David Wilcox also notes, dividing the Age number 2,160 by four you can get close to a year span of 539 years, which other authors and historians have shown to occur within repeating historical cycles[5]. That is, almost to the day, events from 539 years ago seem to cause the same type of event to repeat on a regular cyclical basis. Refer to Chapter 19 in his book for more information.

These divisions of time have been investigated and generally accepted as being a part of existence. There are Ages, there are noticed and repeating cycles, and there are anomalies within time that cause people to stop and evaluate the meaning for them of progress and personal development.

Insight, Perhaps

What the chart data degree anomalies could be showing then is that life is not an orderly and peaceful progression. The Age factor and the repeating historical events show this. There are a purposeful set of "bumps," if you will, within time and space to making personal and spiritual progress for humanity a challenge, and not a given. Maybe life is not expected to proceed in an orderly manner, but in a way to show each of us that we have to constantly grow and adapt to life's changes, challenges and circumstances. Perhaps what we each need to learn is that it is not "others" who cause change, but it is ourselves reacting to the imposed outer energies and forces of the Universe which cause life to move on.

Perhaps this is what the unexpected distribution of statistical highs and lows by degree is showing us. Life is not supposed to be orderly and even; it seems to be designed to impose stops and starts that can cause us to pause, take note, and evaluate before progressing with personal development. The uneven placements shout to say that we need to be prepared for the unexpected from life, and that "norms" do not provide a platform for pause while expecting peace.

Degree Meanings

Do the degree interpretations by the various authors "work"? I leave that for each individual to answer. To me every once in a while an interesting hit is made by an author's degree interpretation that seems to validate their statement for degree results, but this does not "prove" that degree statements in general are helpful and belong with astrological interpretations. They may remain useful to a part of the mind, but may not to the person insisting on traditional chart interpretation.

Degree symbolisms are not a part of traditional horoscopic astrology. Interpretation of the planets, signs, etc., within chart patterns can often tell a traditional astrologer much more than a psychically inspired degree symbolism description and meaning. Individual degree symbolism and commentary remain an interesting part of divinatory astrology, and as such retain usefulness there. Horoscopic astrology remains aligned with Uranus, while divinatory astrology remains aligned with Neptune.

Both horoscopic and divinatory astrology carry validity for their practitioners. Each in their own way show that life and the progression of life on a daily basis is founded on change, even disorder at times. Expect the unexpected is what conclusion can be drawn from this study, and be ready to adapt as necessary to move forward with your life.

Modern Science

Cosmology is an accepted academic study of how the Universe works, was formed, and is developing and evolving. There are many brilliant academics and others working on developing cosmological theory. Out of these studies, which today are still incomplete, comes string theory, or M-theory, theories that hold there could be at least fourteen dimensions within space and time, of which we as humans are only capable of sensing three—up and down, left and right, back and forth. But the mathematics behind their explanations indicates that *if* such extra dimensions exist, then a more acceptable mathematical order to cosmic evolution is described. By some interpretations there may be an infinite number of added dimensions, not just fourteen.[6]

Accepting extra, even an infinite number of dimensions and universes within the reality of our existence, brings mathematical equations that balance and better explain the cosmos and its origin and evolution. If there are an infinite number of dimensions to space and time, then maybe the degree interpretation authors and creators access, even create, their own unique space and time situations/dimensions with their degree descriptions.

Maybe that is what asymmetrical degree distributions are showing. Maybe each author creates a reality for their view of astrology, and their followers then enhance or detract from that reality by their application of the original author's ideas. Thus there may be more than one astrology; in fact there may be an infinite number of astrologies that can be considered. Each individual and published degree interpretation may add content, and at the same time create an alternate dimensional universe for that astrology.

Horary astrology is a practice that takes an asked question, and using the date, time and place the question is asked erects a chart drawn using that data. There are unique and consistent rules for judging Horary charts. Many books and authors have written on how to interpret horary charts. Thousands and thousands of valid horary chart explanations and answers to questions exist. Learning good Horary interpretations takes much practice and skill. But the answers received can be enlightening. It is my opinion that horary astrology could not work if the Universe was a consistent and orderly place. Horary work needs the randomness of time and space.

One insight from examining degree distributions could be that we continually create and recreate our own unique reality through our thoughts and actions. As our lives move on we are constantly challenged to grow and develop as persons. In other words astrology is not a static practice, but it invites personal development and expansion to fit in with the circumstances and times.

Astrology seems to be formed from a living field of consciousness or energy that grows and adapts to each person's needs or expectations. The thoughts and idea of practitioners, as well as skeptics, form their basis from this field of consciousness. Astrology should not be thought of as a one-dimensional thing, but as a living entity that adapts and changes to each user's time, need and culture.

Endnotes

[1] Here are some of the degree interpretation sources used in this study in their date of publication order. Many of these works are out of print and can be difficult to locate.

The Degrees of the Zodiac Symbolised, Charubel (with Sepharial's comments)
The Degrees of the Zodiac Symbolised, La Volasfera (with Sepharial's comments) (1898 ?)
The Sabian Symbols in Astrology, Marc Edmund Jones (1925)
An Astrological Mandala," Dane Rudhyar (1935)
Zodiacal Symbology and its Planetary Power, Isidore Kozminsky (1936 ?)
The Degrees of Life, Chandra Dhi Manthri (1938)
The Three Hundred Sixty Degrees of the Zodiac, Adriano Carelli (?)
Astrology for the 21st Century, David Cochrane (2002)
Degrees of the Zodiac, Donna Walter Henson (?)
Zodiac Degrees, Peter J. Weber (?)
Fixed Stars and Degrees of the Zodiac Analyzed, E. C. Matthews (1947)
The Degrees of the Zodiac Analyzed, Ada Muir (1967)
Degrees of the Zodiac, Esther V. Leinbach (1973)
Degrees of the Zodiac Magnified, Mohan Koparkar, Ph. D. (1976)
Degree Areas of the Zodiac, Carol Rushman (1988)
360 Degrees of Wisdom, Lynda Hill (2004)
Medical Correspondences to the Degrees, Reinhold Ebertin, as translated by Mary L. Vohryzek (1964 ?)

[2] *Moment of Astrology, Origins in Divination*, Geoffrey Cornelius; 2005; ISBN-13: 978-1902405117

[3] *Lost Star of Myth and Time*, Walter Cruttenden; St. Lynn's Press, 2006, ISBN 0-9767631-1-7

[4] *The Synchronicity Key*, David Wilcock, Dutton Publishers, 2013; ISBN 978-0-525-95367-8

5e.g., Anatoly T. Fomenko, *Empirico-Statistical Analysis of Narrative Material and Its Application to Historical Dating, Vol. 1*; Kluwer Academic Publishers, New York, 1994; also, following volumes.

6A very readable layman's book on the complicated subject of Cosmology and String Theory is *The Elegant Universe*, 1999, 2003. 2010 by Brian Greene; W. W. Norton & Co., New York, 2010; ISBN 0-393-05858-1

Monomoiria, a Lost Essential Dignity...?

By Ancuta Catrinoiu

ABSTRACT: Despite the vast research of Hellenistic astrology, little is known about the *monomoiria*, meaning assigning each degree of a zodiacal sign one of the seven heavenly bodies. It is the objective of this study to present an understanding of *monomoiria* by analyzing ten (10) birth charts of twins. It is a qualitative research that seeks to understand the underlying reasons and nuances of how twins can become completely different persons, while having almost the same birth chart, the same angles and so on. How can astrology account for two identical charts bringing different outcomes? This study covers one of the possible explanations, which is related to *monomoiria* of either the Ascendant, Midheaven, Moon or Part of Fortune in the birth chart of twins. In addition, there could be also other parts or lots which change within minutes in a chart, but I have selected only the one mentioned above, which together with the Moon, Midheaven and Ascendant brings a deep and complex understanding of a chart. Therefore, in order to have very accurate data I have selected only birth charts that have either AA or A Roden rating; all birth charts being selected from www.astro.com. The first part of the paper (Introduction) outlines the theoretical principles of monomoiria doctrine as explained in Paulus Alexandrinus's *Introductory Matters*. A connection with the ancient Egyptian horoscope recently discovered is also made, since the horoscope presents monomoiria of planets. Part I contains information regarding the calculation of monomoiria and Part II presents the astrological meaning of it. Last part, part III presents practical examples using birth charts of famous twins.

Introduction

The *Monomoiria* represents the 360 individual degrees of the sky in Hellenistic astrology. Each was associated with a planet.

The concept was introduced by Vettius Valens's *Anthologies Book IV* (150-175 AD) and Paulus Alexandrinus's *Introductory Matters* written in 378 AD.

Based on Paulus's Introduction we know there were two types of *Monomoiria*, one by sign explained in Chapter 5 and the other one by trigon/triplicity which is discussed in Chapter 32.

Valens uses *Monomoiria* as a method for the distribution of the time-lords according to the seven spheres and this seems to operate under the same rule that Paulus gives for the *Monomoiria* by sign.

However, there are even earlier references to *Monomoiria* by sign, as we know that Vetius Valens attributed it to the 1st century astrologer Critodemus, who was a Greek astrologer: "One of the earliest known authors on astrology."[1] His dates are uncertain but 1st century AD at the latest.

It might be also be the case that the *Monomoiria* doctrine goes back to the ancient Egyptians. The connection could be related with the new discovery of an ancient Egyptian horoscope on a papyrus dating back to 319 AD,[2] a period when Paulus Alexandrinus must have lived, also in Egypt. Among technical information regarding the dignities, the length of life, the lots and the master of nativity, the papyrus also mentions *Monomoiria*, calculated in the same manner as Paulus did, which indicates that it was an important technique for analyzing a natal theme.

Moreover, in Paulus's work the doctrine was presented right after the description of the twelve signs, the terms and faces (decans) of the signs, which might imply that *Monomoiria* used to be an essential dignity that the ancients followed.

Part I, How is Monomoiria calculated?

Paulus Alexandrinus explains that in order to find the planetary ruler of the *Monomoiria* of a degree by sign, one starts with the ruler of that sign:

"The single degree division of the stars must be distributed following their position in the heptazone, assigning the first degree to the star whose sign it is, but the second to the one after it in the order of the heptazone, and so on until you come down to the degree which the star holds, including the minutes as one degree." – Paul of Alexandria, Introduction to Astrology translated from Greek by James Herschel Holden, M.A, Fellow of American Federation of Astrologers.

That star (planet) will rule the first degree of the sign. Thus, for Libra, Venus is the ruler of the first degree. The process continues with the planets in Chaldean order (Saturn, Jupiter, Mars, Sun, Venus, Mercury, Moon) through the rest of the degrees of Libra—the second degree's ruler being Mercury, the third degree's Moon, and so on. At the end of Chapter 5, Paulus also presents the Table of *Monomoiriai* for all the 30 degrees of the twelve signs.

Unfortunately, nor the text nor the Egyptian horoscope nor other horoscopes give us any information regarding the use of the single-degree distribution (*Monomoiria*).

However, in Scholium 15,[3] there is mentioned that *Monomoiriai* (plural form of *Monomoiria*) can connect (by "sympathy") two signs otherwise unrelated to each other, such as Taurus and Libra (both ruled by Venus) which sympathize with each other, whether they are disjunct and averted from each other. It continues on mentioning that "signs that are *homozones* of each other and are lessening their evil, which is when they are found to be in their own domiciles or when are equal rising or configured by aspect. This table of the *Monomoiriai* is useful not only for the applications of the stars by body but probably also for the applications by aspect. For application is twofold—by aspect or by body. For separations of the stars, I do not think this table is useful."

Part II, Astrological Meaning of Monomoiria

The Greek word *Moiria* had two meanings:

1. Degree or apportionment—a standard term for the division of the zodiac in Hellenistic writings and

2. Fate, as it is the singular of *Moirai*, incarnations of destiny, primordial deities (**Clotho**, the spinner, **Lachesis**, the allotter, and **Atropos**, literally "unturnable" but metaphorically "inflexible" or "inevitable," i.e. death). *Moira* is a power acting in parallel with the gods, and even the gods could not alter what was ordained. The ancient Greek writers call this power *Moira* or Ananke[4]. The concept of a universal principle of natural order has been compared to similar concepts in other cultures like the Vedic Rta, the Avestan Asha (Arta) and the Egyptian Maat.

"Moira means that part of the zodiac which we call "a degree," but it more commonly means that portion or allotment which is one's fate."[5]

As Robert Schmidt mentions in the Translator's Preface of Paulus's Introductory Matters, "from the frequency with which it occurs in the astronomical sections of Greek astrological writings, one might argue that

Ancuta Catrinoiu | Monomoira, a Lost Essential Dignity

Moiria had come to simply mean a division of the zodiac, and could be safely translated as "degree." However, Paulus's work is too full of word play on this term and the related vocabulary of allotment, apportionment to think that he was not constantly reflecting on its astrological meaning."

Thus, we may deduct that the significance of *Moiria* was that a certain "fate" was apportioned to a degree. *Monomoiria* was seen as there was a "familiarity" among planets in degrees having the same "fate" because they were interconnected. In addition, *Monomoiria* was useful because it could modify different relations between signs.

In the end of the fragment the commentator mentions that the table of *Monomoiria* is worthwhile only for applying aspects of planets, for the separating aspects being useless.

We can conclude that the Hellenistic astrology was concerned with the symbolic patterns of the fate (Moira) who distributes the fortune of the souls. As they were saying: the Moira is the ultimate "order", which even the gods must surrender to.

We can manipulate our conscience and sometimes use the planets in our favor, in order to change our life, but we cannot control our Fate. What we can do is to look deeper into planetary degrees and see the master plan the *Moirai* laid down on them.

Part III, Astrological Commentary with Examples

In the following paragraphs we will present several examples of twins, individuals born on the same day and place and nearly at the same time. Based on the Part of Fortune, Ascendant, MC and the Moon's Monomoiria we found out why their lives are so different from one another, although they have almost identical birth charts.

1. Moon, Ascendant, Midheaven and Part of Fortune Found in Different Monomoiria

Jean, Prince of Luxembourg was born on 15 May 1957 at 00:40 am at Berg, Luxembourg. He is the second son of Jean, Grand Duke of Luxembourg and Princess Joséphine-Charlotte of Belgium and the twin brother of Princess Margaretha. He is known by the name of Jean Nassau, the one royalty who renounced his right of succession to the Luxembourg throne. On the other hand, his twin sister, Margaretha born 26 minutes afterwards had a very different destiny, we could say, almost opposite as she married another royalty: Prince Nikolaus of Liechtenstein. For the time being, this is the last dynastically equal marriage between two sovereign houses currently reigning in Europe. They have had four children.

After being educated at the University of Geneva, Jean went on working as a financial analyst finance, planning and analysis division of the group W.R. Grace. At present, he works in the water industry as an advisor to the GDF-Suez Group, being also a board member of several financial institutions.

His sister, Princess Margaretha, on the other hand, is fulfilling her monarchal duties by supporting for charity different non-governmental organizations (NGO) in Europe and especially, in Luxembourg.

Her main recreational interests and sport activities include riding, skiing, tennis, hunting, reading, and modern and classical music.

Prince Jean's Ascendant is found at 25 Capricorn in the monomoiria of the Sun, while Princess Margaretha's Ascendant is at 3 Aquarius in the monomoiria of Mars. In the same manner, MC is at 26 Scorpion, monomoiria of Moon—for he has had career in water industry, respectively 3 Sagittarius, in the monomoiria of Sun—she shines as royalty among Europe's monarchs.

Princess Margaretha's Moon is located in Sagittarius, in the monomoiria of Jupiter together with Saturn, indicating that the fulfilling of her main duties brought her a more important destiny by serving the helpless. She identifies herself with this responsibility as Mars, monomoiria of her Ascendant is located in the sixth house, that of service to others. In her case, Part of Fortune is also in the sixth house in the monomoiria of Venus, which rules her fourth house, of family and ninth house of higher learning and principles. For her brother, Part of Fortune is in the monomoiria of Sun, which in his case rules eighth house of spouse's resources, as he was the one who married morganatically in 1987 and later in 2004, divorced.

Although the two brothers were given the same birth right, they have had different fates.

2. Moon, Ascendant and MC Found in Different Monomoiria

Here's a little known fact about the King of Rock and Roll: He was a twin, born in Tulepo, Mississippi, on January 8, 1935. Presley was born at 04:35 AM (CST h6w), 35 minutes after his identical twin brother, Jesse, who sadly was delivered stillborn.

Elvis' Moon was at 3 Pisces in the house of Jupiter and Midheaven at 27 Virgo, both in the *monomoiria* of the Sun. Also, he has Sun and Part of Fortune in the *monomoiria* of Sun. His Ascendant was at 13 Sagittarius in the *monomoiria* of Moon, which is in Pisces, the domicile of the benefic Jupiter. His twin brother had Moon at 2 Pisces in the house of Jupiter but in the *monomoiria* of Mars (Ares), Ascendant at 5 Sagittarius in the *monomoiria* of Mercury (Hermes) and MC at 18 Virgo (*monomoiria* of Jupiter-Zeus). The Midheaven is in the *monomoiria* of Jupiter, which is located in his twelve house, while for Elvis the Midheaven is in the *monomoiria* of the Sun, which was probably his salvation. His Part of Fortune is in Libra together with Mars. His Moon at 2 Pisces is in the *monomoiria* of Mars, ruled by Venus in the sign of Capricorn. The Ascendant is in the *monomoiria* Mercury located also in Capricorn, in the second house, in aversion to the Ascendant, not good for life.

For these twins, a time difference of approx. 30 minutes had a huge impact in their lives being a matter of life and death.

3. Only Moon and MC Found in Different Degrees

Kiefer Sutherland was born December 21, 1966 at 09:00 a.m. at St. Marylebone, England, GMT and Rachel Sutherland was born the same day three minutes afterwards, at 9:03 a.m.

This pair of twins decided to go into the entertainment industry together, but while Kiefer is an actor, Rachel works as a post-production supervisor.

Kiefer's Moon is in the Monomoiria of Mars (15 Aries), which means he will exhibit typical martial behavior, especially when compared to his younger sister, who will be more of a commander, who likes to be in charge as her Moon's degree is ruled by the Sun (16 Aries).

The older one will probably show a more aggressive, assertive, competitive and rash attitude which could lead him into all sorts of public trouble (the ruler of Monomoiria is in the tenth house in his detriment, in Libra). Kiefer is known for his criminal behavior (drunk driving) for which he was arrested several times.

While his sister has the Midheaven in the Monomoiria of Mercury, she is working as a TV producer, behind the scenes as her Mercury, ruler of the Midheaven by Monomoiria is in the twelfth house.

The Ascendant degree in the Monomoiria of Venus should make them both very attractive and involved in the arts. Especially in case of the brother, women will be attracted to him and he will be very women-prone, because the Midheaven also shares familiarity with the Ascendant through the same Monomoiria ruler, Venus, which was useful in his career, for sure.

4. Only Parts of Fortune in Different Degrees

The last one isn't exactly surprising as these two are probably the most famous twins. Since their days as Tanner on Full House, among many other roles, the pair has flourished in the fashion world with their label The Row.

Ashley Olsen, born June 13, 1986 at 9:43 a.m. at Van Nuys, California, and Mary-Kate Olsen, born two minutes later.

They both have Moon at 1 Virgo in the house and in the Monomoiria of Mercury, MC at 7 Taurus, in the *Monomoiria* of the Sun. The Ascendant is at 14 Leo in the *Monomoiria* of Mars. However, what sets them apart is Part of Fortune, which in case of Ashley is at 22 Libra in the Monomoiria of Venus, while Mary-Kate has it at 23 Libra in the Monomoiria of Mercury.

"The Part of Fortune is used to describe the basic way in which the individual is physically connected with the surrounding world. It is one of the significators of the body and health, and it is the primary significator of prosperity, and also career as it relates to prosperity." (Robert Hand, The Lot or Part of Fortune, http://www. astro.com).

Although the twins look alike and have basically lived the same life, they have different personalities and interests. Mary-Kate's academic strength is writing; Ashley's is math. Ashley plans to study psychology in college while Mary-Kate's interests are photography and culinary arts.

Apart from her sister, in 2004 Mary-Kate had treatment for an eating disorder that she had been struggling with for quite some time. Both Venus and Mercury, as rulers of Part of Fortune Monomoiria, are in the twelve house of Cancer. However, Venus in Cancer in a diurnal chart is in her own triplicity being stronger than Mercury which is Peregrine. Thus, the problems of Mary-Kate were related of self-undoing (twelve house) through nutrition or lack of it (Cancer).

5. Ascendant, Midheaven and Part of Fortune in Different Degrees

Robin Gibb was born on December 22, 1949 at 03:15 a.m. at Douglas, Isle Of Man together with his twin-brother, Maurice, born 45 minutes later, at 03:50 a.m. Together with their brother Andy, they are known for forming the Bee Gees in 1960 in Manchester, England. They were awarded the "Most successful family vocal group in history" in the Guinness Book of Records.

The family had emigrated to Australia in 1958. The brothers first performed on stage in their home city as pre-teens, encouraged by their dad, Hugh, a bandleader. After winning a radio talent contest, the three boys graduated to hosting their own TV show. Their first record, "Three Kisses of Love," a single in 1963 was mildly successful. By 1966 they were a top local group but with market limitations. An Australian promoter took the band to the U.K. in 1967 as a challenge to the Beatles. They scored with hits almost immediately.

For a period the three brothers had a falling out and Robin went solo for a while with "Robin's Reign." He reunited with his brothers in late 1970.

In the mid-1970s the disco explosion revived the group and made them superstars. Their authorized biography, *The Illustrated Bee Gees*, was published in 1979.

Robin's Ascendant in Scorpio is in the *monomoiria* of Mars, ruled also by Mars. This should have made him individualistic, and/or self-interested compared to his brother who had the Ascendant in the *monomoiria* of Jupiter. They both have had MC in Leo, Robin's in the monomoiria of Jupiter and Maurice in that of the Sun. They both enjoyed great fame and fortune. However, their health was not so good, as both suffered from blocked intestines.

Robin survived the surgery for this condition while his brother, Maurice died unexpectedly following surgery. Robin's Part of Fortune is in Virgo the monomoiria of Moon, while his brother's is in the monomoiria of Mars, in the sign of Libra.

It seems that an invisible thread is weaved into our lives by destiny personified by the three Moirai. In ancient mythology they were mostly described as cold, unfeeling old crones who inspired fear and acted independently of the Gods. Despite this, we, as astrologers, must find their true meaning and purpose in order to guide people according to their Fate for a more fair and just world.
practice.

Endnotes
[1]Neugebauer, H. B; Van Hoesen, H. B. (1987). Greek Horoscopes, Volume 48. Philadelphia: The American Philosophical Society. p. 185.

Degree	♈ ♏	♉ ♎	♊ ♍	♋	♌	♐ ♓	♑ ♒
1	♂	♀	☿	☽	☉	♃	♄
2	☉	☿	☽	♄	♀	♂	♃
3	♀	☽	♄	♃	☿	☉	♂
4	☿	♄	♃	♂	☽	♀	☉
5	☽	♃	♂	☉	♄	☿	♀
6	♄	♂	☉	♀	♃	☽	☿
7	♃	☉	♀	☿	♂	♄	☽
8	♂	♀	☿	☽	☉	♃	♄
9	☉	☿	☽	♄	♀	♂	♃
10	♀	☽	♄	♃	☿	☉	♂
11	☿	♄	♃	♂	☽	♀	☉
12	☽	♃	♂	☉	♄	☿	♀
13	♄	♂	☉	♀	♃	☽	☿
14	♃	☉	♀	☿	♂	♄	☽
15	♂	♀	☿	☽	☉	♃	♄
16	☉	☿	☽	♄	♀	♂	♃
17	♀	☽	♄	♃	☿	☉	♂
18	☿	♄	♃	♂	☽	♀	☉
19	☽	♃	♂	☉	♄	☿	♀
20	♄	♂	☉	♀	♃	☽	☿
21	♃	☉	♀	☿	♂	♄	☽
22	♂	♀	☿	☽	☉	♃	♄
23	☉	☿	☽	♄	♀	♂	♃
24	♀	☽	♄	♃	☿	☉	♂
25	☿	♄	♃	♂	☽	♀	☉
26	☽	♃	♂	☉	♄	☿	♀
27	♄	♂	☉	♀	♃	☽	☿
28	♃	☉	♀	☿	♂	♄	☽
29	♂	♀	☿	☽	♀	♃	♄
30	☉	☿	☽	♄	☿	♂	♃

Table of Single Degree Divisiono (Monomoiria)

[2]P.Berl. 9825: An elaborate horoscope for 319 CE and its significance for Greek astronomical and astrological [3]Scholia means commentary notes made either by copyists or other users of the manuscript.

[4]In Plato's Republic the Three Fates are daughters of Ananke (necessity), primeval goddess of inevitability who is entwined with the time-god Chronos, at the very beginning of time.

[5]Paulus Alexandrinus, Introductory Matters translated by Robert Schmidt, Edited by Robert Hand, Project Hindsight, Greek Track, Volume I, pg. XI.

Mercury Retrograde in Disasters

By Alan Annand

ABSTRACT: This article presents the resuls of research undertaken to test the widely-held belief that Mercury retrograde periods enjoy a significant correlation with the misfortunes of man. Specifically, this study focuses upon those very events—disasters—the etymology of which implies that these "ill-starred" calamities have their root causes in the heavens. Accordingly, the research examines the astrological charts for 60 disasters— natural, maritime, railway, and aviation—spanning centuries and accounting for almost nine million lives lost.

The charts are presented in the sidereal zodiac and whole-sign house system, utilizing sign-to-sign "aspects" and in the absence of trans-Saturnian planets. The study not only assesses the frequency of Mercury retrograde among these disasters but for comparison purposes includes the analysis of "hard aspects" between the Moon, Sun, Mars, Jupiter, Saturn and the nodal axis. In lieu of a proper statistical method, the author has employed a simple mathematical "index of significance" to determine that, although Mercury retrograde appears in disasters more often than expected by chance, its role is quaternary compared with hard aspects between Moon-Jupiter, Moon-Sun, and Sun-Saturn.

Mercury Retrograde in Disasters

A commonly-accepted notion in Western astrology is that when Mercury turns retrograde, as happens three times a year for roughly three weeks at a time, things go terribly wrong for people. But if that's really true, shouldn't it be reflected in events when hundreds—perhaps thousands, or even hundreds of thousands—of people had a really bad day, so bad they died?

Not knowing what I'd find, I examined the 60 worst disasters on record to see if there were any common astrological factors, particularly whether Mercury was retrograde at the time of the event. And by "worst" I mean those with the highest death tolls within each category of disaster.

Disasters and Their Data

Concerning disasters, there are four major types:

1. Natural disasters comprise earthquakes, typhoons, floods and tsunamis. These are the most deadly natural phenomena, and in the top 15 natural disasters of all recorded time, they've claimed 138,000 to 3.7 million victims per event, for a total of 8.7 million fatalities.

2. Maritime disasters involve loss of life on passenger ships and ferries. The *Titanic* is only the most famous, not the most deadly, of such tragedies. The top 15 maritime disasters have drowned 1,000 to 4,386 people per sinking, for a total of 27,000 deaths at sea.

3. Rail disasters typically involve the derailment of passenger trains, or their head-on collision with other trains. In the past 100 years, these major mishaps have killed anywhere from 320 to 1,700 people per train wreck, for a total of 9,000 fatalities.

4. Air disasters typically involve the downing of commercial airliners. These have all occurred within the past 45 years, during which the size of aircraft has placed larger numbers of passengers at risk. These crashes have killed anywhere from 261 to 583 travelers per incident, for a total of almost 5,000 deaths.

For more information on disasters, including dates, times, death tolls and other circumstantial details, see: Wikipedia.org/wiki/List_of_natural_disasters_by_death_toll and Wikipedia.org/wiki/List_of_accidents_and_disasters_by_death_toll

Methodology and Analysis

I first identified the top 15 disasters (ranked by death toll) within each of these four categories: natural, maritime, railway, and aviation. I then prepared charts for each event and ranked by frequency the astrological features for these events, first within their respective categories, and subsequently in total for all disastrous events in the study. I used sidereal positions, but since my analysis involved only aspects and retrogression, the results are (largely) independent of zodiacal sign.

In total, I examined 16 different astrological factors across these 60 disasters. Mercury retrograde is just one of those factors. The other 15 are the "hard" aspects between the Sun, Moon, Mars, Jupiter, Saturn, and the nodal axis.

Hard aspects comprise conjunctions, squares or oppositions. Most astrologers agree that "soft" aspects—sextiles and trines—correlate with benign conditions and circumstances, whereas hard aspects typically accompany difficulties of some kind, eg, disasters.

I did *not* include Mercury and Venus in the catalog of hard aspects with other planets. Because Mercury and Venus are both "inferior" planets whose orbits lie closest to the Sun, their movements from our perspective on Earth are not entirely independent of the Sun. For example, when the Sun is conjunct Jupiter, opposite Saturn, square the nodal axis, etc, Mercury and Venus are frequently in the same relationship with that other planet, especially when using sign-to-sign "aspects."

In this study, I also chose *not* to apply Ptolemaic aspects within orbs, but simply noted sign-to-sign aspects as used in both Hellenistic and Vedic astrology. So, for example, if the Sun and Moon are both in Aries, no matter their respective degrees, they're considered here to be associated, i.e. "conjunct." Or if the Sun is in any degree of Aries while the Moon is in any degree of Cancer, they're considered to be "square." And so on for "oppositions."

Although one could argue that the exclusion of hard aspects to Mercury and Venus constitutes something less than a full review of the astrological factors in disasters, my rationale was as follows. First, I was primarily interested only in knowing how prevalent was Mercury retrograde in these events, and to do that, I needed only a modest number of other factors for comparison purposes. To add more planets (inferior or trans-Saturnian) or use Ptolemaic aspects would only serve to complicate the matter.

In a nutshell, popular astrological wisdom says that bad things happen during Mercury retrograde. The purpose of this study was simply to test that thesis.

Expectations

On average, Mercury goes retrograde three times a year, with each period lasting about three weeks. More specifically, we're informed in Jeff Mayo's *The Astrologer's Astronomical Handbook* that "in a synodic period of 116 days, Mercury retrogrades for an average of 22 days." That's roughly 19% of the time. Therefore, in 60 disasters, we'd expect to see Mercury retrograde in about 11 of them (60 at 19 percent = 11.4).

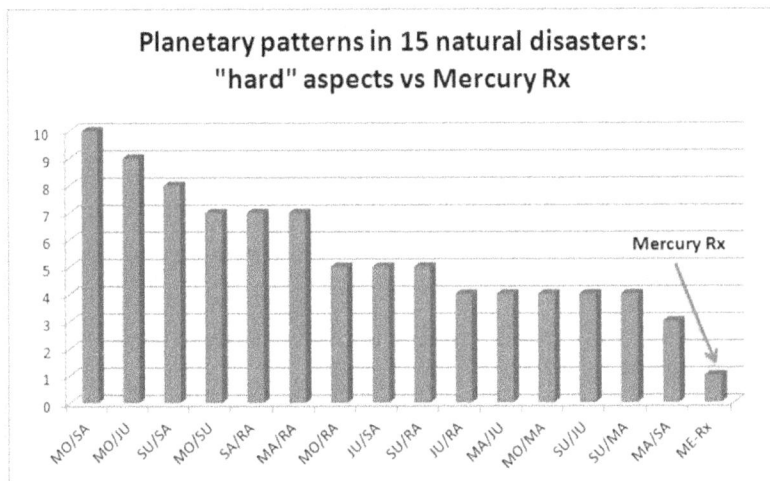

Graph 1: Planetary patterns in 15 natural disasters

The other astrological factors considered in this study are the hard aspects between the Sun, Moon, Mars, Jupiter, Saturn, and the nodal axis. Therefore, in order to subsequently assess the results, we must consider how frequently they occur on average. For instance, if we take Saturn as a stationary object, how often will those other planets form a hard aspect with it, i.e. a conjunction, square, or opposition?

If Saturn sits in Libra, for example, the Sun will form a hard aspect with it four times in a year—an opposition from Aries, squares from Cancer and

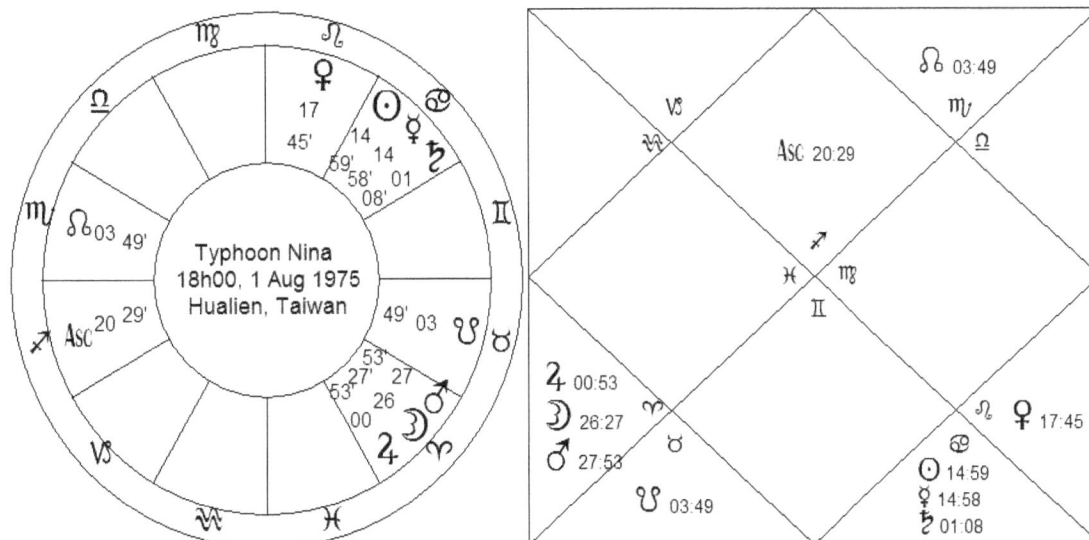

Chart 1: Representative natural disaster: Typhoon Nina

Capricorn, and a conjunction in Libra. In other words, the Sun will form a hard aspect from four signs out of 12, i.e. one in three, or 33 percent of the time. And in fact, these odds are more or less the same for any faster-moving planet in its orbital cycle to form a hard aspect with any slower-moving planet.

Therefore, if we have 60 events, it would be normal to see hard aspects between any chosen pair of planets 33 percent of the time, or 20 occurrences for each pair.

Natural Disasters

Of the 15 natural disasters included in this study, Mercury was retrograde in only one of those events, and was in fact the least-occurring astrological factor among those included for analysis.

Recall that Mercury is retrograde roughly 19 percent of the time; therefore in 15 events it should have turned up roughly three times (15 at 19 percent = 2.85).

As for "hard aspects" between planets, recall also that for any two planets to form a sign-to-sign hard aspect, the chances are 33 percent. So in 15 events, we would expect five occurrences for any given pair of planets.

As we can see from Graph 1, hard aspects between Moon-Saturn, Moon-Jupiter, and Sun-Saturn were more predominant in natural disasters.

Can we draw any conclusions from this observation? Only that the Moon is the greatest influence on tides of atmosphere, ocean and tectonic plates, and that Saturn rules earth-shaking events.

Known in the Philippines as Typhoon Bebeng, Nina was the fourth-deadliest tropical cyclone on record. After making landfall in Taiwan with winds of 115 mph and gusts of 138 mph, it crossed the Formosa Strait to mainland China. Blocked by a cold front, it became a stationary thunderstorm whose 3-day torrential rains overwhelmed the Banqiao Dam which received 1-in-2000-year flood conditions. Like dominoes, 61 other regional dams collapsed, killing 229,000 people. See Chart 1 on the previous page.

The Moon is in a tight conjunction with Mars in Aries. Jupiter is associated with them in the same sign. All three are in sign-to-sign square with Sun and Saturn in Cancer.

Maritime Disasters

Of the 15 maritime disasters included in this study, Mercury was retrograde in six of those events, twice as prevalent as the three occurrences expected on average.

Although hard aspects between Sun-Rahu, Moon-Mars, and Moon-Jupiter were actually more predominant in maritime disasters, we must also keep in mind that, notwithstanding their frequency, they are somewhat less than twice as prevalent as expected on average.

If we can conclude anything from this observation, it is that Mercury retrograde seems to have played an outsized role in maritime disasters.

On December 20, 1987, the Philippine passenger ferry *Doña Paz* collided with an oil tanker carrying a cargo of gasoline. Seriously overcrowded, the ferry had no radio, and its life jack-

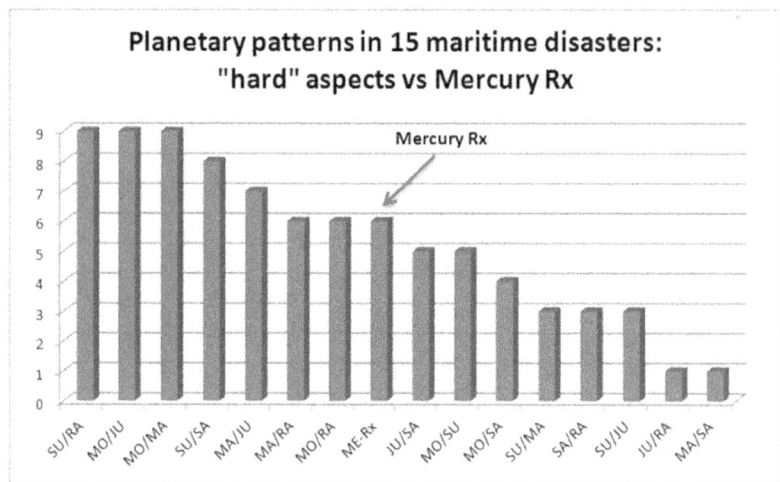

Graph 2: Planetary patterns in 15 maritime disasters

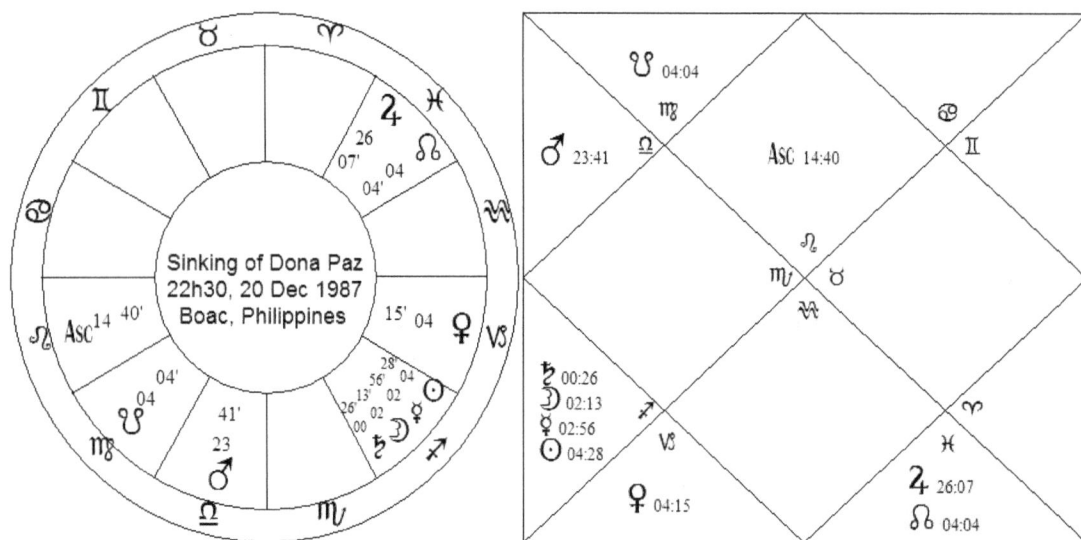

Chart 2: Representative maritime disaster, Sinking of the Doña Paz

ets were all locked up. Upon collision, the tanker's cargo ignited and spread to the ferry, which sank within two hours.

Passengers were forced to leap into shark-infested waters, struggling to stay afloat in a sea of dead bodies and burning gasoline. With an estimated death toll of 4,386 people and only 24 survivors, it was the deadliest peacetime maritime disaster in history.

The Sun, Moon, and Saturn were in the same sign, all square to Jupiter (in its own sign) and the nodal axis.

Railway Disasters

Of the 15 railway disasters included in this study, Mercury was retrograde in four of those events, slightly more than expected on average.

Hard aspects between Sun-Moon, Sun-Jupiter, and Moon-Jupiter lead the pack in railway disasters, only the first of which is twice as prevalent as expected on average.

Hard aspects between Mars/Saturn come in fourth. Although mechanical failures (track infrastructure, signal systems, brakes, etc) are often to blame in railway accidents, this astrological factor is nonetheless scarcely above the average expected.

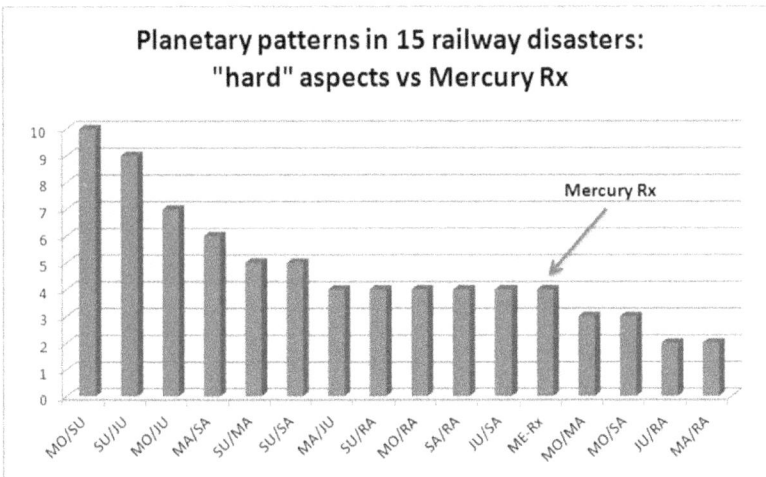

Graph 3: Planetary patterns in 15 railway disasters

In December 1917, a troop train was carrying 1,000 French soldiers home for Christmas leave from the Italian front in WW1. Short of locomotives, the commanding officer for rail traffic coupled 19 coaches to a single engine. The train driver refused to drive the overloaded train, but was forced at gunpoint by the officer to proceed.

As the train descended the Maurienne valley, the brakes had no effect on the heavy load, and the driver lost control. After rocketing down the

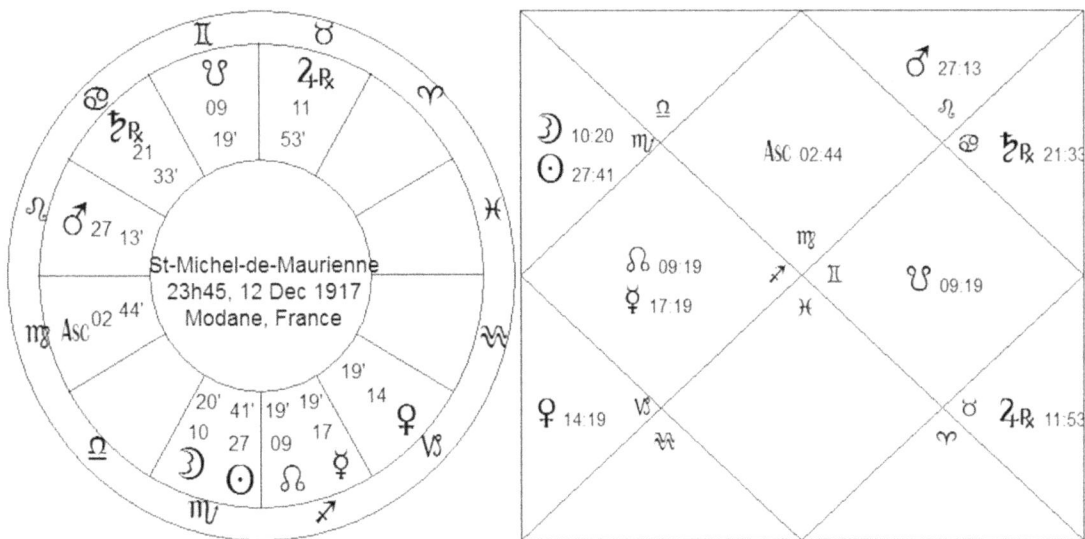

Chart 3: Representative railway disaster, St-Michel-de-Maurienne

mountain at up to 84 mph, the first coach derailed, causing a massive pile-up and resultant fire, killing 700 troops.

The Moon was dark and waning, in the same sign with the Sun. Both were opposed Jupiter, and all three in sign-to-sign square with Mars, which was in mutual reception with the Sun.

Aviation Disasters

Of the 15 aviation disasters included in this study, Mercury was retrograde in only two of these events, less than expected on average.

Hard aspects between Moon-Jupiter and Moon-Rahu are the most commonly-occurring aspects in aviation disasters, yet neither is significantly more prevalent than was expected on average. Hard aspects between Sun-Moon and Saturn-Rahu follow close behind, but again with unremarkable significance.

Notwithstanding this lacklustre showing, we might still note the participation of the Moon's nodes (Rahu and Ketu, North and South Node, respectively) in two of the four most common factors. The North Node Rahu is commonly associated with aviation, as well as sudden events.

On August 12, 1985, on a domestic flight from Tokyo to Osaka, an explosive decompression on a Boeing 747 ripped off a large portion of its tail. The plane lost its hydraulic controls and crashed, killing 520 people on board.

The accident was attributed to a faulty repair performed by Boeing after a tail-strike incident during a landing seven years earlier. It is the deadliest single-aircraft incident in history, and the second-deadliest aviation accident, behind the 1977 Tenerife disaster when PanAm and KLM airliners collided on the airport runway.

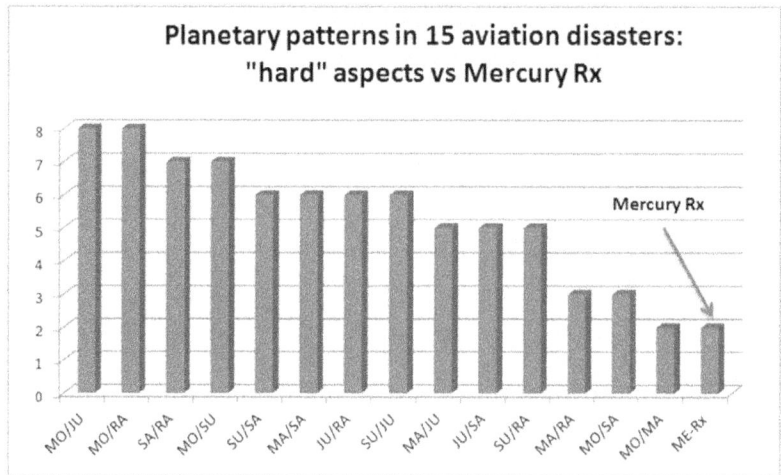

Graph 4: Planetary patterns in 15 aviation disasters

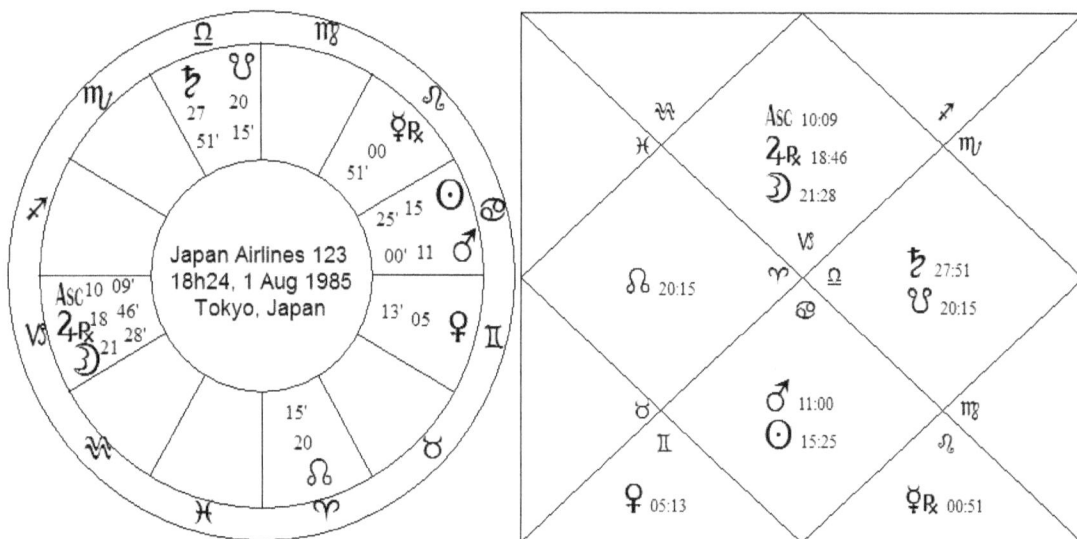

Chart 4: Representative aviation disaster, Japan Airlines Flight 123

The crash chart features a full moon, a debilitated Mars and Jupiter, and an exalted Saturn, all in mutual hard aspect with the Sun and the nodal axis. Mercury is also retrograde.

Overall Observations

To summarize the results of these four disaster categories, the astrological factors in play are presented by order of frequency in Graph 5 below. The first thing we should note is that Mercury retrograde is one of the least-frequently-occurring of the 16 astrological factors present at the time of a disaster. But how "infrequent" is that?

As it turns out, Mercury was retrograde during 13 of these 60 disasters. This is a relatively small sample when compared to rigorous statistical studies, but we can still apply simple math to get a rough idea of its significance. Recall from the earlier section on *Expectations* that, in 60 disasters, we expected to see Mercury retrograde in about 11 of them (60 at 19 percent = 11.4). In other words, with Mercury retrograde in 13 of these incidents, against an expectation of 11 such occurrences, we could say that Mercury retrograde has exceeded expectations by 18 percent.

How does that compare in significance to the other 15 astrological factors, ie, the hard aspects among the Sun, Moon, Mars, Jupiter, Saturn and the nodal axis? Again, referring back to the section on *Expectations*, we noted that any of these planetary pairs would form a hard aspect 33 percent of the time. In 60 events, that means we'd expect Sun/Moon, or any other planetary pair for that matter, to form a hard aspect 20 times.

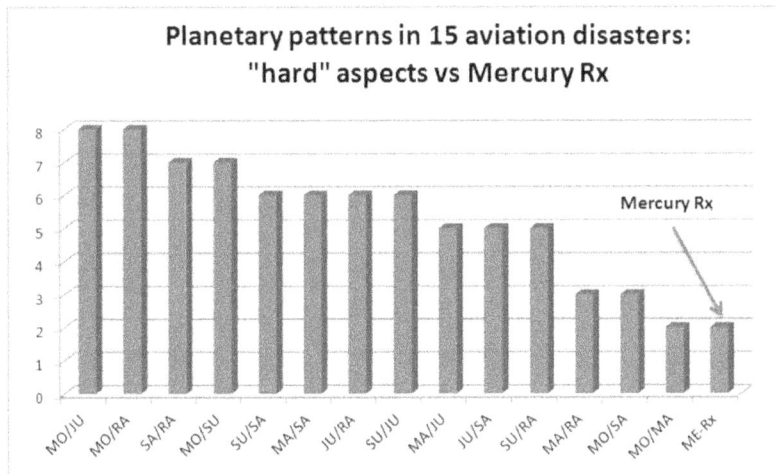

Graph 5: Planetary patterns in 60 disasters

If we examine Graph 5, we see that roughly half of the planetary pairs appear as per average expectations (n=20), give or take an event. Three of these planetary pairs (Moon-Jupiter, Moon-Sun and Sun-Saturn) appear with greater frequency, while two pairs (Mars-Saturn and Jupiter-Rahu) appear with less frequency.

Now, instead of looking only at the raw number of occurrences (i.e. hard aspect of some planetary pair vs Mercury retrograde) over these 60 events, I re-plotted this data in Graph 6 to illustrate a "significance" index. This acknowledges the fact that we expect Mercury to be retrograde 11 times in a study of 60 events, but we expect a hard aspect between any planetary pair to occur 20 times in 60 events. In other words, based on pure numbers alone, a hard aspect between any planetary pair is on average twice as likely as Mercury being retrograde.

Thus, the "significance" index for a planetary pair is equal to X observed occurrences of a hard aspect between

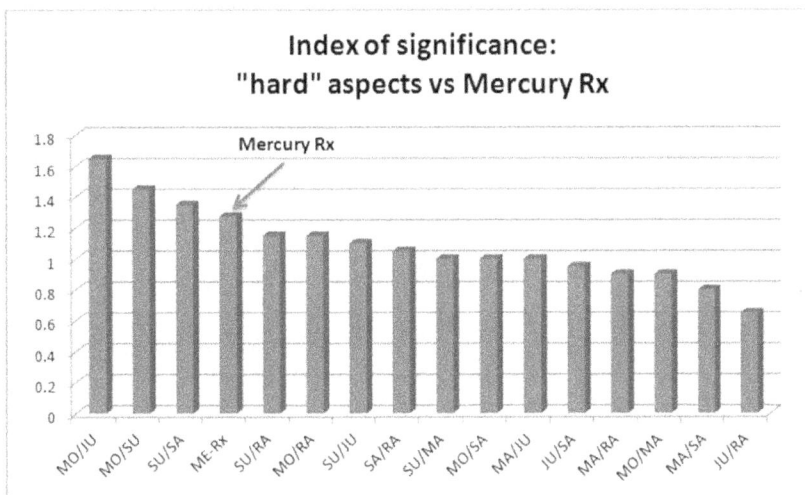

Graph 6: Significance of planetary patterns in 60 disasters

that pair, divided by 20, the expected number of occurrences for a study of this size (n = 60). Similarly, the "significance" index for Mercury retrograde is equal to Y observed occurrences of Mercury retrograde, divided by 11, the expected number of occurrences in a study this size.

If we now compare these two preceding graphs—the raw numbers of planetary patterns occurring, and their significance relative to expectations—we can make some meaningful observations:

As can be seen from Graph 6, the most significant astrological feature in disasters is a hard aspect—conjunction, square or opposition—between the Moon and Jupiter (n = 33). This pattern was present in 55 percent of these disasters. Furthermore, these Moon/Jupiter aspects occurred 65% more frequently than expected.

The second most significant astrological feature is a hard aspect between the Sun and Moon (n = 29). This pattern was present in 48 percent of these disasters, and occurred 45 percent more frequently than expected.

The third most significant feature is a hard aspect between the Sun and Saturn (n = 27). This was present in 45 percent of these disasters, and occurred 35 percent more frequently than expected.

The fourth most significant feature is Mercury retrograde (n = 13). Although this occurred in only 22 percent of these disasters, it was observed 18 percent more frequently than expected.

Meanwhile, at the far end of the scale, the *least* significant feature is a hard aspect between Jupiter and the nodal axis (n = 13). This was present in only 22 percent of these disasters, and occurred 35 percent *less* frequently than expected.

Conclusions

Admittedly, this is a relatively small (n = 60) number of events upon which to draw any firm conclusions. However, as a test of the thesis—*Is Mercury retrograde significant in disastrous events?*—this study would seem to suggest a very modest correlation. Mercury retrograde was present in 13 out of 60 disasters, which is roughly 18 percent more often than expected.

However, other astrological factors appear to be *more* significant. Hard aspects between Moon/Jupiter, Moon/Sun and Sun/Saturn appeared even more frequently than expected—55 percent, 45 percent, and 35 percent, respectively.

Are these numbers statistically significant? To answer that question may require a statistician (which I am not) and a study that incorporates a much larger number of disasters.

In the meantime, however, we may wish to comfort ourselves that the regular recurrence of Mercury retrograde in our astrological calendars should not provoke the anxiety that is so typically stoked by some practitioners.

We might just as well fear hard aspects between the luminaries and the two largest planets. For those of morbid inclination, we can now envision a "disaster clock" in which there are four hands—Saturn, Jupiter, Sun, and Moon. When the hands align, oppose or square each other, trouble looms.

Jupiter and Saturn are in hard aspect for a year at a time. Within that year, the Sun will be in hard aspect with both Jupiter and Saturn every three months—for a month at a time. Within any of those months, the Moon will be in hard aspect with all three—Sun, Jupiter, Saturn—for a couple of days each week.

But if Mercury is retrograde at the same time, maybe you should stay home.

Appendix of Disastrous Events

Natural	Deaths	Date	Local time	Location
China Floods	3,700,000	23 Aug 1931	12h00	Nanjing, China
Yellow River flood	900,000	28 Sep 1887	12h00	Zhenzhou, China
Shaanxi quake	830,000	23 Jan 1556	06h00	Shanxi, China
Tangshan quake	650,000	28 Jul 1976	03h43	Tangshan, China
Bhola cyclone	500,000	12 Nov 1970	12h00	Tazumuddin, Bangladesh
Coringa cyclone	300,000	26 Nov 1839	12h00	Coringa, India
Calcutta cyclone	300,000	7 Oct 1737	12h00	Calcutta, India
Haiyuan quake	273,400	16 Dec 1920	19h23	Haiyuan, China
Antioch quake	250,000	24 May 526	10h00	Antioch, Turkey
Indonesian tsunami	230,000	26 Dec 2004	07h58	Phen, Thailand
Nina typhoon	229,000	7 Aug 1975	18h00	Hualien, Taiwan
Haiti quake	160,000	12 Jan 2010	16h53	Port-au-Prince, Haiti
Kanto quake	142,000	1 Sep 1923	11h59	Sagami-machi, Japan
Bangladesh cyclone	138,866	29 Apr 1991	18h09	Chittagong, Bangladesh
Nargis cyclone	138,000	2 May 2008	18h11	Labutta, Burma

Maritime	Deaths	Date	Local time	Location
Dona Paz	4,386	20 Dec 1987	22h30	Boac, Philippines
Kiangya	3,335	4 Dec 1948	12h00	Shanghai, China
Mont-Blanc	2,000	6 Dec 1917	09h05	Halifax, Canada
Le Joola	1,864	26 Sep 2002	23h00	Serrakunda, Gambia
Sultana	1,800	27 Apr 1865	02h00	Memphis, USA
Neptune	1,700	16 Feb 1993	12h00	Port-au-Prince, Haiti
Tek Sing	1,600	6 Feb 1822	12h00	Koba, Indonesia
Spice Islander	1,573	10 Sep 2011	01h00	Kangani, Tanzania
Titanic	1,514	15 Apr 1912	23h40	St. John's, Canada
Taiping	1,500	27 Jan 1949	00h01	Zhoushan, China
Salem Express	1,400	17 Dec 1991	01h00	Yanbu, Saudi Arabia
Toya Maru	1,159	26 Sep 1954	22h43	Hakodate, Japan
Empress of Ireland	1,024	29 May 1914	02h00	Rimouski, Canada
General Slocum	1,021	15 Jun 1904	10h00	New York, USA
Al Salam Boccaccio	1,012	3 Feb 2006	23h00	Duba, Saudi Arabia

Railway	Deaths	Date	Local time	Location
Tsunami Sri Lanka	1,700	24 Dec 2004	09h30	Peraliya, Sri Lanka
Ciurea Romania	800	13 Jan 1917	13h20	Ciurea, Romania
St-Michel-de-Maurienne	700	12 Dec 1917	23h45	Modane, France
Vereshchyovka	700	24 Jan 1944	12h00	Moscow, Russia
Bihar India	650	6 Jun 1981	12h00	Mansi, India
Guadalajara	600	22 Jan 1915	12h00	Guadalajara, Mexico
Ufa Russia	575	4 Jun 1989	01h15	Asha, Russia
Balvano Italy	560	3 Mar 1944	00h01	Balvano, Italy

Awash Ethiopa	428	14 Jan 1985	13h40	Awash, Ethiopia
Al-Ayatt Egypt	383	20 Feb 2002	02h00	Al-Ayatt, Egypt
Torre-del-Bierzo	375	3 Jan 1944	13h20	Torre del Bierzo, Spain
Chengdu-Kunming	360	9 Jul 1981	01h47	Hanyuan, China
Firozabad	358	20 Aug 1995	02h55	Firozabad, India
Rongjiawan	338	29 Apr 1997	12h00	Rongjiawan, China
Nishapur	320	18 Feb 2004	03h00	Khayyam, Iran

Aviation	*Deaths*	*Date*	*Local time*	*Location*
PanAm-1736 & KLM-4805	583	27 Mar 1977	15h00	Las Palmas, Spain
Japan-123	520	12 Aug 1985	18h24	Tokyo, Japan
Saudi-763 & Kazak-1907	349	12 Nov 1996	18h40	Charkhi Dadri, India
Turkish-981	346	3 Mar 1974	12h40	Paris, France
Air India-182	329	23 Jun 1985	08h15	Cork, Ireland
Saudi-163	301	19 Aug 1980	15h15	Riyadh, Saudi Arabia
Malaysia-17	298	17 Jul 2014	15h15	Donets'k, Ukraine
IranAir-655	290	3 Jul 1988	13h56	Bandar Abbasi, Iran
Iran-AF	275	19 Feb 2003	18h24	Kerman, Iran
AA-191	273	25 May 1979	15h02	Chicago, Illinois
PanAm-103	270	21 Dec 1988	19h03	Lockerbie, Scotland
Korean Air-007	269	1 Sep 1983	06h26	Dolinsk, Russia
American Airlines-587	265	12 Nov 2001	09h16	Belle Harbor, USA
China Airlines-140	264	26 Apr 1994	20h16	Nagoya, Japan
Nigeria Airways-2120	261	11 Jul 1991	12h00	Jeddah, Saudi Arabia

The Astrology of Mass Shooting Events

By Glenn E. Mitchell II, Ph.D.

ABSTRACT: This report studies the statistical relationship between Mass Shooting Events (MSEs) in the United States and astrological factors. Every mass shooting in the U.S. between the Welding Shop Shooting in Miami, Florida in August 1982 and the Rancho Tehama Shooting in California in November 2017 were included. The only requirement was the availability of timed data for each event. 86 out of 99 MSEs met this qualification.

Introduction

Mass shooting events (MSEs) have been a common phenomenon in recent U.S. history. Not only are MSEs becoming more frequent, they are becoming increasingly deadly as the recent mass shooting in Las Vegas demonstrates. This exploratory research attempts to determine astrological factors highly associated with MSEs.

One common approach to Exploratory Data Analysis (EDA) is to take a "shotgun" approach and literally try thousands of astrological factors to determine which are statistically significant and then report. This *is not* the approach taken in this report.

The problem with the shotgun approach to EDA is that lots and lots of astrological factors will appear to be statistically significant by random chance alone. Let's assume that we examine 1,000 astrological measures and we use the scientific norm of a 0.95 level of statistical significance. That means, we can expect 50 of those astrological measures to falsely be associated with MSEs just by random chance.

A long-standing problem with statistical research in astrology is its general atheoretical nature. Correlations and other measures of association like chi-square statistics are frequently interpreted as demonstrating causation. Correlation is one of the requirements to prove causation (we statisticians like to say, correlation is a necessary condition to prove causation). Correlation is *not the only* requirement for proving causation (here, we say, correlation is not a sufficient condition to prove causation).

Time sequence is critical to demonstrate causation. If A causes B, then A needs to change before B changes. We can meet this requirement with event data for MSEs under the assumption that the astrological factors in the event chart precede (perhaps almost simultaneously) the mass shootings themselves.

We also require a theoretical relationship between the astrological factor(s) under consideration and MSEs. If we want to demonstrate causation, we need a story for why we expect A to affect B.

A practical example follows. The Sun tends to appear in houses VII through XII for MSEs. Much more seldom in houses I through VI. The theoretical explanation is basic. Most MSEs occur at work, at school, and at churches. In other words, most MSEs occur during daylight. Not all. Most.

Literature Review

Fort Hood, Aurora, Orlando, Virginia Tech, Sandy Hook, and now Las Vegas: one record-breaking MSE after another has left the American public wondering why mass killings continue and when they will end. More than 33,000 people per year killed by gun violence in this country. The N.R.A.'s recent begrudging concession to support new restrictions on so-called "bump stocks" will likely do little to curb the spiraling gun violence.[1]

CNN asks, "Why is there always a man behind these shootings? And why is it almost always a young man?"[2] One answer is evolutionary psychology.

Psychologists Joseph Vandello and Jennifer Bosson have coined the term "precarious manhood" to describe the theory that manhood is widely viewed as a status that is elusive (it must be earned) and tenuous (it must be demonstrated repeatedly through actions). Self-worth is tied to being perceived as a "real man."[3] There are sound evolutionary reasons why younger men find themselves especially concerned with status and dominance.[4] This includes the Young Male Syndrome, a tendency for some young men to engage in risky, aggressive behavior.[5]

"Young male violence is most likely to be initiated by young men who don't command respect from others. They'll often feel like slighted outcasts, deprived of what they want or feel they deserve."[6] The media often describes mass shooters and terrorists as misfits or loners. In many cases, quite so.

Threat assessment focuses heavily on violence prevention. There is no consistent path to prediction. Instead, there is a variety of theories to predict violence. The psychopathology model is currently the best way to predict violence.[7] Prediction and prevention of violence involves analyzing warning behaviors and spotting red flags. This article uses astrological factors to identify warning behaviors and red flags.

Data

Mother Jones published an article in July 2012 with the title "A Guide to Mass Shootings in America." That article contained some basic statistics on mass shootings in America. An update was published online in 2017 which included downloadable data (in various formats). Subsequent MSEs were appended to the *Mother Jones* data for this study by the author.

http://www.motherjones.com/politics/2012/12/mass-shootings-mother-jones-full-data/

The original *Mother Jones* data and its subsequent update used the following definitions:

- The perpetrator took the lives of at least four people. This is consistent with the FBI definition of a mass shooting to distinguish them from serial killings.

- The killings were carried out by a lone perpetrator. Two exceptions were the killings at Columbine High School and Westside Middle School.

- The shootings occurred in a public place. Except for a party on private property in Crandon, Wisconsin and another in Seattle, Washington, where crowds of strangers had gathered.

- Perpetrators who died or were wounded during the attack were not included in victim counts.

- A "handful" of cases were spree killings. Cases where killings occurred in more than one location over a relatively short period of time.

Crimes related to gang activity and armed robbery are not included. Neither are mass killings in a private home of a domestic nature.

Methodology

This study is a theory-guided EDA. The goal is to identify the major astrological factors associated with MSEs. The major bells.

Two pieces of software were used. JigSaw from Esoteric Technologies was used to construct the random control group for the study. Analysis of the data was done with Air Software's Fast Research program.

JigSaw was used to generate events for random times and places for every date between August 1982 and November 2017, the range of dates covered by the MSE data. The locations were constrained to the approximate longitudes and latitudes of the fifty United States. There were 13,235 control group charts generated for this study, constrained to the dates and approximate geographic area covered by MSEs.

Univariate analysis was undertaken with Fast Research. There were 86 analysis charts.

As Alphee Lavoie, the programmer of FAST Research, likes to point out, if it moves under the sky, Fast Research can study it. Hyperbole, yes. But, the astrological factors covered by the Fast Research software are very broad. Literally, tens of thousands of astrological measures can be studied.

Two principles guided this "first look" at MSCs. First, the research had to be theoretically-driven. Second, only the really significant factors would be included.

A set of theory-driven, astrological keywords related to MSEs was derived from Alfred Witte and Hermann Lefeldt's *Rules for Planetary Pictures: The Astrology of Tomorrow*. For example, mass shooters tend to be socially isolated individuals. There are keywords for *Lonesome*, *Separation* and *Shunned* to capture dimensions of social isolation. In some cases, an aspect or midpoint falls under multiple, theoretically-relevant keywords.

A 99 percent level of probability for each measure was used. The level of probability to use is arbitrary. 95 percent is more conventional in scientific research. Even at 99 percent, the number of significant results was overwhelming. A 99 percent probability would focus in on astrological factors with measures of association so strong, they provide compelling evidence.

The so-called Uranian planets, also called Trans-Neptunian Planets (or TNPs) were used in this study. These eight planets remain hypothetical to this very day.

Alfred Witte was a founder of the "Hamburg School" of astrology.[8] He was summoned to the Russian front during WWI to forecast the moments of artillery bombardments. He failed with traditional astrology. He, thus began his own practical researches and "discovered" the first four TNPs. His student and collaborator, Friedrich Sieggrün, derived the locations of the other four TNPs. Witte used the TNPs to predict bombardments and scenes of mass carnage with success.

TNPs are used in this study for the same reason they were used by Witte and Sieggrün and by modern Uranian astrologers. For the practical reason, they work. The results from this study demonstrate that the fit between the data and model results improves markedly when TNPs are included in the analysis.

When it comes to aspects, the focus was on aspects between any planet (and ASC, MC, North Node) with Mars, Saturn, Uranus, Neptune, Pluto, Hades, Zeus, Chronos, Appollon, Admetos, or Poseidon.

Midpoints likewise involve any planet (and ASC, MC, North Node) as a focal planet, with Mars, Saturn, Uranus, Neptune, Pluto, Hades, Zeus, Chronos, Appollon, Admetos, or Poseidon midpoints.

Results

A common idea is that nothing significant happens without the angles of the horoscope being involved. There's scant evidence for that point-of-view in the mass shooting data. The only planet approaching the required level of probability is Saturn (at 96.5 percent probability). The Sun seldom is involved with the angles in these cases (only 3 out of 86 instances). By random chance alone we would expect the Sun to be conjunct an angle a minimum of 7.1 times.

There is an unmistakable generation effect to MSEs. The earliest MSE in this study occurred in 1982. The next two in 1984. One in 1986. Another in 1987. Etc. This contrasts with more recent years. So far in 2017 (late November), we have experienced ten MSEs. Six in 2016. Seven in 2015. Etc. An undeniable increase in the incidence of MSEs over the years.As a consequence of the increasing numbers of MSEs in recent years, Pluto in Capricorn and Aquarius in Aries were included as predictors. Pluto in Capricorn occurred in 48 of the MSEs. By random chance alone, the expectation would be 22.8 instances. The chi-square statistic was 28, a 100%

probability. Uranus in Aries occurred in 41 of the MSEs, compared with an expectation of 16.3, a chi-square of 37.2, and a probability of 100 percent. Parsimony is an important consideration in scientific research. It is the idea that a model should be no more complicated than is required to explain the phenomenon. This study applies the so-called "Rule of 3." [9] Donna Cunningham expressed this rule succinctly. This ". . . old rule says that for an astrological interpretation to be true, you must be able to see it expressed three ways in the chart. If you see it once, it is only a possibility; if you see it twice, it becomes more likely; but if you can see the same theme a third time, that interpretation then becomes a probability." [10] This study retains themes that appear at least three times as aspects or midpoint pictures.

The astrological keywords for aspects and midpoints meeting the study criteria are listed below:

		Chi²	Prob.
• Autocratic			
Mercury = Zeus		7.7	99.4%
Mars = Midheaven	SELDOM[11]	6.5	99.0
Mars + Kronos = Zeus		6.7	99.1
Pluto + Midheaven = Zeus		7.0	99.2
• Compulsion			
Moon + Mercury = Zeus		14.6	100.0
Mercury + Poseidon = Vulcanus		7.0	99.2
Neptune + Kronos = North Node		8.6	99.7
Pluto + Zeus = Uranus		16.7	100.0
Zeus + Poseidon = Vulcanus		11.8	99.9
• Death			
Mercury = Admetos		12.7	100.0
Uranus = Neptune	SELDOM	38.5	100.0
Moon + Admetos = Uranus		15.9	100.0
Uranus + Neptune = North Node		24.3	100.0
Uranus + Poseidon = Saturn		17.2	100.0
• Deception			
Neptune = Apollon		16.1	100.0
Neptune = Vulcanus		13.3	100.0
Uranus + Vulcanus = North Node		12.1	100.0
Neptune + Poseidon = Kronos		9.1	99.7
• Destruction			
Mars + Uranus = Hades		18.1	100.0
Jupiter + Admetos = Uranus		8.1	99.6
Hades + Zeus = North Node		31.2	100.0
• Determination			
Moon = Admetos		7.6	99.4
Mercury = Admetos		12.7	100.0
Zeus = Kronos	SELDOM	8.2	99.6
Sun + Midheaven = Mars		8.9	99.7
Uranus + Midheaven = Zeus		11.0	100.0
Saturn + Pluto = Mars		6.7	99.1

	Chi^2	Prob.
• Enraged		
Mercury + Midheaven = Uranus	23.9	100.0%
Mercury + Poseidon = Mars	9.4	99.8
Admetos + Ascendant = Uranus	9.4	99.8
• Evil		
Hades = Kronos	23.8	100.0
Hades + North Node = Apollon	7.0	99.2
Hades + Zeus = Mars	9.4	99.8
Hades + Kronos = Pluto	8.6	99.7
• Excited		
Mercury + Midheaven = Uranus	23.9	100.0
Uranus + Ascendant = Midheaven	15.9	100.0
Uranus + Midheaven = Hades	15.9	100.0
Admetos + Ascendant = Uranus	9.4	99.8
• Government		
Mars + Neptune = Kronos	13.0	100.0
Mars + Zeus = Ascendant	11.6	99.9
Pluto + Hades = Zeus	17.2	100.0
• Haughtiness		
Ascendant + Midheaven = Kronos	15.5	100.0
Moon + Midheaven = Admetos	7.9	99.5
Mercury + Venus = Admetos	8.2	99.6
Zeus + North Node = Pluto	7.4	99.3
• Hindrances		
Sun + Vulcanus = Hades	7.9	99.5
Sun + Zeus = Hades	12.1	99.9
Saturn + Midheaven = Poseidon	7.4	99.3
Saturn + Pluto = Mars	6.7	99.1
Saturn + Pluto = Hades	11.1	99.9
Saturn + Zeus = Midheaven	10.4	99.9
Saturn + Zeus = Hades	26.7	100.0
Saturn + Admetos = Neptune	16.1	100.0
Saturn + Vulcanus = North Node	28.3	100.0
Uranus + Vulcanus = Saturn	13.0	100.0
Neptune + Hades = Saturn	21.4	100.0
Zeus + Ascendant = Saturn	11.6	99.9
Kronos + Poseidon = Saturn	7.7	99.4
• Lonesome		
Sun + Saturn = Zeus	7.4	99.3
Venus + Saturn = Ascendant	19.0	100.0
Uranus + Admetos = Cupido	22.0	100.0

	Chi²	Prob.
• Enraged		
Mercury + Midheven = Uranus	23.9	100.0%
Merucry + Poseidon = Mars	9.4	99.8
Admetos + Ascendant = Uranus	9.4	99.8
• Evil		
Hades + Kronos	23.8	100.0
Hades + North Node = Apollon	7.0	99.2
Hades + Zeus = Mars	9.4	99.8
Hades + Kronos = Pluto	8.6	99.7
• Excited		
Mercury + Midheaven = Uranus	23.9	100.0
Uranus + Ascendant + Midheaven	25.9	100.0
Uranus + Midheaven + Hades	15.9	100.0
Admetos + Ascendant = Uranus	9.4	99.8
• Government		
Mars + Neptune = Kronos	13.0	100.0
Mars + Zeus = Ascendant	11.6	99.9
Pluto + Hades = Zeus	17.2	100.0
• Haughtiness		
Ascendant + Midheaven = Kronos	15.5	100.0
Moon + Midheaven = Admetos	7.9	99.5
Mercury + Venus = Admetos	8.2	99.6
Zeus + North Node = Pluto	7.4	99.3
• Hindrances		
Sun + Vulcanus = Hades	7.9	99.5
Sun + Zeus = Hades	12.1	99.9
Saturn + Midheaven = Poseidon	7.4	99.3
Saturn + Pluto = Mars	6.7	99.1
Saturn + Pluto = Hades	11.1	99.9
Saturn + Zeus = Midheaven	10.4	99.9
Saturn + Zeus = Hades	26.7	100.0
Saturn + Admetos = Neptune	16.1	100.0
Saturn + Vulcanus = North Node	28.3	100.0
Uranus + Vulcanus = Saturn	13.0	100.0
Neptune + Hades = SAturn	21.4	100.0
Zeus + Ascendant = Saturn	11.6	99.9
Kronos + Poseidon = Saturn	7.7	99.4
• Lonesome		
Sun + Saturn = ZEus	7.4	99.3
Venus + Saturn = Ascendant	19.0	100/0
Uranus + Admetos = Cupico	22.0	100.0
Admetos + North Node = Cupido	6.8	99.1

	Chi²	*Prob.*
• Love and Lovability		
Sun + Venus = Admetos	10.8	99.9%
Venus + North Node = Admetos	8.5	99.6
Venus + Vulcanus = Neptune	8.2	99.6
• Mental Illness		
Sun + Uranus = Pluto	8.5	99.6
Moon + Mercury = Midheaven	9.7	99.8
Moon + Poseidon = Hades	12.2	100.0
Mars + Saturn = Poseidon	12.5	100.0
• Murder		
Uranus = Admetos	6.5	99.0
Mercury + Hades = Mars	11.6	99.9
Mercury + Zeus = Hades	12.5	100.0
Mars + Uranus = Hades	18.1	100.0
Mars + Hades = Vulcanus	6.8	99.1
Uranus + Midheaven = Hades	15.9	100.0
• Poverty		
Jupiter + Hades = Saturn	9.7	99.8
Saturn + Pluto = Hades	11.1	99.9
Saturn + Hades = Admetos	13.5	100.0
Saturn + Zeus = Hades	26.7	100.0
Neptune + Vulcanus = Hades	20.8	100.0
Hades + North Node = Cupido	10.5	99.9
Hades + Admetos = North Node	11.6	99.9
Pluto + Cupido = Hades	16.4	100.0
Apollon + Vulcanus = Neptune	34.5	100.0
• Separation		
Mars = Saturn	7.0	99.2
Uranus = Admetos	6.5	99.0
Sun + Ascendant = Admetos	6.8	99.1
Sun + Saturn = Zeus	7.4	99.3
Sun + Admetos = Ascendant	8.5	99.6
Moon + Mars = Saturn	7.4	99.3
Venus + Mars = Neptune	7.0	99.2
Venus + Neptune = North Node	7.0	99.2
Mars + North Node = Saturn	20.4	100.0
Jupiter + Ascendant = Saturn	16.6	100.0
Jupiter + North Node = Neptune	8.1	99.6
Jupiter + Cupido = Admetos	7.7	99.4
Saturn + Ascendant = Zeus	7.0	99.2
Saturn + Cupido = Mars	9.4	99.8
Saturn + Cupido = Apollon	8.5	99.6

		Chi²	Prob.
Saturn + Apollon = North Node		8.1	99.6%
Uranus + North Node = Saturn		10.8	99.9
Neptune + North Node = Mars		6.8	99.1
Neptune + North Node = Admetos		8.0	99.5
Neptune + Cupido = North Node		9.4	99.8
Neptune + Cupido = Apollon		9.1	99.7
Cupido + Admetos = Ascendant		8.6	99.7
Cupido + Admetos = Saturn		8.9	99.7
Cupido + Admetos = Vulcanus		6.6	99.0
Admetos + North Node = Midheaven		7.0	99.2%
Admetos + North Node = Cupido		6.8	99.1
Vulcanus + North Node = Neptune		7.7	99.4
• Shunned			
Venus + Saturn = Ascendant		19.0	100.0
Jupiter + Ascendant = Saturn		16.6	100.0
Uranus + Admetos = Cupido		22.0	100.0
Cupido + Admetos = Saturn		8.9	99.7
• Tension			
Uranus = Vulcanus		46.9	100.0
Moon + Uranus = Ascendant		23.9	100.0
Uranus + Vulcanus = Apollon		14.7	100.0
• Transformation			
Uranus = Pluto	SELDOM	11.7	99.9
Saturn + Admetos = Uranus		18.9	100.0
Neptune + Admetos = Uranus		18.9	100.0
Pluto + Kronos = Admetos		18.7	100.0
Pluto + Apollon = Uranus		18.3	100.0
Pluto + Vulcanus = Uranus		8.2	99.6
Pluto + Poseidon = Vulcanus		21.8	100.0
Vulcanus + Midheaven = Pluto		17.3	100.0
• Victim			
Mars + Vulcanus = North Node		13.0	100.0
Jupiter + Hades = Poseidon		8.8	99.7
Saturn + Poseidon = Hades		7.0	99.2

There is ample evidence of strong associations between astrological factors and MSEs. The categories have what statisticians refer to as face validity. This means, that a reasonable observer would conclude that these categories tap into important motivations why some individuals engage in mass shootings.

It was previously mentioned, for example, that MSE perpetrators tend to be socially isolated. We see confirmatory evidence under keywords for Lonesome, Separation, and Shunned.

The findings presented above are univariate. Each astrological factor is evaluated in isolation from other factors.

Air Fast Research includes the capacity to evaluate multivariate models, where each criterion in the model is assigned its own weight. A score for each observation is calculated. What we expect to find with MSEs is a largely homogenous set of scores for the observed MSEs. Extreme variations in the data would suggest that the model does not fit the data well.

When the model excludes the TNPs, the predictions for individual MSEs vary considerably. From a score of 0 to a score of 5. If a model predicts well, we expect much more uniformity in the predictions. The results below suggest that traditional astrological factors alone do not explain MSEs. In some individual cases, the predictions are good; in other cases, not so good; in a few cases, the predicted weight was zero.

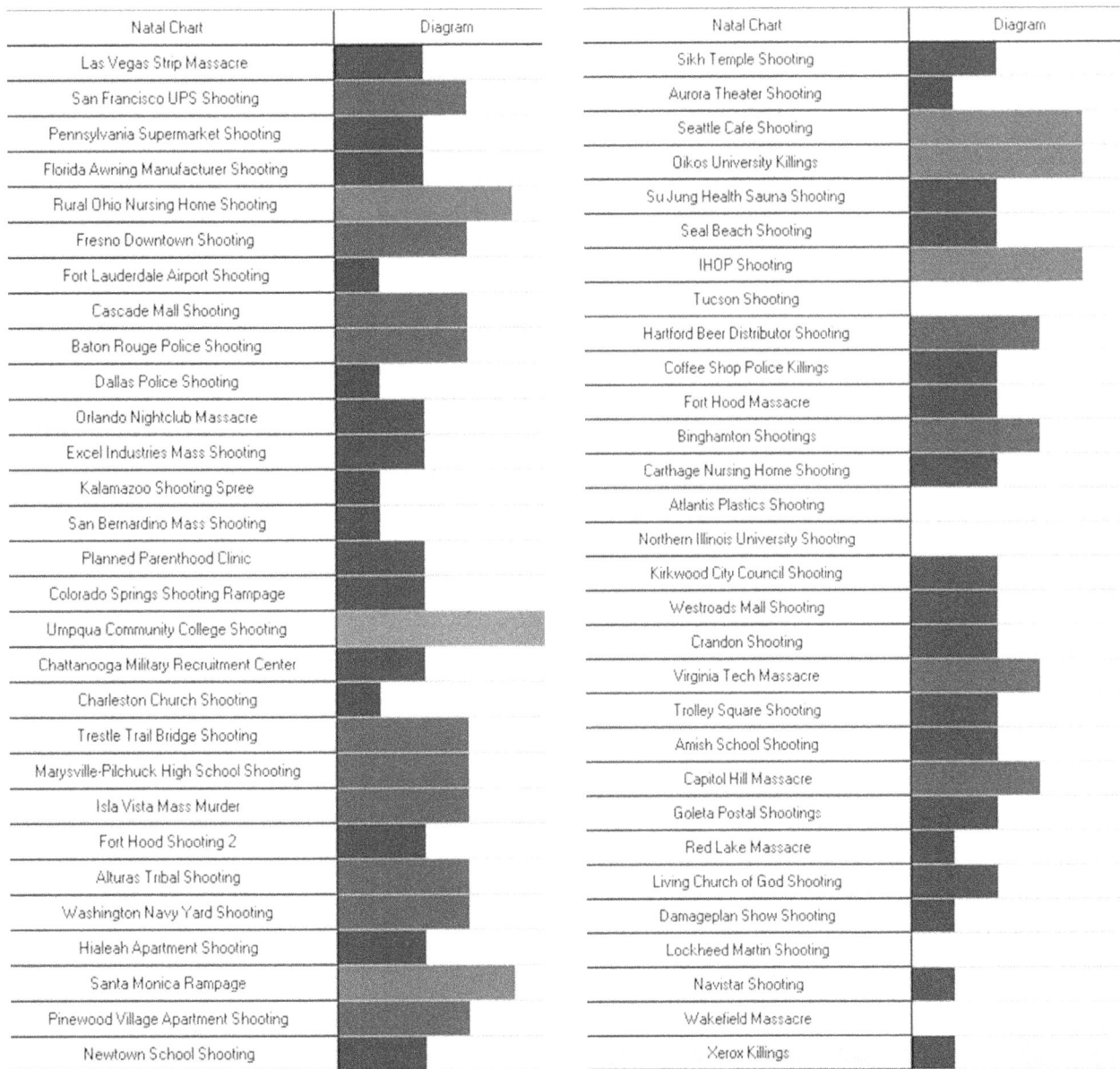

Natal Chart	Diagram		Natal Chart	Diagram
Las Vegas Strip Massacre			Sikh Temple Shooting	
San Francisco UPS Shooting			Aurora Theater Shooting	
Pennsylvania Supermarket Shooting			Seattle Cafe Shooting	
Florida Awning Manufacturer Shooting			Oikos University Killings	
Rural Ohio Nursing Home Shooting			Su Jung Health Sauna Shooting	
Fresno Downtown Shooting			Seal Beach Shooting	
Fort Lauderdale Airport Shooting			IHOP Shooting	
Cascade Mall Shooting			Tucson Shooting	
Baton Rouge Police Shooting			Hartford Beer Distributor Shooting	
Dallas Police Shooting			Coffee Shop Police Killings	
Orlando Nightclub Massacre			Fort Hood Massacre	
Excel Industries Mass Shooting			Binghamton Shootings	
Kalamazoo Shooting Spree			Carthage Nursing Home Shooting	
San Bernardino Mass Shooting			Atlantis Plastics Shooting	
Planned Parenthood Clinic			Northern Illinois University Shooting	
Colorado Springs Shooting Rampage			Kirkwood City Council Shooting	
Umpqua Community College Shooting			Westroads Mall Shooting	
Chattanooga Military Recruitment Center			Crandon Shooting	
Charleston Church Shooting			Virginia Tech Massacre	
Trestle Trail Bridge Shooting			Trolley Square Shooting	
Marysville-Pilchuck High School Shooting			Amish School Shooting	
Isla Vista Mass Murder			Capitol Hill Massacre	
Fort Hood Shooting 2			Goleta Postal Shootings	
Alturas Tribal Shooting			Red Lake Massacre	
Washington Navy Yard Shooting			Living Church of God Shooting	
Hialeah Apartment Shooting			Damageplan Show Shooting	
Santa Monica Rampage			Lockheed Martin Shooting	
Pinewood Village Apartment Shooting			Navistar Shooting	
Newtown School Shooting			Wakefield Massacre	
			Xerox Killings	

When TNPs are included in the model, the predictions improve markedly. Much of the variation in predicting individual MSEs disappears. The results are much more homogenous. The minimum prediction weight is 111 and the maximum is 147.

Natal Chart	Diagram
Las Vegas Strip Massacre	
San Francisco UPS Shooting	
Pennsylvania Supermarket Shooting	
Florida Awning Manufacturer Shooting	
Rural Ohio Nursing Home Shooting	
Fresno Downtown Shooting	
Fort Lauderdale Airport Shooting	
Cascade Mall Shooting	
Baton Rouge Police Shooting	
Dallas Police Shooting	
Orlando Nightclub Massacre	
Excel Industries Mass Shooting	
Kalamazoo Shooting Spree	
San Bernardino Mass Shooting	
Planned Parenthood Clinic	
Colorado Springs Shooting Rampage	
Umpqua Community College Shooting	
Chattanooga Military Recruitment Center	
Charleston Church Shooting	
Trestle Trail Bridge Shooting	
Marysville-Pilchuck High School Shooting	
Isla Vista Mass Murder	
Fort Hood Shooting 2	
Alturas Tribal Shooting	
Washington Navy Yard Shooting	
Hialeah Apartment Shooting	
Santa Monica Rampage	
Pinewood Village Apartment Shooting	
Newtown School Shooting	
Accent Signage Systems Shooting	

Atlanta Day Trading Spree Killings
Columbine High School Massacre
Thurston High School Shooting
Westside Middle School Killings
Connecticut Lottery Shooting
Caltrans Maintenance Yard Shooting
Fort Lauderdale Revenge Shooting
Air Force Base Shooting
Chuck E. Cheese's Killings
Long Island Rail Road Massacre
101 California Street Shootings
Lindhurst High School Shooting
Royal Oak Postal Shootings
University of Iowa Shooting
Luby's Massacre
GMAC Massacre
Standard Gravure Shooting
Stockton Schoolyard Shooting
ESL Shooting
Shopping Centers Spree Killings
United States Postal Service Shooting
San Ysidro McDonald's Massacre
Welding Shop Shooting
Maryland Office Park Shooting
First Baptist Church Shooting

Summary

This report studies the statistical relationship between Mass Shooting Events (MSEs) in the United States and astrological factors. Every mass shooting in the U.S. between the Welding Shop Shooting in Miami, Florida in August 1982 and the Rancho Tehama Shooting in California in November 2017 with timed data were included. Univariate analysis was undertaken with Fast Research. There were 86 analysis charts.

Prediction and prevention of violence involves analyzing warning behaviors and spotting red flags. This article uses astrological factors to identify those warning behaviors and red flags. A number of astrological keywords for aspects and midpoints were developed for the study criteria. These are based on theory. Air Fast Research includes the capacity to evaluate multivariate models, where each criterion in the model is assigned its own weight.

Using traditional astrological criteria, the associations between astrological factors and MSEs is somewhat less than overwhelming. When TNPs are added, there is ample evidence of strong associations between these astrological factors and MSEs.

Sikh Temple Shooting
Aurora Theater Shooting
Seattle Cafe Shooting
Oikos University Killings
Su Jung Health Sauna Shooting
Seal Beach Shooting
IHOP Shooting
Tucson Shooting
Hartford Beer Distributor Shooting
Coffee Shop Police Killings
Fort Hood Massacre
Binghamton Shootings
Carthage Nursing Home Shooting
Atlantis Plastics Shooting
Northern Illinois University Shooting
Kirkwood City Council Shooting
Westroads Mall Shooting
Crandon Shooting
Virginia Tech Massacre
Trolley Square Shooting
Amish School Shooting
Capitol Hill Massacre
Goleta Postal Shootings
Red Lake Massacre
Living Church of God Shooting
Damageplan Show Shooting
Lockheed Martin Shooting
Navistar Shooting
Wakefield Massacre
Xerox Killings

Atlanta Day Trading Spree Killings
Columbine High School Massacre
Thurston High School Shooting
Westside Middle School Killings
Connecticut Lottery Shooting
Caltrans Maintenance Yard Shooting
Fort Lauderdale Revenge Shooting
Air Force Base Shooting
Chuck E. Cheese's Killings
Long Island Rail Road Massacre
101 California Street Shootings
Lindhurst High School Shooting
Royal Oak Postal Shootings
University of Iowa Shooting
Luby's Massacre
GMAC Massacre
Standard Gravure Shooting
Stockton Schoolyard Shooting
ESL Shooting
Shopping Centers Spree Killings
United States Postal Service Shooting
San Ysidro McDonald's Massacre
Welding Shop Shooting
Maryland Office Park Shooting
First Baptist Church Shooting

Endnotes

[1]https://www.vanityfair.com/news/2017/10/the-psychology-behind-mass-shootings-hive-podcast

[2]http://www.cnn.com/2016/07/08/health/psychology-mass-shootings/index.html

[3]Bosson, J.K., Vandello, J.A. (2011). "Precarious Manhood and Its Links to Action and Aggression," *Current Directions in Psychological Science*, Vol 20, Issue 2, pp. 82-6.

[4]http://www.cnn.com/2016/07/08/health/psychology-mass-shootings/index.html

[5]Wilson, M., Daly, M. (1985). "Competitiveness, risk taking, and violence: the young male syndrome," *Ethology and Sociobiology*, Vol. 6, Issue 1, pp. 59-73.

[6]http://www.cnn.com/2016/07/08/health/psychology-mass-shootings/index.html

[7]https://www.psychologytoday.com/blog/why-bad-looks-good/201711/the-psychology-mass-shootings-how-see-red-flags

[8]https://astrologer.ru/Witte/biography_eng.html

[9]Frank C. Clifford, *Getting to the Heart of Your Chart: Playing Astrological Detective*, London, UK: Flare Publications, 2012

[10]https://skywriter.wordpress.com/2009/02/07/spotting-themes-in-a-birth-chart-the-rule-of-three/

[11]SELDOM means that the relationship is inverse. Instead of the astrological factor showing up significantly more often than chance, it instead shows up significantly less often than chance. Whether a given measure shows up more often than expected or less often than expected, is important information to learn.

America's True Horoscope: Can the Las Vegas Shooting Tragedy Help Solve the Debate?

By Pamela Rowe, LPMAFA

ABSTRACT: The horoscope and especially the time of birth of a country is often debated by astrologers. Examining the astrological patterns of historic events can help us decide which chart works best for us. There are amazing links between the tragic Las Vegas USA shooting of October 1, 2017, which left 58 innocent people dead and 489 injured and the Gemini Ascendant natal chart of the USA. Using traditional astrology and Cosmobiology the natal chart, secondary progressions, directions and transits, plus some relevant planetary cycles and a lunar return are described. The natal chart of the shooter Stephen Craig Paddock reveals an interesting but conflicted personality, with a sad personal history and wasted potential. Reviewing his secondary progressions and directions with the transits of the event gives the reader some insight into his mental state at the time of the shooting. People whose lives have an impact on the U.S. people (for better or worse) will have natal charts with strong links to the U.S. chart. Comparing Paddock's chart with the natal U.S. Gemini Ascendant chart, it is no surprise that there are significant links. Outstanding is the first house dynamic, pioneering character of the U.S. and its people, who also demand the right to carry arms. Paddock's aggressive actions highlight this pattern, but misinterpret its positive expression. Consequently his actions have reinforced arguments to question this right.

At 10:05 p.m. on October 1, 2017, at the annual Route 91 Harvest Country Music Festival, a crazed gunman sent a barrage of bullets from his room on the 32nd floor of the Mandalay Bay Hotel, Paradise, Las Vegas into the large crowd below. The venue was a 15 acre lot, 450 metres from the hotel. 58 innocent people aged between 20 and 67 years old died and 489 received non-fatal injuries before the gunman committed suicide. It was the deadliest mass shooting committed by an individual in the U.S.

According to reports, the gunman, 64-year-old Stephen Paddock, had checked into the hotel on September 25, 2017 with more than 10 suitcases holding 23 guns for his evil, premeditated act. On that day Saturn was square Mercury = serious plans, depression, blocking of the nervous system.

Why? we ask. How can normal people understand such action?

Can astrology ascertain that the location was unsafe and that those affected, through fate or circumstance, had somehow tapped into the astrological scenario of that moment?

Without the birth charts of the victims we can only consider the astrological patterns at the time of the shooting. Also the U.S. horoscope and whether this and other recent events may bring about eventual changes in the law, or generate other safety measures to help prevent further such episodes.

Las Vegas Shooting starts
Natal Chart
1 Oct 2017, Sun
10:05 pm PDT +7:00
Paradise, Nevada
36°N07 115°W08
Geocentric
Tropical
Placidus
Mean Node

Fig. 1

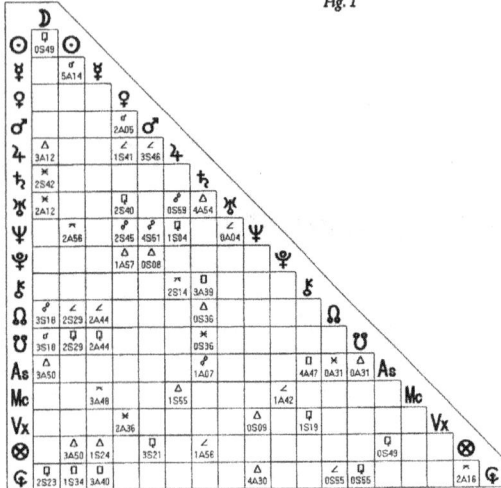

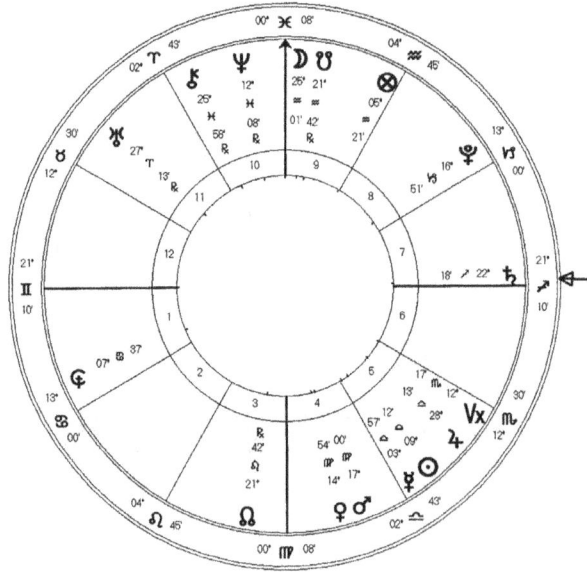

Start of Las Vegas Shooting

The mundane traditional chart for the event is calculated for 10:05 pm, the time shooting into the crowd started (Fig. 1). The most outstanding feature of the chart is Saturn at 22 Sagittarius 18 in the seventh house and opposition the 21 Gemini 10 Ascendant. The Ascendant represents the people in the environment and the seventh house represents open enemies, war, loss and limitation generated by a public enemy.

In fact, Saturn was on the Descendant during the whole time of the shooting, which ended at 10:15 p.m.

The Midheaven at 0 Pisces 08, a sensitive, artistic sign, was semi-square Pluto in the eighth house of the death.

Neptune, the ruling planet of the tenth house (government, national prestige) was placed in the tenth house opposition Venus and Mars in the fourth, semi-square Uranus in the eleventh, sesquiquadrate Jupiter (co-ruler of Pisces) in the fifth and quincunx the Sun in the fifth (describing the musical setting, romantic and happy people, and the male "outsider").

Hypothetical Hades is rising and square the Sun (the destructive masculine power of the past, deficiencies from a previous life).

The Jupiter-Uranus opposition had recently coincided with sudden unexpected shocks on a world level and the involvement of Neptune emphasizes the confusion and deception necessary for the gunman to stage this event.

Shooting Started , the 90-Degree Cosmogram

(Fig. 2) Mars = Saturn Ascendant/Neptune = Mercury/Midheaven = Sun/Moon = an aggressive act as a result of paranoia, mental or physical illness affecting partners and families.

Sun = Saturn Ascendant/Jupiter Uranus = severe tests of strength, a dangerous environment, use of technology, broken relationships.

Saturn Ascendant = Moon/Pluto = depression, causing many upsets and a violent reaction in the environment.

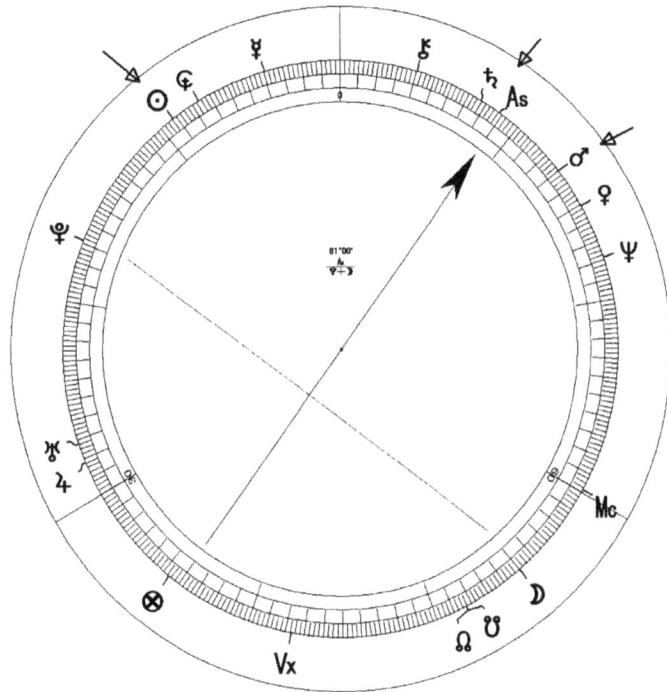

Las Vegas Shooting starts
Natal Chart
1 Oct 2017, Sun
10:05 pm PDT +7:00
Paradise, Nevada
36°N07' 115°W08'
Geocentric
Tropical
Placidus
Mean Node

Fig. 2

USA
Natal Chart
4 Jul 1776 NS, Thu
2:14:16 am LMT +5:00:40
Philadelphia, USA
39N57 075°W10'
Geocentric
Tropical
Placidus
Mean Node

Fig. 3

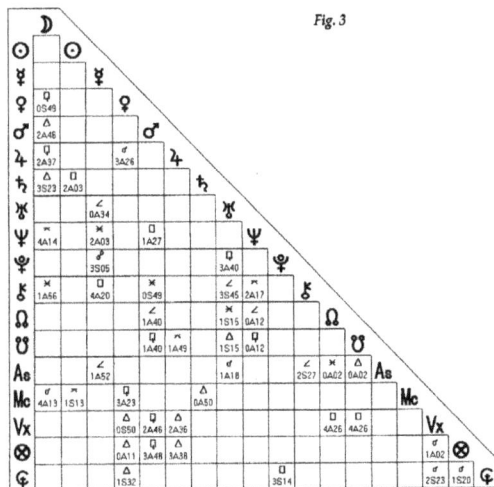

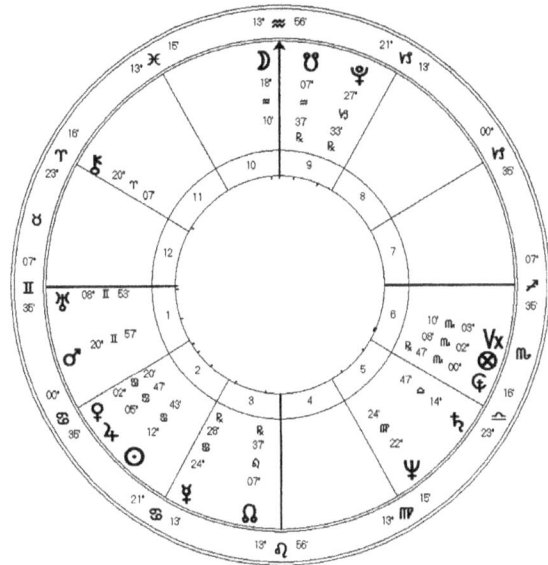

The Traditional U.S. Horoscope of the U.S.

Fig. 3. Because more than one time of birth of a country is often discussed and debated, we as astrologers must select a chart which, after research, works for us. I have always favored the July 4, 1776, 2:14:15 a.m. LMT Philadelphia chart, which I believe is the one favored by famous early American astrologer Evangeline Adams.

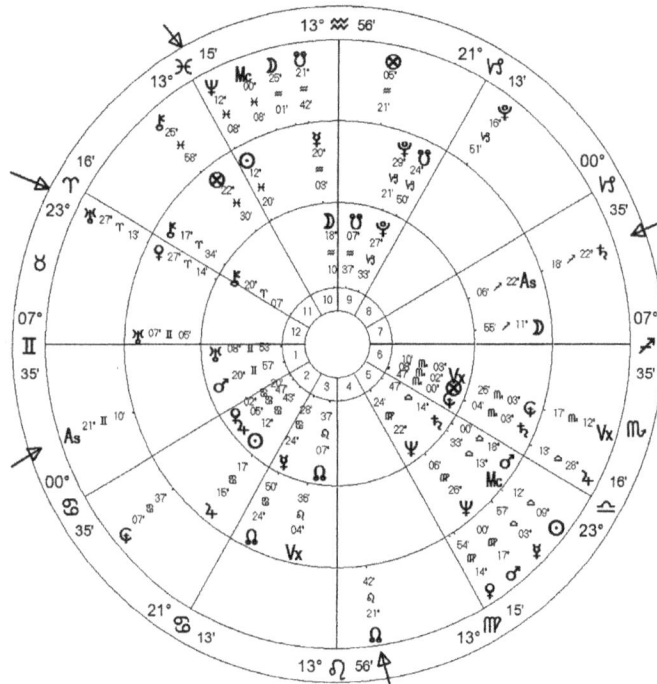

Fig. 4

Who knows why the American Declaration of Independence was signed at 2:14:15 a.m.? We will never know for sure and can only compare this chart with historical U.S. events. However, it would not be the first or last time a document was signed at an unusual time.

The Ascendant of this early morning chart is 7 Gemini 35 conjunction Uranus. In addition, the chart ruler Mercury is in close semi-square to Uranus.

As a resident of another country who has traveled the U.S. extensively and made many friends there, I see the U.S. as representative of high level communication, invention, technology, theatre, and film making. And who can forget the extraordinary technological advancement made by the U.S. as a result of the Moon landing in 1968?

Tri-wheel Usa Natal, Secondary Progressions & Transits October 1, 2017

In Fig. 4, the center wheel is the U.S. natal chart and the middle wheel is the U.S. natal chart progressed using secondary progression, SA in longitude to the date of the shooting and using the natal location for the progression. The outside wheel shows the transits for the commencement of the shooting in Las Vegas.

Amazing Links to U.S. Chart

This chart combination is amazing and aptly describes the event. Victims of this crime will have natal, progressed, or directed horoscope positions aspecting more than one of the dangerous patterns present. The strong Jupiter (protective) involvement suggests that although the event was shocking, it could have been worse with even more death and injury.

1. The SP (secondary progressed) Sun (12 Piisces 20) is conjunct transiting Neptune (12 Pisces 08) within minutes, both trine natal Sun (12 Cancer 43) = a weak, sensitive male, artistic environment.

2. The SP Ascendant at 22 Sagittarius 06 is conjunct transiting Saturn at 22 Sagittarius 18 and opposition natal Mars (20 Gemini 57) and transiting Ascendant (21 Gemini 10). This important opposition is in a T-square to natal Neptune (22 Virgo 24) = death, cutting of ties as a result of illness, paranoia, but positively expressed as compassion and support by the masses.

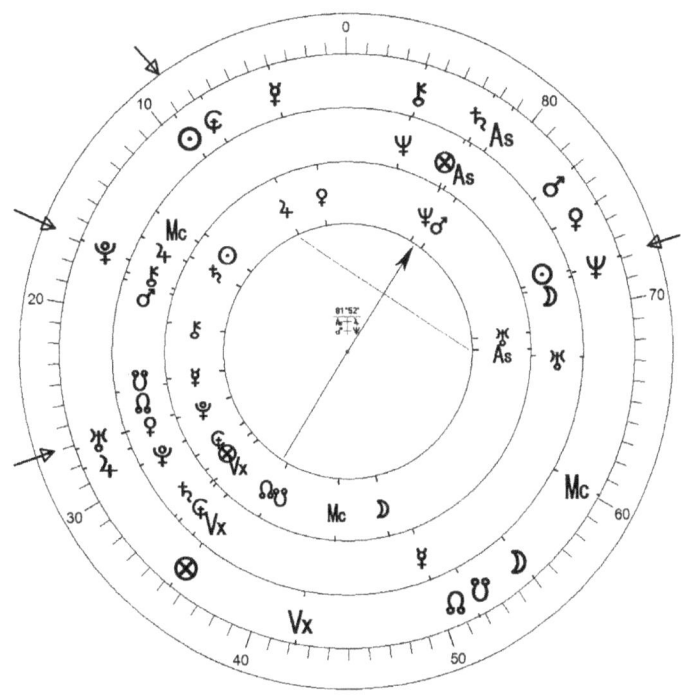

Fig. 5

Inner Wheel
USA
Natal Chart
4 Jul 1776 NS, Thu
2:14:15 am LMT +5:00:40
Philadelphia, USA
39°N57' 075°W10'
Geocentric
Tropical
Placidus
Mean Node

Middle Wheel
USA
Sec.Prog. SA in Long
1 Oct 2017, Sun
0:00 am LMT +5:00:40
Philadelphia, USA
39°N57' 075°W10'
Geocentric
Tropical
Placidus
Mean Node

Mean Node
Placidus
Tropical
Geocentric
36°N07' 115°W08'
Paradise, Nevada
10:05 pm PDT +7:00
1 Oct 2017, Sun
Natal Chart
Las Vegas Shooting starts
Outer Wheel

What is really interesting is that the SP Ascendant in Sagittarius is in the sign opposite to its natal Gemini position and moving through the U.S. seventh house of partners, allies, and open enemies. This suggests a period of courageous reflection and reassessment in these areas. The core values of the people have been highlighted, along with the current trend to expose and deal with those who have inflicted past as well as recent crimes.

Many astrologers "sense" the current Sagittarius SP Ascendant and others argue in favour of a U.S. natal Sagittarius Ascendant.

Naturally, because of our limited lifespan, we as individuals will never experience our personal SP Ascendant moving through our seventh house, but can observe and learn from the events occurring in countries that do, such as the U.S., whose official birth date is July 4, 1776.

3. Transiting Mars (17 Virgo 0) was semi-square SP Saturn (3 Scorpio 04) = death, cutting of ties.

4. SP Venus (27 Aries 14) was conjunct transiting Uranus (27 Aries13) and both are in opposition to transiting Jupiter (28 Libra 13) . Transiting Uranus conjunction SP Venus was also in close square to natal Pluto (27 Capricorn 33) = sudden events, shocks and transforming events, release of tension involving loved ones and the arts.

5. The transiting lunar nodal axis (21 Leo-Aquarius 42) is conjunct SP Mercury (20 Aquarius 03). The SP lunar Nodes (24 Cancer-Capricorn 50) were conjunct natal Mercury (Mercury is the natal and transit chart ruler) = world news, karmic message.

6. Transiting Pluto (16 Capricorn 51) formed a T-square with SP Mars (18 Libra 00) opposition SP Chiron (17 Aries 34) = extraordinary force, obsession, violent assaults.

7. The U.S. was coming into its last quarter SP lunar phase = reactionary, inflexible, philosophical viewpoints.

There are other links that will enhance the story. See what you can find.

Tri-dial U.S. Natal, Secondary Progressions and Transits October 1, 2017

The tri-dial (Fig. 5) works best with minimum orbs so that the most active aspects and tightest orbs are visually apparent. The 90-degree cosmogram is an excellent tool for the intuitive astrologer, whereas the traditional chart moves through the steps created by our astrological forefathers and mothers to create a clear, logical picture.

The inner dial is the U.S. natal chart, middle dial the U.S. secondary progressed chart, and outer dial the transits for the event.

The tri-wheel pinpoints the U.S. natal Mars rising square natal Neptune (conjunctions, squares, and oppositions are placed together on the cosmogram), powerfully linking to the U.S. secondary progressed Ascendant and Part of Fortune, plus the transiting Saturn-Ascendant pattern. On the other side of the dial (semi-square or sesquiquadrate) we see the U.S. natal Vertex = SP Vertex = SP Hades = transiting Part of Fortune.

This is indeed a dangerous pattern suggesting a period of loss, endings and new beginnings, health issues and undermining factors.

Natal Pluto = SP Venus, Sun and Moon = transiting Jupiter, Uranus and Neptune = disruption and deception, transformation in partnerships and in life of a loved one, fate and destiny. Spiritual journey.

The Jupiter = Pluto and Pluto = Jupiter patterns are present = important legal matters, big losses.

So it appears that as well as the tragic personal losses there will be large financial issues.

When the fast-moving points Ascendant and Midheaven join the slow-moving planets that form difficult or dangerous patterns, they act as triggers.

Therefore the location for the event in Las Vegas was not a safe place for many people to be at 10:05 p.m. on October 1, 2017.

Note: At 9:59 p.m., six minutes before he commenced his rampage, Paddock fired more than 200 rounds through his door, wounding security guard Jesus Campos in the thigh.

At that time the fast-moving Ascendant was at 19 Gemini 42 and the Midheaven at 28 Aquarius 34, which means that the Ascendant had moved 1 degree, 28 minutes and the Midheaven 1 degree, 34 minutes by the time the rampage on the crowd commenced.

This made little difference to the chart, in particular the setting Saturn, which had set by the time the shooting ended at 10:15 p.m.

The Shooter, Nature Versus Nurture

Stephen Craig Paddock, the shooter-perpetrator of the massacre, was born April 9, 1953 at 11:05 a.m. CST, Clinton, Iowa. He was the eldest of four sons of Benjamin Hoskins Paddock, a convicted bank robber who escaped prison in 1969 and was on the FBI most wanted list until 1977.

Stephen Paddock graduated from the John H. Francis Polytechnic High School in 1971 and from California State University Northridge in 1977 with a degree in business administration. He worked for the federal government between 1975 and 1985 and became highly successful as a real estate owner, investor, and speculator.

Traditional Chart of Stephen Paddock

Paddock's natal chart (Fig. 6) signature is cardinal fire (Aries), with the Sun, Venus, and Midheaven in Aries, indicating a successful solo worker and influential leader. Ambition and friendships were grounding influences (Mars, Jupiter, and Fortunae in Taurus in the eleventh house); but his powerful, aggressive, and unharnessed impulses were a danger to himself and others..

His chart has a cardinal grand cross. The Aries Sun is in a wide conjunction to Venus in the tenth house and opposition the Saturn-Neptune conjunction in the fourth house, suggesting negativity and ill health stemming from parents and/or ancestors, aptly describing his father's notorious history, plus physical childhood insecurity and negativity. This opposition forms the grand cardinal cross with the Cancer Ascendant opposition Chiron in the sixth house conjunction the Descendant = disappointments and wounding experiences through his partners

Fig. 6

Stephen Craig Paddock
Natal Chart
9 Apr 1953, Thu
11:05 am CST +6:00
Clinton, Iowa
41°N50'40" 090°W11'19"
Geocentric
Tropical
Placidus
Mean Node

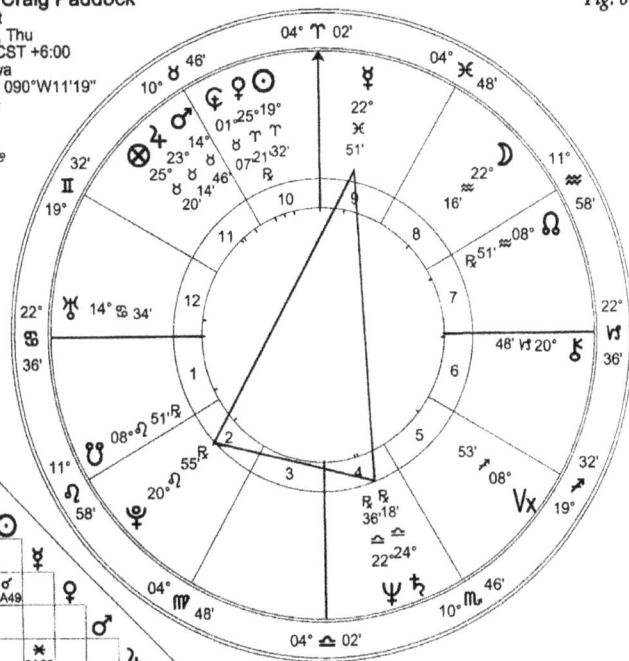

and other people in general, as suggested by his two failed marriages.

At its best this pattern would have enabled Paddock to be a caretaker of others, provided he could find a strong enough ally to help strengthen his tendency to be swayed by negative influences within himself or by those in his immediate circle.

Stephen's brother Eric denied that there was any influence from the father, who was arrested in 1960 when Stephen was seven-years-old, because their mother told them the father was dead. However it is generally accepted that the first seven years of a child's life form the foundation of his or her later years. Astrologers in particular would mark this period as the waxing square of Saturn in its 29.5-year cycle.

Stephen's Cancer Ascendant and Mercury in Pisces are two important water points. First, the Cancer Ascendant represents the importance of home and family history. Cancer the Crab clings to and reveres the past and its heroes, so was Stephen's intelligence and education enough to contain his aggressive emotional blueprint?

Mercury in Pisces in the ninth house trine the Ascendant and sextile Jupiter and Chiron indicate an opportunity to attain higher education and make a success of life. Jupiter in Taurus in a T-square to the Moon opposition Pluto across the second and eighth money houses, which Reinhold Ebertin describes as "great success, lucky chances," suggesting financial success, which he did achieve. Luck was on Stephen's side when despite normal security measures, he was able to blatantly fulfil his deadly murder plan.

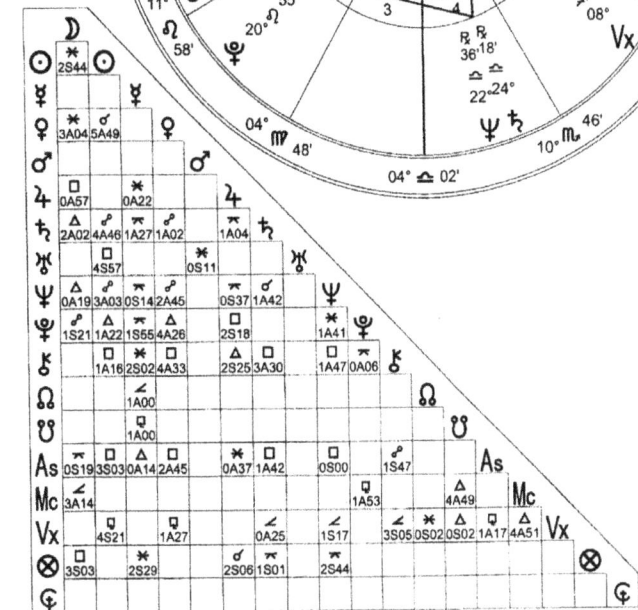

Much has already been written by astrologers on the hard aspects between the Moon and Pluto, which describes the power and intensity of the emotions, expressed through obsessive and often creative action.

Mercury in Pisces is sensitive and vulnerable so it would be an inner battle for a tough, militant gunman to deal with such depth of emotion. Mercury forms a Yod to Pluto in the second house (values, priorities) and the Saturn-Neptune conjunction in the fourth (harking back to hereditary and family values). In Stephen's case the total pattern indicates a propensity to mental illness, based on obsessive tendencies—an inner split.

Tri-wheel—Paddock's Secondary Progressions and Transits for Event (Fig. 7)

Stephen was still in his secondary progressed New Moon phase, with the SP Moon in Cancer conjunction SP Mercury = new plans based on emotional childhood experience, a trip back in time. Mercury is the ruler of the SP chart (Fig 7).

Stephen's SP Jupiter was fewer than two degrees from his SP Midheaven. This important SP conjunction was

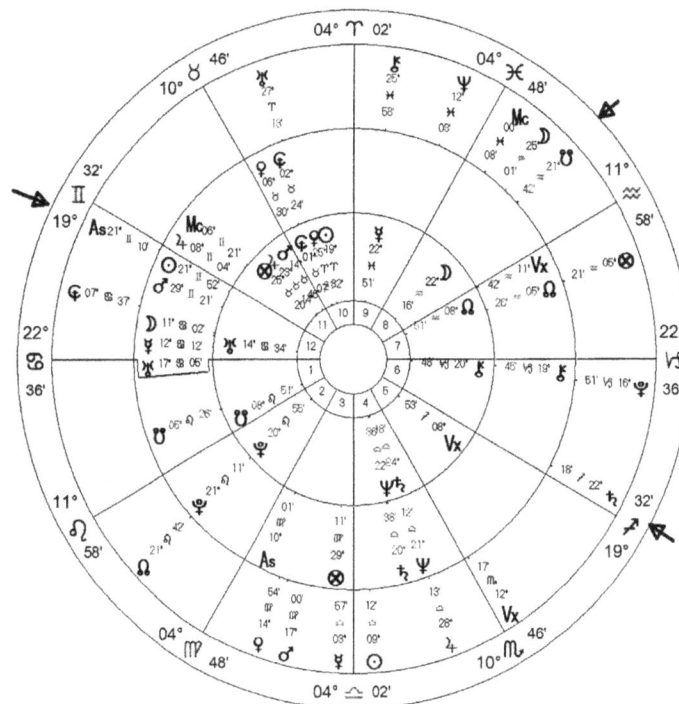

Inner Wheel
Stephen Craig Paddock
Natal Chart
9 Apr 1953, Thu
11:05 am CST +6:00
Clinton, Iowa
41°N50'40" 090°W11'19"
Geocentric
Tropical
Placidus
Mean Node

Middle Wheel
Stephen Craig Paddock
Sec.Prog. SA in Long
1 Oct 2017, Sun
0:00 am CST +6:00
41°N50'40" 090°W11'19"
Geocentric
Tropical
Placidus
Mean Node

Mean Node
Placidus
Tropical
Geocentric
36°N07' 115°W08'
Paradise, Nevada
10:05 pm PDT +7:00
1 Oct 2017, Sun
Natal Chart
Las Vegas Shooting starts
Outer Wheel

Fig. 7

conjunct the U.S. natal Ascendant and Uranus = opportunity for plans to manifest, sudden release targeting the American people, attracting the public eye.

When the shooting started, transiting Ascendant (21 Gemini10) was conjunct Stephen's SP Sun in the twelfth house trine SP Saturn-Neptune in the fourth and square his natal Mercury in the ninth. The square to Mercury triggered the natal mental split mentioned above. Transiting Saturn at 22 Sagittarius 18 opposed the SP Sun and transiting Ascendant.

Shortly before the event Stephen experienced a lunar return in his natal eighth house, with the transiting Moon conjunction the transiting lunar Node axis, conjunction his natal Moon opposition Pluto = karmic life and death experience.

Tri-dial—Paddock's Natal/Secondary Progressions and Transits for Event

All of the above patterns and more can be seen on the tri-dial (Fig. 8). Transiting Pluto in close opposition to SP Uranus in the twelfth house reinforces the validity of transits to secondary progressions. Stephen was determined to transform his life and make his mark on history at the expense of others' lives, whereas in addition to the tragedy, his actions increased debate on the U.S. gun laws.

Tri-dial Paddock's Natal/Solar Arc and Transits for Event

There is additional information on this solar arc tri-dial to accurately describe the event … (Fig. 9)

Mars (transit) conjunction Uranus (S Arc) = Hades (natal) = well planned violence to maximize damage in a public place.

Pluto (transit) opposition Mars (S Arc) = Sun/Uranus Midpoint (natal) = sudden violent action, a radical reformer.

Mercury (transit) = Hades (S Arc) = Midheaven (natal) = Mars/Pluto Moon (natal) = Fanatical realization of plans, mental disintegration.

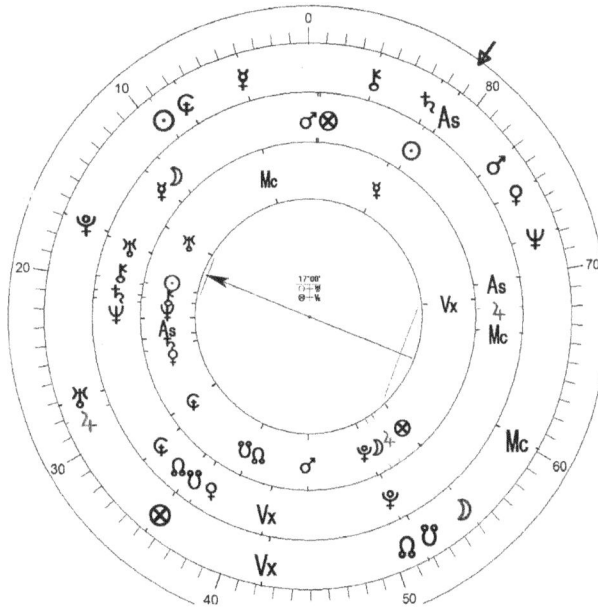

Fig. 8

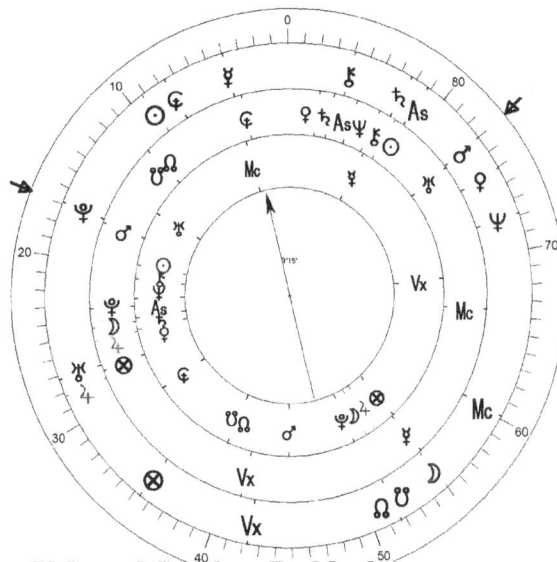

Fig. 9

Comparison Natal Charts—U.S. and Stephen Paddock

Stephen's links with the U.S. chart are unmistakable, but unfortunately they emphasize his notoriety rather than productive contribution. Venus, Hades, Mars, Jupiter and Fortunae fall in the U.S. twelfh house = success with behind-the-scenes activities and through institutions.

Stephen's grand cross (Sun Venus opposition Saturn Neptune square Ascendant opposition Chiron) = the U.S. Mercury in the third house square Chiron in the eleventh = plans to wound friends and neighbours, victims and victimization, brooding over the past, physical and mental pain, sending a message.

U.S. Pluto in the ninth house taps into the grand cross through its opposition to natal Mercury (conjunction Stephen's Ascendant square his Saturn Neptune) = powerful communication, mental trauma, in-depth research, destructive effects on others.

Reinhold Ebertin describes the Saturn-Pluto combination as "a fanatical adherence to one's principles once they have been adopted, the mass murderer." However, this combination can also be seen in the personal charts of highly disciplined, hardworking people, often of a spiritual or religious nature.

Stephen's Uranus conjunction U.S. Sun in the second house square U.S. Saturn in the fifth house = sudden shift in priorities, rebellion against tradition, sudden separations, breaking new ground.

Stephen's Moon conjunction U.S. Moon in the tenth house (4 degree orb) = desire to be famous, gaining recognition.

Stephen's lunar Node axis conjunction reversed U.S. lunar Node axis = destiny encounters, fait accompli (action completed before those affected are in a position to query or reverse it).

Stephen's Sun in Aries square natal Chiron in Capricorn = U.S. Chiron in Aries in the eleventh = warped perception of "necessary wounds." In his book *Chiron, the New Planet in Your Horoscope*, Richard Nolle states that those with Chiron in Capricorn "tend to be attracted to older mentors" and "measure their own self-worth through the eyes of others." He believes that these people have a strong desire to conquer time.

Stephen's Mercury in Pisces opposition U.S. Neptune in Virgo in the fifth house = abundant imagination, self-deception, faulty judgement, loss of power to feel or sense, disturbances originating in the subconscious, out of perspective.

Inner Chart
USA
Natal Chart
4 Jul 1776
2:14:15 AM
LMT +05:00:40
Philadelphia
USA
75w10'00 39n57'00
Geocentric
Tropical
Placidus
Mean Node

Outer Chart
Stephen Craig Paddock
Natal Chart
9 Apr 1953
11:05:00 AM
CST +06:00:00
Clinton
USA
90w11'19 41n50'40
Geocentric
Tropical
Placidus
Mean Node

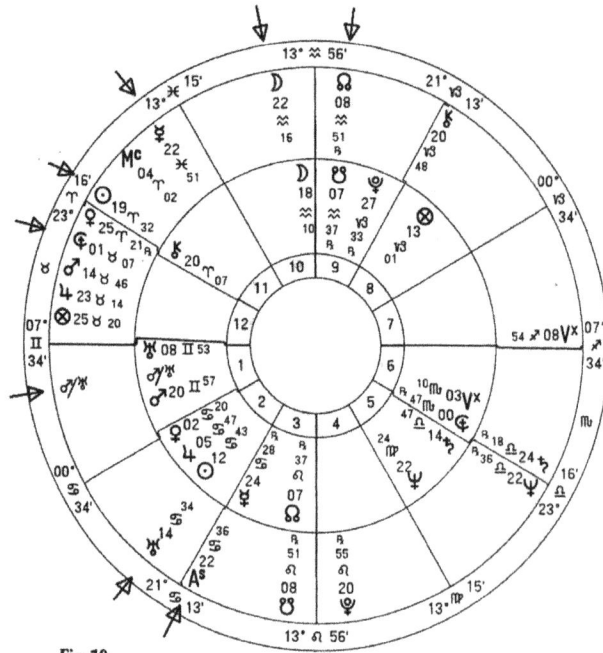

Fig. 10

Stephen's Hades in Taurus opposition U.S. Hades in the sixth house in Scorpio = destroying powers of the past, revenge.

An unusual contact is Stephen's Mars/Uranus midpoint (14 Gemini 40) conjunction U.S. Mars/Uranus midpoint (14 Gemini 55) in the U.S. first house of the people. We all have this midpoint in our charts. It demonstrates our determination, willpower and potential for aggressive action, plus energy events such as operations and accidents. In the case of the U.S. natal chart it may suggest fighters of freedom, sporting prowess and the right of the people to carry arms.

In Paddock's case his aggression was directed toward the people (U.S. first house) as an expression of his paranoid memories, revenge and a distorted viewpoint of authority and how it affected his role in society. At that time his mental split dictated that he could no longer maintain the control necessary to continue cultivating positive opportunities for himself.

The timing and astrological action of the event suggests that it may be pivotal in future US reviews and reassessments of policies.

References

Wikipedia; *Combination of Stellar Influences* by Reinhold Ebertin; *Rules for Planetary Pictures* by Ludwic Rudolph; *Chiron: The New Planet in Your Horoscope* by Richard Nolle.; www.astrodatabank; Solar Fire and Janus 5 for chart wheels.

Voyager Mission: Infinity and Beyond

By Marilyn Muir

ABSTRACT: In 1957, the Soviet Union launched Sputnik and the race for space moved into high gear. In 1961, President John F. Kennedy ramped up the U.S. space program with the objective to land a man on the Moon by the end of that decade. On July 20, 1969, that mandate was achieved as astronauts Neil Armstrong and Edwin "Buzz" Aldrin spent 21 hours on the surface of the Moon, two hours of which were outside their capsule. Space achievements came rapid fire as we moved from our system's inner space to the outer space of the cosmos . . . Voyagers' twin mission. Two space probes were launched in 1977, just 16 days apart, with twin yet different missions to explore the outer planets and beyond. These still operating probes just celebrated 40 years in space. An investigation of the launches and main events in their timelines to date offered the opportunity to view both the sameness and the differentness of their twin but unique mission. Using traditional astrological tools: planets, signs, houses, aspects and major configurations, the basis for comparison was both established then verified with very tight orbs. The probes twin-ness and their individuality can be clearly seen, one still within our solar system's boundaries, one now traveling in interstellar space . . . the Cosmos.

On August 20, 1977, the space probe Voyager II was launched from Cape Canaveral, Florida sent out by NASA to study the solar system's outer planets. On September 5, 1977 its twin, Voyager I, was launched with a similar mission, study of the outer planets. Both Voyager space probes carried the Golden Record of our world into the Cosmos. Because of differing mission directives and trajectories, Voyager I actually encountered two of the outer planets before Voyager II and thereby became more prominent in our news reporting. Voyager II actually visited four outer planets: Jupiter, Saturn, Uranus, and Neptune and completed its primary mission. It now has an "extended mission to study the outer reaches of our Solar System." While it is in a conserve power mode it has completed 40 years of continuous flight and operation as of August 20, 2017. It is currently in the helioshield area of our outer solar system and has not crossed the heliopause threshold for interstellar space.

Voyager I, because of its mission directive and trajectory, was the first to fly by Jupiter, its closest approach on March 5, 1979. Voyager I continued on to Saturn and did its flyby of both Saturn and its moon Titan on November 12, 1980. As close as I can tell from the NASA reported timeline, Voyager I completed its passage of the heliopause where the outgoing energy (the solar wind) from our Sun gives way to the incoming energies (the interstellar wind) from outer space, on August 25, 2012, at a distance of 121 AU (18 billion km from the Sun). Voyager I crossed into interstellar space into the cosmos.

Again, for energy conservation, Voyager I's main thrusters were shut down November 8, 1980. As time, travel, and space itself wore down the directional thrusters, it became necessary to see if the main thrusters could be re-fired and substituted in service. On November 28, 2017, 37+ years after shutdown, those primary

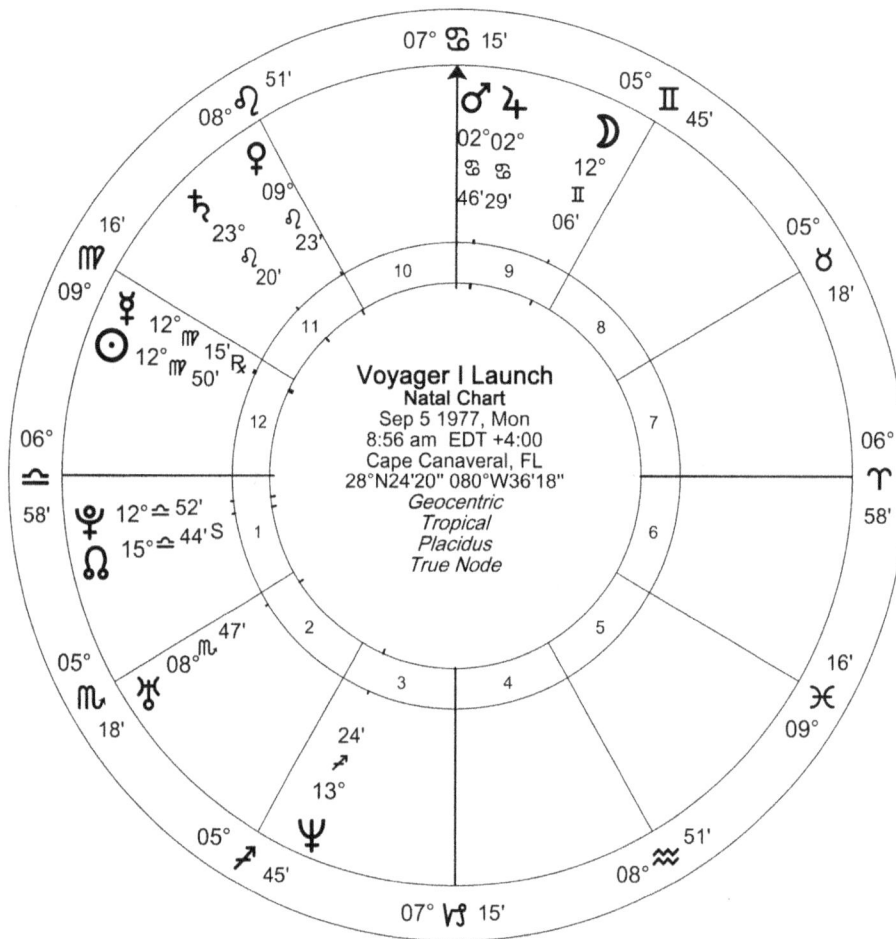

Voyager I Launch
Natal Chart
Sep 5 1977, Mon
8:56 am EDT +4:00
Cape Canaveral, FL
28°N24'20" 080°W36'18"
Geocentric
Tropical
Placidus
True Node

thrusters were once again fired and will be pressed into directional service. The maneuver worked! Now the same procedure is under consideration for Voyager II in order to prolong the life of the equipment, the mission and the amazing scientific information that can still be contributed by both probes, one in actual interstellar space, one approaching it through the helioshield. Both probes are still functioning and able to contribute, and the science lab has prolonged their usefulness for a few more years. YES!

I wondered about the launches and how those flyby activations would look astrologically. I chose Voyager I to research first since it has already crossed into interstellar space. We have an accurate launch time and five active dates to examine. The same procedure will be done for Voyager II in part 2 of this study.

Voyager I launch

- The launch chart has 6 Libra 58 is rising, with Pluto in the first house at 12 Libra 52 and the North Node close by, also in the first house at 15 Libra 44.

- The four angles complete a tight grand cross, Midheaven 7 Cancer 16, conjunction Mars-Jupiter in the ninth house at 2 Cancer 29-46.

- This is a space shot to our solar system's outer limits and beyond: cardinal (initiation) on the angles and with a Mars-Jupiter conjunction in the house of long distance travel (Jupiter's semi-major axis is 778.57 million km from the Sun and it was the nearest of the four bodies).

- Exploring the unknown (unconscious) is very Plutonian and the Nodes give a character of karma or destiny.

- The chart ruler is Venus at 9 Leo 23 square Uranus at 8 Scorpio 47, the Uranus challenge to invent, reveal,

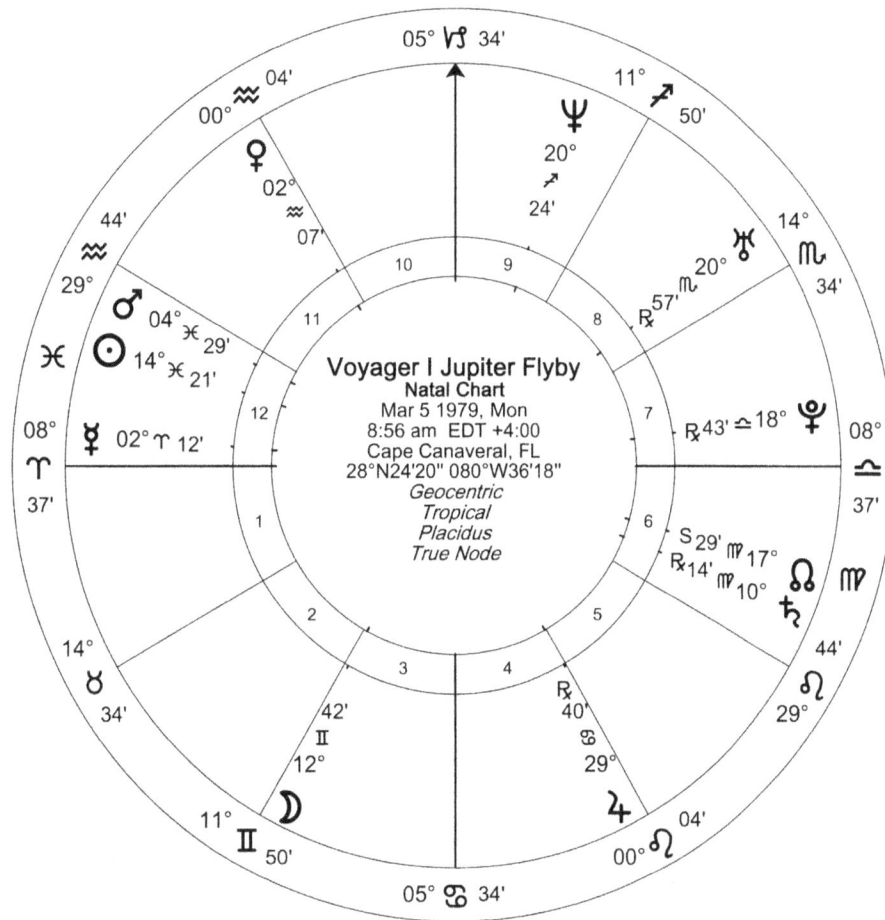

Voyager I Jupiter Flyby
Natal Chart
Mar 5 1979, Mon
8:56 am EDT +4:00
Cape Canaveral, FL
28°N24'20" 080°W36'18"
Geocentric
Tropical
Placidus
True Node

open new horizons pushing the very social lady Venus in the eleventh house of group efforts, the science team.

- One more pattern dominates this chart: a mutable T-square involving four planets with Moon at 12 Gemini 06 in the ninth house opposition Neptune at 13 Sagittarius 24 in the third (travel houses) square Mercury at 12 Virgo 15 retrograde and Sun at 12 Virgo 50 in the twelfth house. So much of the flight was very twelfth house—time/duration/silence, behind-the-scenes work.

- Perhaps the retrograde Mercury was evidenced by the twin probes launched within such a short time of one another (16 days), each with a unique mission. This flight was number 2 in launch, number 1 by designation.

What about the ongoing events? I use diurnals to illustrate the activity. (To calculate a diurnal chart, use the natal chart data, changing only the date for the activity itself. Change nothing else! This provides a personal transit chart for that event, complete with Ascendant and Midheaven.)

Jupiter Flyby

Do not change the time standard from the natal launch chart.

The closest approach to Jupiter was March 5, 1979, only 1.5 years after the launch. The flyby angles happen to be quite close to the launch chart.

- Flyby Midheaven is at 5 Capricorn 34 and the Ascendant at 8 Aries 37.

- Flyby Mercury at 2 Aries 12 is tightly square the launch Mars-Jupiter conjunction. Chart-wise Jupiter is involved in its own flyby.

13° ♍ 56'

15° ♎ 19'

09° ♌ 24'

☿ ♄ ♃
06° 03°
♀ ♎ ♎
15° 04° 01'
22° ♎ 52'
48'

14° ♌ 41' ℞

05° ♋ 42'

♏ 55'
11°

☿ 03° ♏
59' S

10   9

11   8

☉ 20° ♏ 18'
⛢ 25° ♏ 31'

12   7

05° ♐ 04'

Saturn/Titan Flyby
Natal Chart
Nov 12 1980, Wed
8:56 am EDT +4:00
Cape Canaveral, FL
28°N24'20" 080°W36'18"
Geocentric
Tropical
Placidus
True Node

05° ♊ 04'

1   6

♆ 21° ♐ 14'
♂ 22° ♐ 49'

2   5

05° ♑ 42'

☽ 12° ♑ 51'

3   4

55'
♉ 11°

09° ♒ 24'

15° ♈ 19'

13° ♓ 56'

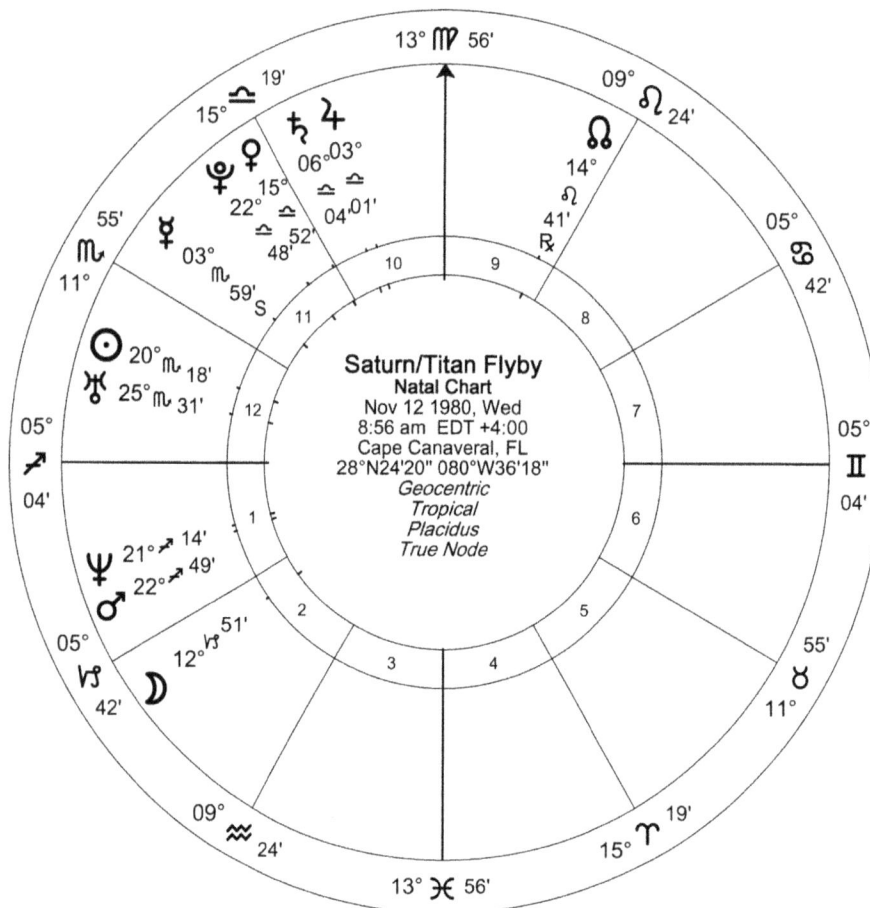

- Venus, the launch chart ruler, is at 2 Aquarius 07 in the diurnal chart, opposition retrograde Jupiter at 29 Cancer 40. Transiting Jupiter is specifically involved in the Jupiter flyby again!

- Remember the launch Moon-Neptune opposition? There it is again, 1.5 years later, with the flyby Moon within a half-degree of its launch position.

- For this flyby event, the Moon position of the Moon-Neptune opposition is also square the Sun at 14 Pisces 21 and South Node aat 17 Pisces 29.

- Back to the mutable T-square. It was now strengthened with the addition of retrograde Saturn at 10 Virgo 14. Mars, the flyby chart ruler, is in that mutable complex but quite wide in orb at 4 Pisces 29 in the twelfth house with Pisces intercepted. This was a scientific achievement, photos, data, not as much as spotlight.

Voyager I had a close encounter with Jupiter as the event ruling Venus opposed Jupiter and the event Mercury triggered the natal Jupiter-Mars as the Sun occupied Pisces.

Saturn/Titan Flyby

Do not change the time standard from the launch chart.

Saturn's semi-major axis is 1,433.53 million km from the Sun. The closest approach for both Saturn and Titan was collective on November 12, 1980.

- Flyby Midheaven at13 Virgo 56 conjunction the launch Sun-Mercury conjunction and tightly square the launch Moon-Neptune opposition.

- Flyby Jupiter at 3 Libra 01 conjunction Saturn 6 Libra 04 is conjunct the launch Ascendant.

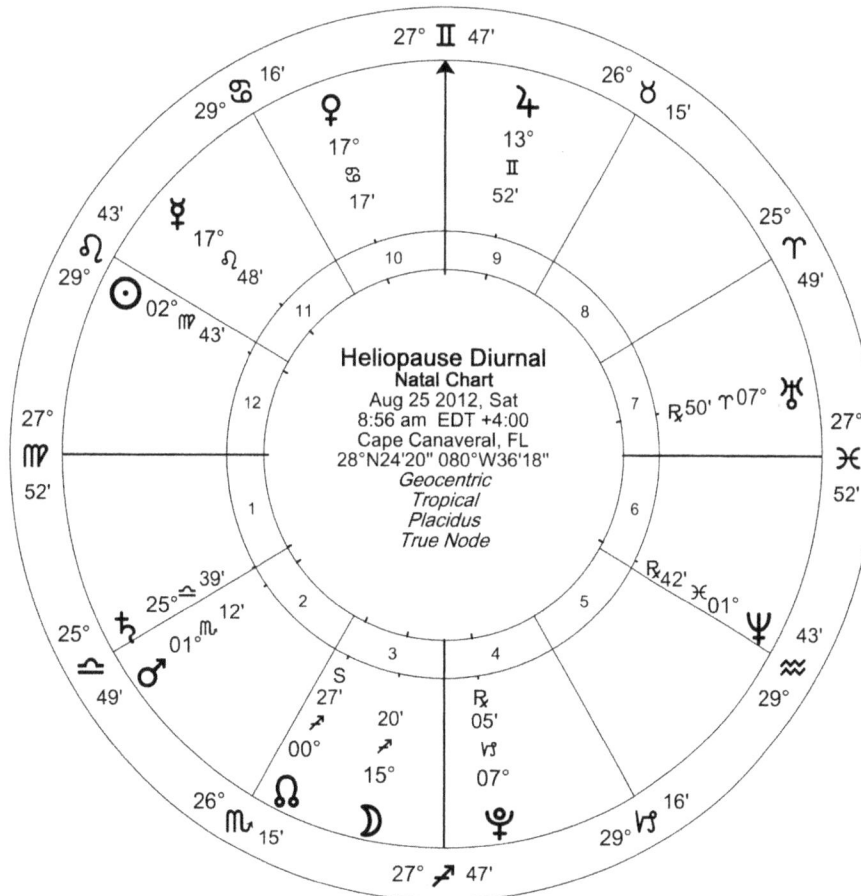

Heliopause Diurnal
Natal Chart
Aug 25 2012, Sat
8:56 am EDT +4:00
Cape Canaveral, FL
28°N24'20" 080°W36'18"
Geocentric
Tropical
Placidus
True Node

- Flyby Moon is tightly square launch Pluto.

- Flyby Venus is tightly conjunct launch the Pluto-North Node conjunction.

- This is a Saturn flyby so it is not a surprise that the flyby Sun-Uranus conjunction is tightly square the launch Saturn (Saturn was the traditional ruler of Aquarius, the sign of the flyby South Node).

Heliopause

There was some confusion but the official NASA date is August 25, 2012.

How in this world do we decide what represents the place where our Sun's control over our system switches to intergalactic energy? Where do we locate that astrologically? How about the black hole at the very center of our Milky Way Galaxy's center (Sagittarius A), approximately 28 Sagittarius *at the time of the launch 40 years ago*?

- Will a tight conjunction to the heliopause chart IC at 27 Sagittarius 47 do it for you?

- Or if that is too speculative how about heliopause retrograde Pluto at 7 Capricorn 05 just 10 minutes from the V-1 launch IC?

- How about a tight Moon 15 at Sagittarius 20-Jupiter at 13 Gemini 52 opposition tightly trigering the launch mutable T-square?

- How about heliopause Venus at 17 Cancer 17 square launch Pluto near the launch North Node?

- How about heliopause retrograde Uranus at 7 Aries 50 conjunction the launch Descendant?

How many tight connections do you need for proof?

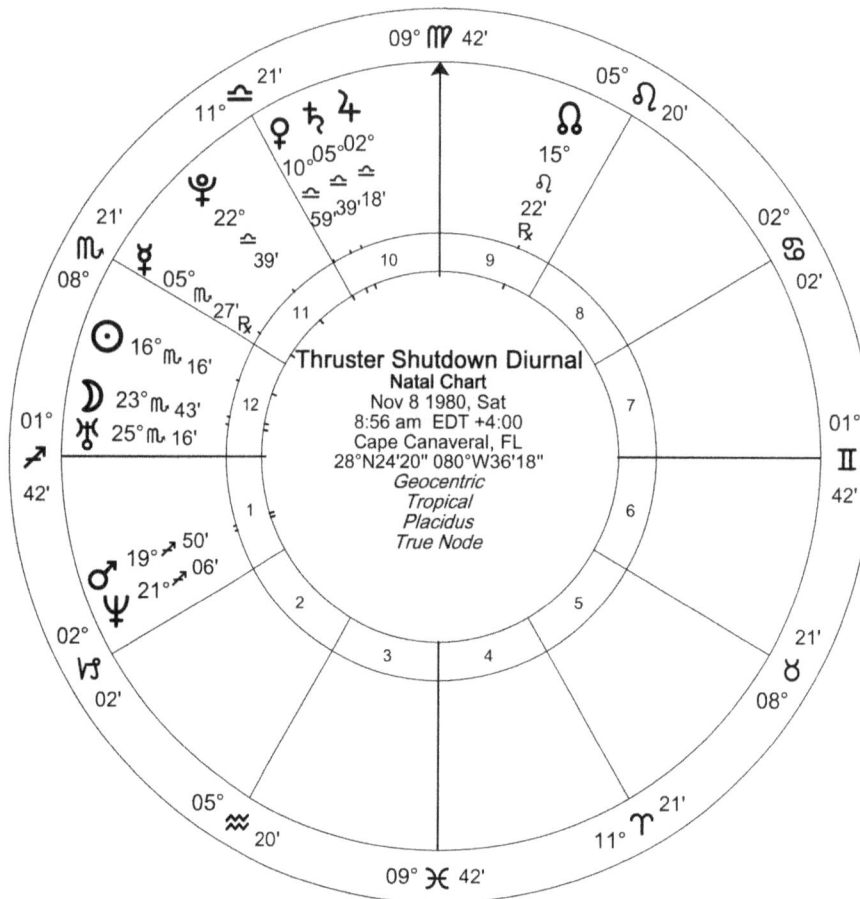

Chart labels:
09° ♍ 42'
11° ♎ 21'
05° ♌ 20'
☊ 15°
♀ ♄ ♃ 10° 05° 02°
♎ ♎ ♎ 59' 39' 18'
♌ 22' Rx
♇ 22°
21°
02°
♏ 08° ☿ 05° 27' Rx
02° ♋ 02°
10   9
11   8
☉ 16° ♏ 16'
☽ 23° ♏ 43'
♅ 25° ♏ 16'
Thruster Shutdown Diurnal
Natal Chart
Nov 8 1980, Sat
8:56 am EDT +4:00
Cape Canaveral, FL
28°N24'20" 080°W36'18"
Geocentric
Tropical
Placidus
True Node
7
01° ♐ 42'
01° ♊ 42'
12   1
6
♂ 19° ♐ 50'
♆ 21° ♐ 06'
2
5
02° ♑ 02'
21° ♉ 08'
3   4
05° ♒ 20'
11° ♈ 21'
09° ♓ 42'

Thrusters: Off Again, On Again

Do not change the launch time standard for these events.

Remember that I mentioned that the main thrusters were shut down November 8, 1980? This was just a few days prior to the Saturn/Titan flyby. Can we see that relatively minor activation to the launch chart from that diurnal?

- The shutdown at Midheaven 9 Virgo 42 tightly triggered the launch mutable T-square.
- Shutdown Jupiter at 2 Libra 18 square the launch Mars-Jupiter conjunction.
- Shutdown Venus at 10 Libra 59 conjunction launch Pluto.

That is a lot of astrological activity for the simple act of shutting off the thrusters. Fast forward *37 years*....

Re-firing of those thrusters occurred November 28, 2017.

- Re-fire Midheaven at 1 Libra 06 square the launch Mars-Jupiter conjunction, joining the re-fire Moon out of sign but about three degrees applying.
- Re-fire Neptune at 11 Pisces 29 triggered the launch mutable T-square.
- Re-fire Pluto at 17 Capricorn 44 square launch North Node.

Perhaps you have noticed that I dwelled on the cardinal and mutable aspects in these charts. That is because they had to do with rulership of events and houses. There were connections between fixed positions as well. I also focused on hard aspects for this initial study: conjunction, square and opposition. Why? I see them as action aspects and the softer aspects as support and flow. This is a man-made probe that sits atop a monster rocket and

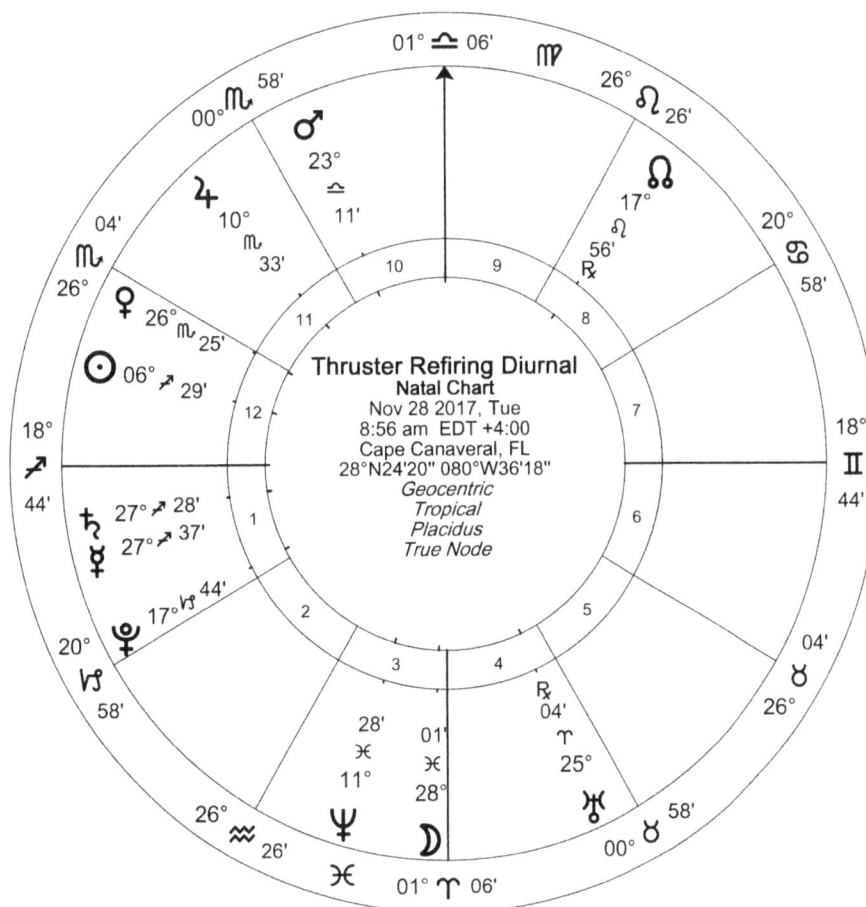

Thruster Refiring Diurnal
Natal Chart
Nov 28 2017, Tue
8:56 am EDT +4:00
Cape Canaveral, FL
28°N24'20" 080°W36'18"
Geocentric
Tropical
Placidus
True Node

gets blasted out into space, to face the unknown with little to no help should anything go wrong. Sextiles and trines just don't do that. They may help succeed, but they do not risk.

Understand also there always is more to see/find. Every time I pick up a chart I see more than I saw initially. This study is enough to show the interconnectedness of the charts from one launch to its five specific activations.

This exercise should also show you that just because something constitutes an event it cannot be separate from the process that engendered that event and its ongoing ramifications. Life is a process, a series of interconnected events and activities, sometimes even a cascading event process. It is not about isolated or unconnected events. Study the *process* inherent in all events.

Part 2, Voyager 2

Now we will look at Voyager 2, which technically was in space prior to Voyager 1, and we will follow the same technical procedure: use the launch for the base chart and flybys of the space probe to the four outer planets that it visited. This will provide us with a comparison to see if the basic principles we developed for Voyager 1 hold up for Voyager 2. To avoid confusion I have marked these new chart positions V-2 or V-1 where necessary to maintain clarity.

Voyager 2 was launched August 20, 1977, 14:29:00 UTC (10:29 a.m. EDT), Cape Canaveral, Florida

Repeating the Voyager 1 launch cardinal angular cross, Voyager 2 angles have somewhat later cardinal degrees also in tight square to one another. The Ascendant is 13 Libra 37, with Pluto in the twelfth house at 12 Libra 21 and the North Node in the first house at 16 Libra 17. Both are square the Midheaven at 14 Cancer 13, with chart-ruler Venus widely conjunction the Midheaven in the tenth house at 20 Cancer 33.

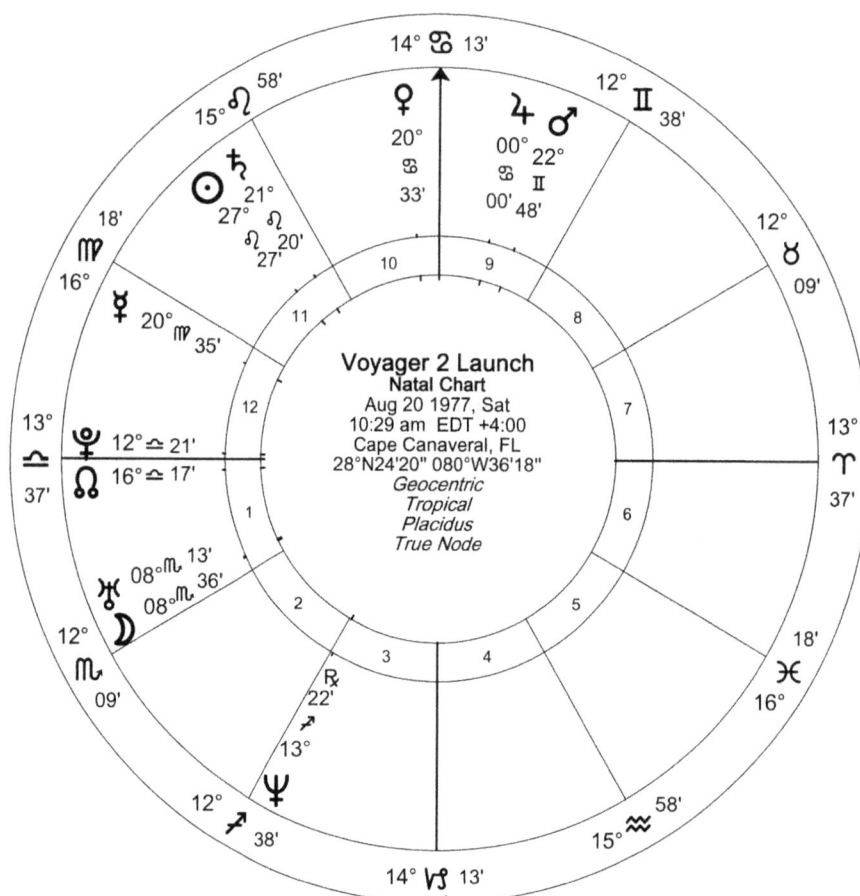

The ruler of the Midheaven, the Moon at 8 Scorpio 36, is tightly conjunct Uranus at 8 Scorpio 13, late in the first house.

There is a wide, separating (weakening) Sun-Saturn conjunction from 21 Leo 20 to 27 Leo 27. Why weakening? The aspect perfected prior to launch: process.

The V-2 Mars/Jupiter launch conjunction evident in Voyager I had not fully formed for this launch, however both planets are again in the ninth house and Neptune is still in the third house, both transportation houses. Understand that V-2 preceded V-1 in launch, but its trajectory made it reach Jupiter and then Saturn-Titan later than V-1. The Mars/Jupiter conjunction was developing for this launch (V-2) and had fully developed and was pivotal for the launch of V-1. V-1 got to the planets first . . . it had the stronger aspect.

The V-2 launch Mars and Mercury are in close applying square with launch Mercury in the twelfth house. So much of what these charts represent are twelfth house energies with the long silence of space and the continual behind-the-scenes activity. Not negative, just indicative of the use and application of these energies.

Voyager 2 Jupiter Flyby

The first planetary flyby for Voyager 2 was Jupiter on July 9, 1979, 22:29:00 UTC (10:29 a.m. EDT).

The launch positions for both probes were based at Cape Canaveral, Florida. The flybys are up close and personal with the planets themselves. We are using diurnals to keep the information and activations between the launch of the individual space probe and its personal experience in outer space. We do have times of encounter for Voyager 2. But if you were to the cast a chart for the flyby of a planet, how do you correlate its location to the Earth date and Universal time? I stayed with traditional diurnals so I would compare apples to apples, one launch at a time.

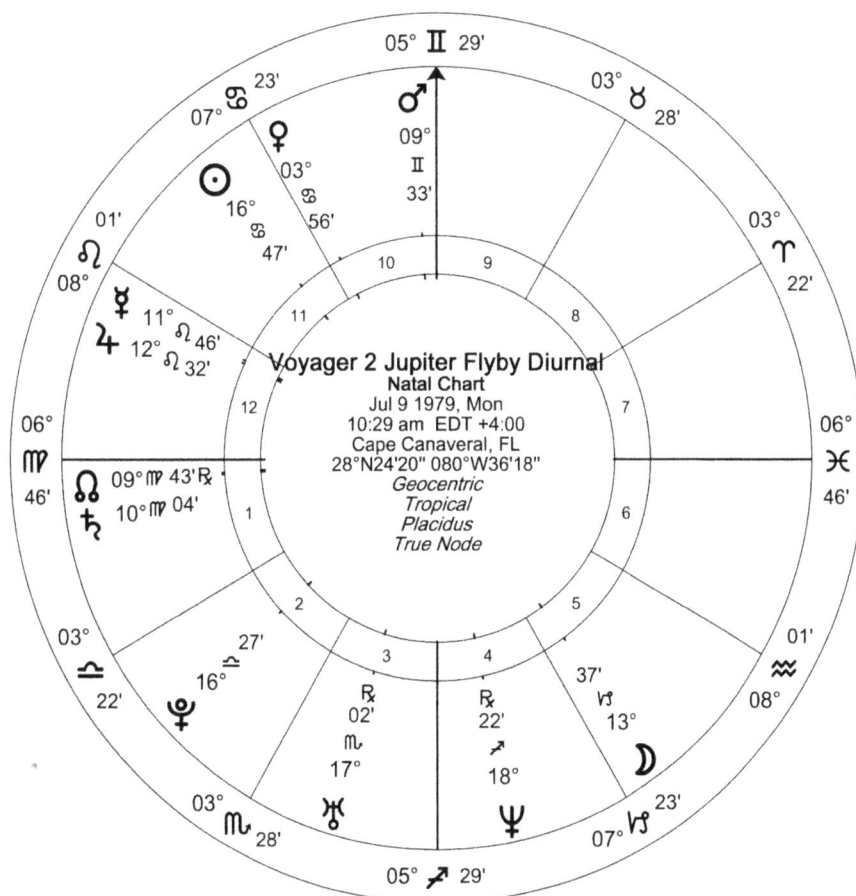

The chart shows:

- 05° ♊ 29'
- 07° ♋ 23'
- 03° ♉ 28'
- ♀ 09° ♊ 33'
- ♂ (at MC area)
- ☉ 16° ♋ 47'
- 03° ♋ 56'
- 03° ♈ 22'
- 01' ♌ 08°
- ☿ 11° ♌ 46'
- ♃ 12° ♌ 32'
- 06° ♍ 46'
- ☊ 09° ♍ 43' ℞
- ♄ 10° ♍ 04'
- 06° ♓ 46'
- 03° ♎ 22'
- ♇ 16° ♎ 27'
- ☋ 08° ♒ 01'
- ℞ ♏ 02° 17'
- ℞ ♐ 22° 18'
- ♑ 37° 13°
- ☽ ♑ 23'
- 03° ♏ 28'
- ♅ ♏
- ♆ 07° ♑
- 05° ♐ 29'

Center text:
Voyager 2 Jupiter Flyby Diurnal
Natal Chart
Jul 9 1979, Mon
10:29 am EDT +4:00
Cape Canaveral, FL
28°N24'20" 080°W36'18"
Geocentric
Tropical
Placidus
True Node

The Voyager 2 launch focused on mid cardinal degrees so we start work there.

- V-2 Jupiter flyby Sun at 16 Cancer 47 opposition Moon at 13 Capricorn 37 (Full Moon) square Pluto at 16 Libra 27, triggering the mid-range cardinal planets in the V-2 launch grand cross.

- V-2 Jupiter flyby Midheaven at 5 Gemini 29 conjunction Mars ay 9 Gemini 33, both square Ascendant at 6 Virgo 46, Norh Node at 9 Virgo 43 and Saturn at10 Virgo 04, a tight active complex relative to this event.

- V-2 Jupiter flyby chart ruler Mercury is 11 Leo 46 conjunction flyby Jupiter at 12 Leo 32. Jupiter is dignified (strong) in the twelfth house. The chart ruler is conjunct the planet being visited . . . definitely appropriate.

- The V-2 launch chart ruler is Venus. The V-2 Jupiter flyby Venus at 3 Cancer 56 is widely conjunct launch Jupiter at 00 Cancer 00.

Remember, first flyby honors for Jupiter and Saturn went to Voyager 1, which did this first.

Voyager 2 Saturn Flyby

Voyager 2's Saturn flyby occurred August 25, 1981, 3:24:05 UTC.

- There are cardinal degrees everywhere, eight of primary 13 positions ranging from eight to 25 degrees with multiple activations.

- Venus is again this chart ruler for the V-2 flyby of Saturn, look first to the Saturn-Venus conjunction at 7 Libra 56 to 8 Libra 22, also conjunction Jupiter at 10 Libra 26, square flyby Moon at 11 Cancer 45, triggering the cardinal degrees previously listed.

- V-2 Saturn flyby Neptune at 22 Sagittarius 06 opposition (triggering) V-2's launch Mars at 22 Gemini 48,

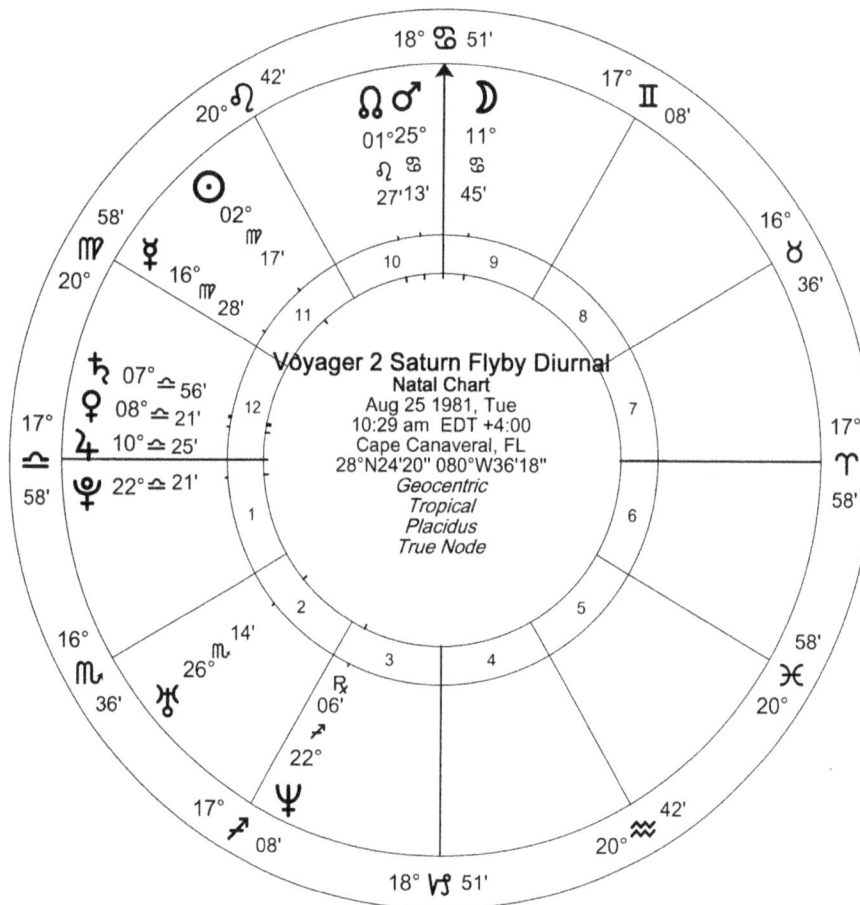

Voyager 2 Saturn Flyby Diurnal
Natal Chart
Aug 25 1981, Tue
10:29 am EDT +4:00
Cape Canaveral, FL
28°N24'20" 080°W36'18"
Geocentric
Tropical
Placidus
True Node

square V-2 launch Mercury at 20 Virgo 35, creating a T-square (action) between the charts.

Now Voyager 2 did some firsts of its own.

Voyager 2 Uranus Flyby

Voyager 2's Uranus flyby occurred January 24, 1986, 17:59:47 UTC. Note: Do not change the launch chart time standard for this diurnal.

- Look at Uranus at 20 Sagittarius 46 directly conjunction the V-2 Uranus flyby Midheaven at 21 Sagittarius 03. As the Midheaven represents the goal or mission of the event, this is specific!

- A Sun-Venus close conjunction (4:19 to 5:30 in Aquarius) is joined by Mercury at 29 Capricorn 18 in a wider and out of sign conjunction. Uranus is the ruler of Aquarius and there are three planets in Aquarius for this rendezvous, with Jupiter as chart ruler in its mundane dignity in the twelfth house. This Jupiter is receiving stimulation from Mars at 24 Scorpio 50 in the late eighth house (destiny) on the ninth house cusp (far journeys).

- What about V-2's launch with Uranus conjunction Moon at 8 Scorpio? V-2's flyby Pluto is 7 Scorpio 18.

- We should not forget the mid-cardinal degrees so strong in the V-2 launch chart. The Uranus flyby Moon is 17 Cancer 40, triggering that entire complex.

Voyager 2 Neptune Flyby

Voyager 2's Neptune flyby is a WOW!

- Mid-cardinal angular cross with a Uranus-Saturn-Neptune conjunction in early Capricorn opposition Jupiter

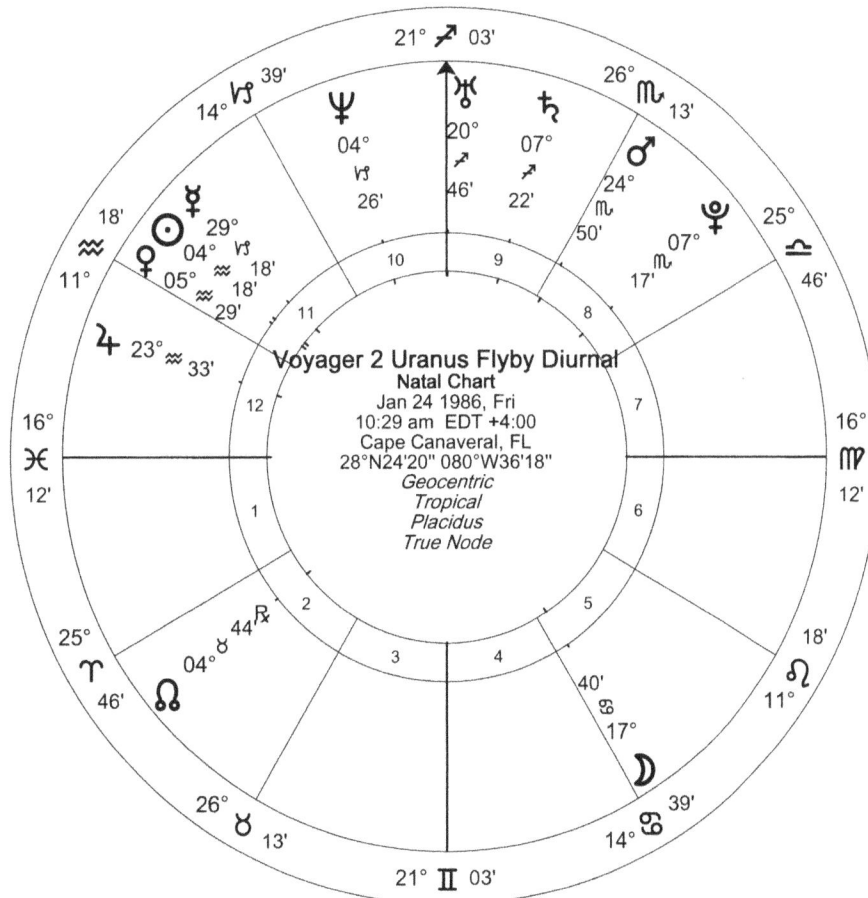

Voyager 2 Uranus Flyby Diurnal
Natal Chart
Jan 24 1986, Fri
10:29 am EDT +4:00
Cape Canaveral, FL
28°N24'20" 080°W36'18"
Geocentric
Tropical
Placidus
True Node

in early Cancer and a wide but applying out-of-sign Moon.

- Remember that a transiting (diurnal) Moon travels one degree of actual motion every two hours on the clock. As the fastest moving body, the Moon at 25 Gemini 40 will move from one to another in this T-square complex within the 24 hours of its originating position. It was square flyby Mercury in the twelfth at 29 Virgo 16. This flyby was technically the end of its stated mission to fly by the four outer planets. Anything past this point becomes part of its extended mission and is still in progress.

- Also note that this flyby Moon had just activated the V-2 launch Mars at 22 Gemini 48 about six hours earlier on the day's clock. V-2 launch Mars was square launch Mercury, both Mercuries in their respective twelfth houses. I read that as technical, detailed, backup and support, transmission of photo and data, all behind the scenes activity.

- V-2 launch Neptune is 13 Sagittarius 22, tightly square Neptune flyby Mars at 13 Virgo 57. Neptune flyby, Neptune trigger.

Because the scientists took advantage of the lineup of the four outer planets, Voyager 2 had a much longer journey and has not yet gone through the heliopause. Both space probes celebrated 40 years in their journey in 2017, amazing feats. They are both functional in a curtailed way to prolong their life cycle and contribution.

Planetary Patterns

I have not done anything with planetary patterns other than the traditional T-squares and grand crosses described throughout.

Now I need to remedy that omission and point out that this V-2 Neptune flyby has a Bowl pattern, with

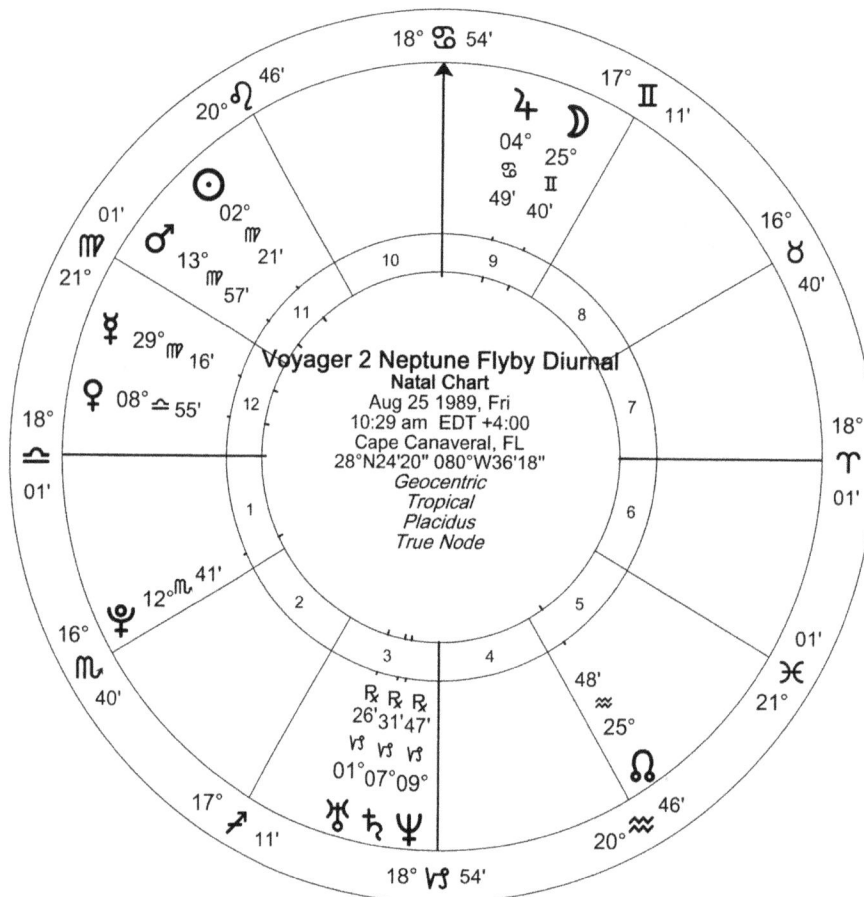

Voyager 2 Neptune Flyby Diurnal
Natal Chart
Aug 25 1989, Fri
10:29 am EDT +4:00
Cape Canaveral, FL
28°N24'20" 080°W36'18"
Geocentric
Tropical
Placidus
True Node

Neptune and the Moon as rim planets that guide and direct the energy of the bodies they contain. I have pointed out that as the Moon travels forward it will trigger first one than another of the major T-square planets… in this order: square Mercury, opposition Uranus, conjunction Jupiter, opposition Saturn, square Venus, opposition Neptune. Later in its passage it will square the Ascendant-Descendant axis and then conjunct the Midheaven and oppose the I.C. This is a perfect example of the process involved in such an event. It is an event, but it is also one moment of a long-term, ongoing process with many parts . . . and this particular process still has life in it!

What about the natal V-2 launch pattern? A Bowl pattern again, with a Neptune-Mars opposition as rim planets. From my understanding, Bowl patterns contain the available energies but need a catalyst to spring into action . . . lots of preparation, with triggers to catapault that preparation into·activity. This pattern has the mutable T-square for a trigger.

Looking back at the Voyager I launch, it has the Moon-Neptune opposition as rim planets and a mutable T-square of planets as trigger.

Voyager 1 Saturn/Titan flyby had the lunar Nodes as rim, what astrologer Connie Cummings termed a nodal barrier in a long ago article. Nodes are points in space, in this instance that serve to contain the energies, not the usual planetary bodies as rim. Cummings described this as a chart and life almost "entrapped" to perform in a certain way, almost karmically bound. The ten bodies contained within the nodal barrier are tightly bundled, within 100 degrees of zodiacal space, a quite single-purpose objective. What do you do if you are a probe in outer space, going "where no man has gone before," robotic or externally commanded in choice? I think this fits the Cummings description of the nodal barrier. V-1 completed its original planetary exploration mission at that point and moved on to experience the outer edges of the solar system where it gives way to interstellar space.

Note: the shutting off of the thrusters for Voyager 1 occurred within four days of the Saturn/Titan flyby, so that chart also has the nodal barrier as rim positions with an even tighter bundling of the physical bodies, all ten contained within 79 degrees! Talk about intended purpose within the nodal boundary (karmic)!

Re-firing of the V-1 thrusters again gives a nearly perfect bowl, all ten bodies within 182 degrees with the tight Mars/Uranus opposition as rim planets. This was something never tried before (Uranus), a re-firing (Mars) of engine (Mars) for power (Mars), again (retrograde Uranus).

V- 2 Saturn flyby was tighter than a bowl, about 160 degrees of space, moving towards a bundle pattern, very dedicated or focused. Again the Moon and Neptune are rim planets.

V-2 Uranus flyby was a lopsided Bucket or Funnel chart with the Moon as singleton widely separating (13 degrees) from the opposition to Neptune. Lopsided strikes me as a good word for a Uranus flyby, considering its polar axis is tilted 98 degrees, resting near the ecliptic (planetary path).

The charts not listed for pattern did not meet the criteria for a specific pattern being more freeform or "splash" in layout.

Stelliums, Clusters

I do constant historical research astrologically. It is my personal experience that planetary stelliums or clusters occur frequently in important happenings or to the people involved in important happenings. I checked all the charts used in this concept. Results:

- V-1 shut thrusters: Libra stellium: Jup, Sat, Ven, Plu; Scorpio stellium: Mercury, Sun, Moon, Uranus; 53 degree cluster: 8 planets.

- V-1 Saturn/Titan flyby: Libra stellium intact, Scorpio: Mercury, Sun, Uranus; 53 degree cluster: 7 planets

- V-1 re-fire thrusters: Sagittarius stellium: Sun, Saturn, Mercury plus Ascendant.

- V-2 Saturn flyby: Libra stellium: Saturn, Venus, Jupiter, Plut plus Ascendant.

- V-2 Neptune flyby: Virgo stellium: Sun, Mars, Mercury; Capricorn stelliium: Uranus, Saturn, Neptune.

Final Notes

We can see many repetitions in each of these intentionally brief descriptions of these twelve events. There is individual definition between the two probes, but they are on a common mission. There are three more commonalities I would point out.

- Pluto is conjunct the Ascendants for both V-1 and V-2 launchs and the V-2 Saturn flyby.

- The North Node is conjunct the Ascendants for both launches and the V-2 Jupiter flyby.

- Venus is amazingly active in both the probe series. Why Venus? Think of the nature of the teamwork necessary to plan, implement, guide the ongoing process for more than 40 years… twin probes on a common mission, each with its own schedule and goal.

I think it is easy to lose sight of the enormity of how these connections work astrologically, beginning in 1977, through all the years of both silence and activity, celebrating 40 years in 2017. The probes are still alive, they are still able to generate, transmit, photograph and function for NASA's scientists while in a carefully selected life preservation mode. V-1 has been in interstellar space for years. V-2 is getting closer to the heliopause and the encounter with interstellar space. Science has to be selective in their use of the probes because they do have a finite life cycle and they are now exploring the infinite. They . . . and we . . . have more work to do.

Note: If someone knows how to acquire the position of Titan for each launch and Saturn flyby, it would be interesting to see if any of that data matches the chart positions used for this study.

Earthquake Prediction Model III-A

By Jagdish Maheshri

ABSTRACT: The objective of this research project is to further continue[1,2,3,4,5] analyzing and investigating correlations between astronomical data and the significant earthquakes of magnitude seven and higher by developing the model using the 110 years (1900-2009) of earthquake data and then predicting the earthquakes for 2011-2017, with the intended goal of predicting future earthquakes with a greater advanced warning and higher degree of accuracy than current technology. Up to this point in research, the Model III[3] seems to perform better than other models. This paper focuses on further exploring the possibility of improving the Model III by analyzing an additional case of the Model III that includes the selection of the angle pairs as independent variables employed in linear regression. As a part of this ongoing research, further research is necessary to build a useful, predictive model that can assess the probability of a given earthquake occurring during a certain time period at a given geographical location on earth. Predicting earthquakes well in advance of the state of the art will promote, protect, and enhance the world economy, potentially saving millions of lives.

Introduction

There is absolutely no precedent in predicting an earthquake solely based on planetary configuration. An occurrence of an earthquake is a random event and it can sometimes occur more frequently than other times. This research began with the idea that planetary positions along the ecliptic, and therefore, their apparent (geocentric) positions as viewed from earth, could potentially correlate with the occurrence of earthquakes. Based on planetary characteristics and a large amount of earthquake data, several hypotheses were tested to see if these correlations actually exist. The results of this exercise indicated that certain planetary configurations seem to correlate reasonably well with earthquakes. This research has evolved from 15-degree multiple angles (Model I) to 12 degree multiple angles (Model II) to the top 16 most frequently occurred longitudinal (Model III) and declination (Model IV) angles.

The intent of this paper is to highlight the initial findings of the extension to the Model III with an additional case of Model III-A, and compare their (Model III and III-A) predictions performance against the actual earthquakes of seven and higher values for 2011-2017.

Independent Variables versus Dependent Variables

As pointed out in the earlier papers[1,2,3,4] one of the challenges involved in developing a correlation between earthquakes and the corresponding astronomical planetary data is to accurately select the independent variables for developing the model.

In order to avoid confusion, the word angle here when used as "angle pair" refers to the description of planets involved in forming that angle (such as Saturn-Jupiter pair as Sa-Ju), and when it is used as just "angle," it refers to the "value" of the angle for that angle pair (such as Sa-Ju30 for Sa-Ju forming a 30-degree angle).

An angle between any two planets is the angle (value) formed by them with respect to the earth. For example, while Jupiter is rising on the eastern horizon and Mars is at the zenith (just above in the sky) the planets are said to form a square aspect (approximately a 90-degree angle) between them. In other words, it is the angle formed by Jupiter and Mars with respect to the earth. And it exactly equals the geocentric longitudinal difference between them along the ecliptic. In the models presented here, the dependent variable is the earthquake magnitude, and the independent variables are the angles of the planetary angle pairs

To further clearly explain this in detail, consider a simple case. Assume that only three planets Saturn, Jupiter and Mars are responsible for an earthquake of significant magnitude M (seven or higher) to occur when they make certain angles between them. Let us assume that their geocentric longitudinal positions to be Sa, Ju and Mr. The respective angle pairs thus formed are Sa-Ju, Ju-Mr and Sa-Mr.

The correlation between M (earthquake magnitude) and the angles is assumed linear, and therefore, mathematically, it can be expressed as:

$$M = a_1 \times (Sa\text{-}Ju) + a_2 \times (Ju - Mr) + a_3 \times (Sa\text{-}Mr) + a_4$$

In the above equation, a_1, a_2, a_3 and a_4 are constants. M, which is on the left hand side of the equation, is a dependent variable while the angles (values of the angles) on the right side are independent variables. It is the variation or change in the angle value of these independent variables dictates the variation in the earthquake value M.

However, it can be shown that information about any two pairs of these angles is sufficient to know the third pair. For example, if we know the angles of Sa-Ju and Ju-Mr then by adding these two angles the angle of Sa-Mr is known. In other words, there are truly only two independent variable angle pairs in the above equation. The challenge then becomes is to decide which of these two variable angle pairs are truly independent or which one is to discard so that the above equation represents the accurate correlation between the earthquake M and the angle pairs.

In general, in theory, for N number of planets, there can be no more than N-1 independent pairs of angles for a given earthquake. In statistical term, one degree of freedom is removed when planets are paired from the list of N number of independent planets. The Model III[3] is based on 11 planets (6 outer planets: Pluto, Neptune, Uranus, Saturn, Jupiter and Mars; 2 inner planets: Venus and Mercury; Sun, Moon and the north lunar node, Rahu). For 11 planets, therefore, a total of 55 angle pairs are possible. However, for a given earthquake, theoretically a maximum of 10 pairs out of these 55 pairs are truly independent.

For each planetary angle pair, the original model III uses the top 16 most frequently occurred angles for the earthquakes of magnitude seven and higher that occurred during the 1900-2009. Consider a typical earthquake that occurred on January 17, 1903 at 16:05 GMT of Magnitude 7.0[7].

The sidereal longitudinal planetary positions on the scale of 0 to 360 degrees for that moment are shown in Table-1. Since our interest is in planetary angles, the difference between the longitudinal positions of the respective planetary pair, the value of planetary angles for any given moment will be the same regardless of the zodiac (tropical or sidereal) used. The planets are listed in the order from the slowest moving planet Pluto to the fastest moving Moon (note that average motion of Venus, Mercury and Sun is about the same as Mercury and Venus always appear closer to Sun from the earth, and therefore are listed in the order: Venus, Mercury and Sun).

Table 1. Sidereal Longitudinal Planetary Positions for January 17, 1903 16:05 GMT

1	Pluto	55.616	85
2	Neptune	69.260	68
3	Uranus	241.06	94
4	Saturn	277.32	26
5	Rahu	177.88	04
6	Jupiter	299.61	27
7	Mars	168.53	78
8	Venus	285.84	16
9	Mercury	292.72	95
10	Sun	273.98	01
11	Moon	149.79	72

In Table 2, all 55 angle pairs along with their respective values are listed for this earthquake. The first two letter mnemonics are used for planets. For example, Pl for Pluto, Ra for Rahu, Ju for Jupiter, Mn for Moon, and so on are employed. The value of angle (difference between the longitudinal positions of the respective planetary pair) is always positive and lies between 0 to 180 degrees. The angle pairs are listed with the the slowest moving planet (such as Pluto) first making angles to other planets, then Neptune with other planets, and finally Sun with the Moon.

Table-2, Fifty-five Planetary Angle Pairs Along with Their Respective Values

1	Pl-Ne	13.64382	11	Ne-Ur	171.8087	20	Ur-Sa	36.25318
2	Pl-Ur	174.5474	12	Ne-Sa	151.9381	21	Ur-Ra	63.18903
3	Pl-Sa	138.2942	13	Ne-Ra	108.6197	22	Ur-Ju	58.5433
4	Pl-Ra	122.2635	14	Ne-Ju	129.6479	23	Ur-Mr	72.53161
5	Pl-Ju	116.0041	15	Ne-Mr	99.27714	24	Ur-Ve	44.77222
6	Pl-Mr	112.921	16	Ne-Ve	143.419	25	Ur-Mc	51.6601
7	Pl-Ve	129.7752	17	Ne-Mc	136.5312	26	Ur-Su	32.91064
8	Pl-Mc	122.8873	18	Ne-Su	155.2806	27	Ur-Mn	91.27223
9	Pl-Su	141.6368	19	Ne-Mn	80.53652			
10	Pl-Mn	94.18034						

28	Sa-Ra	99.44221	35	Ra-Ju	121.7323	41	Ju-Mr	131.0749
29	Sa-Ju	22.29012	36	Ra-Mr	9.342578	42	Ju-Ve	13.77108
30	Sa-Mr	108.7848	37	Ra-Ve	107.9612	43	Ju-Mc	6.883201
31	Sa-Ve	8.519033	38	Ra-Mc	114.8491	44	Ju-Su	25.63266
32	Sa-Mc	15.40692	39	Ra-Su	96.09967	45	Ju-Mn	149.8155
33	Sa-Su	3.342546	40	Ra-Mn	28.0832			
34	Sa-Mn	127.5254						

46	Mr-Ve	117.3038	50	Ve-Mc	6.887883	53	Mc-Su	18.74946
47	Mr-Mc	124.1917	51	Ve-Su	11.86158	54	Mc-Mn	142.9323
48	Mr-Su	105.4422	52	Vn-Mn	136.0444			
49	Mr-Mn	18.74062						
55	Su-Mn	124.1829						

Earlier it was explained that for three planetary angle pairs, information (angle values) about any two angle pairs is sufficient to know the angle of the third pair. In that example we used Saturn, Jupiter and Mars. From Table-2, the angle Sa-Ju equals 22.29; Ju-Mr equals 131.07. Then the third pair, Sa-Mr, can be computed by subtracting 22.29 from 131.07, which equals 108.78. And it agrees with the value in Table-2 for Sa-Mr listed as 108.78.

According to the top 16 most frequently occurred angles for each pair of angles for the earthquakes of magnitude seven and higher during the 1900-2009 [3,8], the following 15 angle pairs are involved for this earthquake (Note that 0.5 orb was employed to calculate the top 16 most frequently occurred angles for each pair) as listed in *Table-* .

Table 3, Fifteen Angle Pairs, Based on the Top 16 Most Frequently Occurred Angles for Each Angle Pair

1	Ne-Ur	172
2	Ne-Sa	152
3	Ne-Ra	109
4	Ne-Ju	130
5	Ne-Mr	99
6	Ne-Mn	81
7	Ur-Ra	63
8	Ur-Mr	73
9	Ur-Su	33
10	Sa-Mr	109
11	Sa-Su	3
12	Ra-Mn	28
13	Mr-Mn	19
14	Ve-Mc	7
15	Mc-Su	19

It is important to note that out of a possible 55 angle pairs, only 15 angle pairs come from the list of the top 16 most frequently occurred angles for each pair.

Now, as stated earlier, for a given earthquake only 10 angle pairs out of these 55 pairs are truly independent if 11 planets are involved. However, Table-3 lists 15 pairs of angles. But with close inspection, for instance, among the three pairs: Ne-Ur, Ne-Ra and Ur-Ra, one of them is dependent and therefore, must be removed.

In order to establish a criterion for removing a dependent pair of angle, an assumption is made that the planets that are closer to the earth are considered more important in contributing to earthquake than the others. With that assumption, the slowest moving planet among the three pairs, Ne-Ur, Ne-Ra and Ur-Ra is Ne-Ur, and it is treated as a dependent variable angle pair. Therefore, it is removed. This criterion is termed here as Top Discard, since the slowest moving planet appears at the top in the list shown in Table-1.

In Table-3, all the planets except Pluto (Pl) are involved. Therefore, there cannot be more than nine independent angle pairs. However, by successively applying the dependent angle pair discarding procedure from top, 11 independent angle pairs are obtained, and they are listed in Table-4.

Table 4, Eleven Independent Angle Pairs After Applying the Top Discard Procedure

1	Ne-Ju	130
2	Ne-Mn	81
3	Ur-Ra	63
4	Ur-Mr	73
5	Ur-Su	33
6	Sa-Mr	109
7	Sa-Su	3
8	Ra-Mn	28
9	Mr-Mn	19
10	Ve-Mc	7
11	Mc-Su	19

The explanation for the 11 independent angle pairs while theoretically only nine independent angle pairs were expected is as follows.

For each angle pair, there can be a maximum of 180 angles possible, and since the model only selects the top 16 frequently occurred angles for each variable of angle pair, some of the angle pairs do not get picked up by the model.

To further explain this, in Table-4, the top two angle pairs are Ne-Ju130 (meaning one of the top 16 angles for the Neptune-Jupiter angle pair is 130 degrees) and Ne-Mn81. The third angle in this case would be Ju-Mn150. However it does not appear in Table-4 since it is not in the list of top 16 angles for the variable angle pair Ju-Mn.[3] It is in fact listed as the 23rd angle in the list of most frequently occurred angles for that pair. Therefore, it doesn't show up in the selection. As a result, the Ne-Ju does not get discarded.

Thus, instead of selecting N-1 angle pairs for N number of planets involved, for some earthquake data points, the number of independent variable angle pairs can exceed N-1 for N number of planets. And because of this limitation, as it will be shown later, despite the theoretically better approach, the performance of this Top Discard based model is somewhat degraded. There are about 400 data points out of 1672 (about 22 percent) which exceed theoretically expected N-1 independent variables.

Since the only major difference between the Model III and the Model III-A is discarding of angle pairs which are deemed to be dependent variables from the list of independent variables, the development of Model III-A is very similar to that of the original Model III.

Therefore, a review of the original Model III is presented here before presenting the Model III-A.

Review of the Original Model III

The original Model III[3] was developed to predict earthquakes of magnitude 7 and higher by accounting the influence of each individual angle pair of planets and weighing them differently. The weighted model was developed using a simple linear regression technique. Thus, in theory, there are 55 different pairs of planets (six outer, two inner, Sun, Moon, and North Node) and 16 distinct angles (from 0 degrees to 180), making a total of 880 maximum possible unique variables that can influence the earthquake occurrence.

Since the Moon's average daily variation is about 13 degrees it can form almost equal number of angles with every other planet during a daily 24-hour period. Nonetheless to test the influence of Moon, two sets of models, one with the inclusion of Moon and the other without were developed.

The earthquakes of magnitude 7 or higher that occurred during January1900-December 2009 were obtained from the USGS[6,8] website. Two data sets of 1900-1972 and 1973-2009 were combined to create one large data set of 1672 points. To avoid the co-linearity in data employed, if there were more than one earthquake of magnitude 7 or higher occurred in one day, the only one with the highest magnitude was selected for that day for this analysis. The accuracy of the data sets was verified against the Centennial Earthquake Catalog[6]. The first step of the analysis was to determine the top sixteen frequently occurred angles during the 1900-2009. Then computations of angles for all the 55 planetary angle pairs were performed. Using an orb of one half degree the planetary data pertaining to the top 16 angles were extracted for all 55 planetary angle pairs for the model. Thus, there are 880 unique variables. A linear model is assumed as follows.

Earthquake Magnitude = $\sum$ Cn * (angle pair)n + constant for n =1 to 880

where Cn is the coefficient of the ^{nth} angle pair; and the nth angle pair equals unity when true and zero otherwise.

For example, Neptune-Saturn 152 degree angle is represented by the $X_{184}{}^{th}$ variable which becomes unity only when the angle between Uranus and Saturn lies between 151.5 and 152.5 degrees. For all other angles between Uranus and Saturn, $X_{184}{}^{th}$ variable equals zero.

Linear regression was performed and all the coefficients were estimated by generalized least squares. A number of coefficients were so small in magnitude that their influence on the model was deemed negligible. The corresponding variables were omitted one at a time and the regression was repeated to confirm that their influence on the model indeed was negligible. As mentioned earlier two sets of the model were developed, one with the inclusion of Moon (referred here as with-Moon model) and the other without Moon (referred here as without-Moon Model). For each of these two sets, two cases were obtained as follows:

The first case for each of these two sets includes all the variables (880 variables for with-Moon Model and 720 variables for without-Moon model)

The second case where the insignificant variables were omitted subject to the criteria of t>=1 where "t" is statistical test that measures the significance of the coefficient. For this case there were 410 variables for with-Moon model and 280 variables for without-Moon model.

The value of the constant in the linear equation of these cases as calculated by robust linear regression ranged between 7.27and 7.30. The simulation results showed that the two cases of each set were almost identical in their performance as the successive omission of coefficients of insignificant magnitude did not seem to degrade the model performance while allowing the data noise reduction.

It must be noted that one of the limitations of these models is that they only apply over a narrow range of seven and higher earthquake magnitude. Therefore, all predicted values for earthquakes below magnitude seven are irrelevant and meaningless since they can be applicable for the entire lower range of earthquake magnitudes from zero to 6.9. The other important limitation to these models is that they are based on only 1672 data points (since earthquakes of magnitude seven and higher occur about a dozen time per year). Thus, for example, for the model of 410 variables, the ratio of data points to model variables is just above four. Consequently, the R-square term, which is a measure of model fit, varied with decreasing amount of variables from 0.51 to 0.45 indicating a fit not so perfect.

Using Greenwich noontime daily planetary positions, each model was then used to predict the earthquakes for the year 2011-2017. A summary of assumptions reflecting the limitations described above form the basis for the model and are listed below:

1. The predicted earthquakes of magnitude less than 7 are ignored since the model is based on the earthquake data set of magnitude 7 and higher. Thus, the prediction dates of an earthquake of magnitude less than 7 also apply for the dates when earthquake did not occur.

2. As pointed out earlier, in order to determine the angles for each angle pair of two sets of models, with-Moon and the without-Moon were developed. The determination of the angles used for each pair of planets was based on the top 16 most frequently occurred angles for earthquakes of seven and higher magnitude during 1900-2009. Thus for each pair of planets, a unique set of 16 angles were used in the models.

3. One half of degree orb is applied for all angles.

4. Since the predictions (or simulations) were computed on a daily basis corresponding to Greenwich noon, prediction is assumed to apply for the entire date (12:00 a.m. to the next 12:00 a.m. of Greenwich Time).

5. The minimum number of angles required to meet the criteria of realizing the earthquake of magnitude seven or higher must be higher than the daily average number of angles for that year.

6. The model cases thus obtained when applied to the daily Greenwich Noon geocentric planetary longitude for 2011-2017 for earthquake predictions, the predicted resulted seem to overestimate the actual earthquakes about by the amount of their corresponding root mean square errors. Therefore, the predictions were corrected with the lower end of the root mean square errors which ranged from 0.28 to 0.33.

7. Out of the four model cases only two, 410-variable with Moon and 720-variable without Moon model cases, were selected as they seem to correlate well with the actual data. In other words, the prediction dates are based on the simulated results provided by these two model cases.

Top Discard based Model III (Model III-A)

Identically following the steps involved in developing the Model III, the Model III-A was developed where linear regression was performed and all the coefficients were estimated by generalized least squares. But before the linear regression was performed the angle pairs which were deemed to be dependent variables from the list of independent variables were discarded by applying the "Top Discard" procedure as described earlier. Thus, two sets of the model were developed, one with the inclusion of Moon (referred here as with-Moon model) and the other without Moon (referred here as without-Moon Model). For each of these two sets, two cases were obtained as follows:

The first case for each of these two sets included all the variables (880 variables for with-Moon Model and 720 variables for without-Moon model)

The second case where the insignificant variables were omitted subject to the criteria of t>=1 where "t" is statistical test that measures the significance of the coefficient. For this case there were 364 variables for with-Moon model and 284 variables for without-Moon model.

The value of the constant in the linear equation of these cases as calculated by robust linear regression ranged between 7.20and 7.298. The R-squared term, which is a measure of model fit, varied with decreasing amount of variables from 0.5 to 0.43. The simulation results showed that the two cases of each set were almost identical in their performance as the successive omission of coefficients of insignificant magnitude did not seem to degrade the model performance while allowing the data noise reduction.

The assumptions involved are identical to the ones that apply for the Model III as listed above. Additional assumptions for the Model III-A are:

1. In order to establish a criterion for removing a dependent pair of angle, an assumption is made that the planets that are closer to the earth are considered more important in contributing to earthquake than the others. This criterion is termed here as Top Discard, as the slowest moving planet in the angle pair is discarded first.

2. The number of angle pairs for N number of planets involved can exceed theoretical limit of N-1 due to the limitation of frequently occurred top 16 angles for each variable angle pair. There are about 400 data points out of 1672 (about 22 percent) which exceed theoretically expected N-1 independent variables.

Results

The Model III which is based on the top 16 most frequently occurred angles for each pair of planetary angle with four different cases was employed for prediction of earthquakes of significant (seven or higher) magnitude for 2011-2017. The prediction days and the corresponding actual dates on which earthquakes occurred are summarized in Table-5 for 2011-2017.

Table 5, Model III Results for 2011-2017

Model Cases	No. of Days (P days)		Number of Hits	Actual No. of Earthquakes	P days/Total	Probability Biinomial
1 880 Variables	618		31	99	0.24169	0.06433
2 410 Variables	826		36	99	0.32303	0.22313
3 720 Variables	707		34	99	0.2765	0.08628
4 280 Variables	882		33	99	0.34494	0.63255
Combined 410/720 variables	1086	55	99	0.42472	0.00593	

Note: Total Number of days for 2011-2017 is 2557

In column 2 of Table 5 the four cases of the model III are listed. The first and the second case are for with Moon set. The first case includes all 880 variable angles while the second one 410 variable angles subject to the criteria of t>=1 where "t" is statistical test that measures the significance of the coefficient. Similarly the third and the fourth are for without Moon set, with all 720 variables angles for the third case and 280 variable angles for the fourth case subject to t>=1.

In column 3 of Table-5, the corresponding total number of prediction dates for 2011-2017 are listed. Note that total number of days for the entire 7-year period is 2557.

The corresponding successful earthquake hits or predictions for all cases are listed in the next column, the column 4, and the actual number of earthquakes that occurred during the seven year period is listed in column 5.

In column 6, the respective ratio of the prediction dates and the total number of dates are shown for all cases. Using the Binomial probability distribution, the last column lists the calculated probability (p-values) for each of these four cases. The lower the probability, the better the performance. When p-value approaches unity, the model performance approaches the total randomness or zero correlation. Usually when the p-value is less than 0.1, the model performance is considered significant enough.

Thus, for 880 variable case (out of four cases), the p- value (probability) as listed in Table-5 is 0.06433 or 6.4 percent. In other words, the case-1 correctly predicts 31 earthquakes out of 99 earthquakes by picking 618 predicted days out of 2557 days of the seven year period. It also means the probability for predicting 31 or higher earthquakes out of 99 earthquakes by picking 618 days out of 2557 days is 6.4 percent.

At the bottom of the Table-5, a combined case of the 410 and 720 variables is listed. This case successfully predicts 55 out of 99 earthquakes by picking 1086 days out of 2557 days and that translates to the p-value of 0.00593 or 0.6 percent probability. Thus the combined case being one order of magnitude better (from 6.4 to 0.6 percent) is very significant.

The performance of Model III-A which is based on the top 16 most frequently occurred angles for each pair of planetary angle and employs the top discard procedure to discard the angle pairs that are deemed not truly independent, is highlighted similar to Model III, with four different cases for predicting earthquakes of significant (seven or higher) magnitude for 2011-2017. The prediction days and the corresponding actual dates on which earthquakes occurred are summarized in Table-6 for 2011-2017.

Table 6, Model III-A Results for 2011-2017

Model Cases	No. of Days (P days)	Number of Successful Hits	Actual No. of Earthquakes	P days/Total	Probability Binomial
1 880 Variables	588	29	99	0.22996	0.0879
2 391 Variables	686	25	99	0.26828	0.67476
3 720 Variables	635	31	99	0.24834	0.0867
4 287 Variables	642	19	99	0.25108	0.93321
Combined					
391/720	990	41	99	0.38717	0.32504

Note: Total Number of days for 2011-2017 are 2557.

As shown in Table-6, for 880 variable case (the case 1), the p- value (probability) as listed in Table-6 is 0.08791 or 8.8 percent. In other words, the case-1 correctly predicts 29 earthquakes out of 99 earthquakes by picking 588 predicted days out of 2557 days of the seven year period. It also means the probability for predicting 29 or higher earthquakes out of 99 earthquakes by picking 588 days out of 2557 days is 8.8 percent.

At the bottom of Table 6, a combined case of the 391 and 720 variables is listed. This case successfully predicts only 41 out of 99 earthquakes by picking 990 days out of 2557 days and that translates to the p-value of 0.32504 or 32 percent probability. Thus the combined case in this case is worse than the case-1 of 880 variables or case-3 of 720 variables. The best case for Model III-A is either 880 variable or 720 variable case.

Conclusions

When compared, the results from Table-5 and Table-6 for Model III and Model III-A, respectively, it is clear that all the cases of the Model III show better performance of predicting earthquakes against the corresponding cases of the Model III-A.

As explained earlier, the poor performance of the Model III-A can be attributed to the fact that for about 22 percent of the earthquake data points, the number of independent variable angle pairs exceed N-1 for N number of planets. This was due to the limitation that the angle pairs that deemed as not truly independent variables could not be discarded as they were not included in the top 16 frequently occurred angles for those angle pairs.

Furthermore, the limit of number of angles for the top frequently occurred angles cannot be increased since it would worsen the already poor ratio of 880 variables for 1672 data points for linear regression. Thus despite the theoretically better approach, the performance of this Top Discard based model is degraded due to unsuccessful discarding of the angle pairs that were deemed not independent.

Additionally, the assumption of "Top Discard," the criterion for removing a dependent pair of angle, may sometimes remove the truly independent variable instead of dependent one.

The better performance of the Model III over the Model III-A can also be attributed the fact that the degradation due to retaining the dependent variables for Model III may not be as significant as that due to degradation of the Model III-A where inadverantly the a true independent variable might be removed.

It is important to recognize that model performance varies from one year to the next. The performance of Model III is significantly enhanced for 2014 by correctly predicting 11 out of 12 earthquakes by picking 148 days out of 365 for that year. However, the performance of Model III was severely degraded by predicting only 3 out of 7 earthquakes by picking 200 predicted days out of 365 for 2017. Therefore, the performance of the Model III and Model III-A as well may need to be observed over a long period of time to confirm the consistency of their performance.

For the improvement of the Model III-A more research is warranted, perhaps by effectively discarding the unwanted angle pairs for each of the earthquake data point, and also perhaps by redistributing the number of top angles among all the angle pairs instead of 16 top angles for all angle pairs.

Finally, for the model to be applied for earthquakes of magnitude 7 and higher to predict over a narrower range of days and locations would require further research work.

Acknowledgements

The author wishes to acknowledge the U.S. Geological Survey Web site for availability of downloading the earthquake data.

References

Earthquake Prediction Model presented at the NCGR (National Council for Geocosmic Research) Research Symposium. National Conference: Baltimore, Maryland, March 2007

Earthquake Prediction Model II, *NCGR Research Journal*, Volume 3, Fall/Winter 2012-2013

Earthquake Prediction Model III, *NCGR Research Journal*, Volume 5, Fall 2015

Earthquake Prediction Model IV, *Journal of Research of the American Federation of Astrologers*, Volume 17, February 2016

Earthquake Prediction Model III Performance, *NCGR Research Journal*, Volume 7, Fall 2017

Centennial Earthquake Catalog, Engdahl and Villaseñor, 2002

Declination Aspects Research

By John Halloran

ABSTRACT: Working with 22 large chart collections of timed birth charts, a total of 35,000 charts, a research the project found meaningful variations in frequency of planetary declination aspects between the 22 trait and vocational categories represented by the collections. A good research project should provide information that is real and meaningful. One can only be sure of that when one is comparing apples to apples. This paper will describe how one project achieved that.

Unpredictable astronomical factors are the biggest source of uncertainty and error when one goes looking for astrological correlations. Because of this, it is problematic to compare the frequency of one aspect to the frequency of other aspects in a particular set of charts, such as in a collection of alcoholics. There could be unsuspected astronomical reasons why more of one aspect is found than another. As Scott G. Vail and Mark Pottenger showed with their *Tables for Aspect Research* book [1986, ACS Publications, Inc.], the frequency of an astrological aspect in a set of charts can depend upon the years in which the subjects were born. This is most likely to be true when the charts are not spread out over a number of years but are for an occupation such as computer programmer that is tied to a particular historical development. One could try to tabulate the birth years of one's charts and compare to the astronomical frequencies in this book, but the book only has angular separations in the zodiac and it does not cover all chart points. It would also be an excessively detailed and left-brained approach to something that can be done better by using a holistic approach that just bypasses the issue of astronomical frequencies.

I embarked upon this research project in a quest to find the astrological meaning of each declination parallel and contraparallel aspect. I designed the project so that the meaning would naturally emerge from the project results. These results are helping me to write a complete set of declination aspect interpretations, separate for males and females, for which I am also reading biographical summaries.

The project worked with separate chart collections for 22 categories of people. The number of charts in the different collections range from a high of 4839 charts for Athletes to a low of 326 charts for Computer Programmers. The mean or average number of charts per collection is 1573 charts. The average number of charts in these 22 collections found to have a particular declination aspect, such as Jupiter parallel Neptune within 1 degree, is approximately 67 charts per collection. The research project looked for declination aspects between Sun, Moon, Mercury, Venus, Mars, Jupiter, Saturn, Uranus, Neptune, Pluto, Ascendant, Midheaven, Moon's North Node (mean), Chiron, East Point, and Black Moon Lilith (mean) - a total of 16 chart points, giving a total of 240 possible parallel and contraparallel aspects. This means that the average person's chart has approximately 10 declination aspects within 1 degree of orb when the above chart points are turned on. In practice, the aspects that are close to being exact will be much stronger than are the aspects that are more than 30 minutes apart.

The project makes use of birth data assembled by Michel Gauquelin and Lois Rodden. Ten years ago a customer converted Gauquelin data to the Halloran chart format in exchange for an updated copy of *AstrolDeluxe ReportWriter*. The customer sent me 10 files with timed birth data, for Actor, Alcohol, Deranged, Military, Murder, Musician, Painter, Politico, Science, and Writers. To these 10 chart collections, I have added 12 additional collections extracted from version 4 of Lois Rodden's *Astrodatabank* - Astrologers, Athletes, Businessfemale, Businessmale, Computer, Engimech, Healers, Lawyers, Life-80s [Octogenarians], Pilots, Psychol, and Teacher.

From the *AstrolDeluxe Platinum* release notes:

Version 9.7.6 adds to the **By Aspect** search at **Options, Research Charts**, **Search Two**, a checkbox '**Append percentage found to text file**', where the program creates the name of the file from the name of the currently loaded charts file. If the currently loaded charts file is alcohol.cht, then if this checkbox is checked, the results of the aspect search will be appended to the file alcoholpct.txt. Each appended line will look like this: Moon parallel (000.000) Venus using an orb of 1° 68 1793 0.0379. This means that out of 1793 charts, 68 charts, or 3.79%, met the criteria. By manually performing all of the aspect searches in which one is interested on the currently loaded charts collection, a text file can be built up fairly quickly. The search results for this collection can then be compared to the same search results found for other chart collections. This lets one see if a particular aspect is found more frequently or less frequently among different types of people.

At the end of doing this for all 22 chart files, I had 22 new files ending with 'pct.txt', each with 240 lines for the 240 possible aspects. I then wrote a Parallels Table program that automatically went through all 22 'pct.txt' files and extracted the same aspect line from each file, one aspect at a time, to a listbox that was sorted by the found percentage. The program then appended that aspect's sorted list to a Table text file, before moving on to the next aspect. The result is the Table shown below.

The amount of the aspect found percentage is not what matters, as that could be related to astronomical factors. What matters is the amount of the spread or difference between the chart collections. We are looking at the actual frequency with which the same aspect occurred among different types of people. This is what I mean about the project comparing apples to apples.

The astrologer can look at the order in which occupations are listed to see what occupations a particular declination aspect favors. This gives an overview of aspect strengths and weaknesses.

The astrologer who wants to use this table is not completely out of the woods when it comes to astronomical factors. The astrologer must be aware that the Gauquelin chart collections come from an older time period than do the Astrodatabank chart collections. If you see all the Gauquelin collections and the file of octogenarians clustered together, there is probably an astronomical reason for it. It is most likely when two slow moving outer planets are involved. To illustrate two collections, here are the Historical Frequency Graphs for Gauquelin's collection of Scientists and Rodden's collection of Healers.

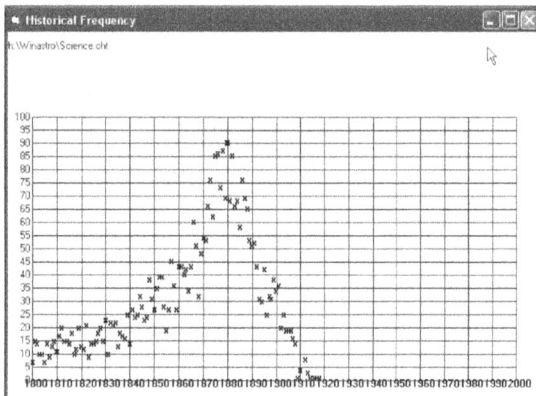

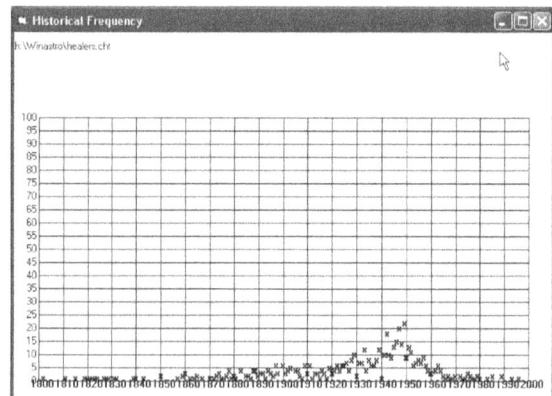

Moon Parallel Uranus—the Healer

The occupation of Healer was the most popular occupation relative to all 22 occupations when looking for charts with Moon parallel Uranus. Here are the search results for that aspect:

Moon parallel Uranus using an orb of 1°	33	555	0.0595	Healers
Moon parallel Uranus using an orb of 1°	16	326	0.0491	Computer
Moon parallel Uranus using an orb of 1°	54	1206	0.0448	Astrologers
Moon parallel Uranus using an orb of 1°	113	2604	0.0434	Businessmale
Moon parallel Uranus using an orb of 1°	210	4839	0.0434	Athletes
Moon parallel Uranus using an orb of 1°	16	374	0.0428	Psychol
Moon parallel Uranus using an orb of 1°	62	1472	0.0421	Painter
Moon parallel Uranus using an orb of 1°	50	1248	0.0401	Musician
Moon parallel Uranus using an orb of 1°	85	2171	0.0392	Teacher
Moon parallel Uranus using an orb of 1°	24	619	0.0388	Engimech
Moon parallel Uranus using an orb of 1°	32	876	0.0365	Deranged
Moon parallel Uranus using an orb of 1°	51	1408	0.0362	Actor
Moon parallel Uranus using an orb of 1°	26	726	0.0358	Lawyers
Moon parallel Uranus using an orb of 1°	18	509	0.0354	Businessfemale
Moon parallel Uranus using an orb of 1°	71	2026	0.0350	Writers
Moon parallel Uranus using an orb of 1°	62	1793	0.0346	Alcohol
Moon parallel Uranus using an orb of 1°	14	418	0.0335	Pilots
Moon parallel Uranus using an orb of 1°	20	622	0.0322	Murder
Moon parallel Uranus using an orb of 1°	87	2723	0.0320	Life-80s
Moon parallel Uranus using an orb of 1°	32	1002	0.0319	Politico
Moon parallel Uranus using an orb of 1°	107	3646	0.0293	Science
Moon parallel Uranus using an orb of 1°	89	3438	0.0259	Military

Famous women born with this aspect within an orb of 15 minutes include:
Elizabeth Barrett Browning
Amanda Bynes
Irene Cara
Skeeter Davis
Chaka Khan
Christina Ricci
Condoleeza Rice
Simone Simon
Leigh Taylor-Young
Kristi Yamaguchi

The interpretation for this parallel aspect for females is a synthesis of what is in these famous women's biographies and the distribution of aspect search results. Here is the interpretation:

Freedom is important to you. You don't respond well to having people try to control you. You can overcome barriers and limits. You tend to be articulate and outspoken. You could display your independence by having different personal idiosyncrasies. You can adopt an outrageous, non-conformist style of dress. You can be at-home in and travel between different worlds. You do not like feeling confined. You would prefer an occupation that gives you individual freedom, such as astrologer, healer, or individual athlete (e.g., tennis player or ice-skater).

Moon Parallel Chiron—the Scientist

The occupation of Scientist was the most popular occupation relative to all 22 occupations when looking for charts with Moon parallel Chiron. Here are the search results for that aspect:

Moon parallel Chiron using an orb of 1°	164	3646	0.0450	Science
Moon parallel Chiron using an orb of 1°	80	1793	0.0446	Alcohol
Moon parallel Chiron using an orb of 1°	22	509	0.0432	Businessfemale
Moon parallel Chiron using an orb of 1°	23	555	0.0414	Healers
Moon parallel Chiron using an orb of 1°	36	876	0.0411	Deranged
Moon parallel Chiron using an orb of 1°	106	2723	0.0389	Life-80s
Moon parallel Chiron using an orb of 1°	48	1248	0.0385	Musician
Moon parallel Chiron using an orb of 1°	14	374	0.0374	Psychol
Moon parallel Chiron using an orb of 1°	27	726	0.0372	Lawyers
Moon parallel Chiron using an orb of 1°	80	2171	0.0368	Teacher
Moon parallel Chiron using an orb of 1°	51	1408	0.0362	Actor
Moon parallel Chiron using an orb of 1°	36	1002	0.0359	Politico
Moon parallel Chiron using an orb of 1°	22	622	0.0354	Murder
Moon parallel Chiron using an orb of 1°	70	2026	0.0346	Writers
Moon parallel Chiron using an orb of 1°	14	418	0.0335	Pilots
Moon parallel Chiron using an orb of 1°	115	3438	0.0334	Military
Moon parallel Chiron using an orb of 1°	161	4839	0.0333	Athletes
Moon parallel Chiron using an orb of 1°	34	1206	0.0282	Astrologers
Moon parallel Chiron using an orb of 1°	73	2604	0.0280	Businessmale
Moon parallel Chiron using an orb of 1°	9	326	0.0276	Computer
Moon parallel Chiron using an orb of 1°	17	619	0.0275	Engimech
Moon parallel Chiron using an orb of 1°	40	1472	0.0272	Painter

Famous men born with this aspect within an orb of 12 minutes include:
Henry Cisneros
Jim Clark
Bob Dylan
Stephen Jay Gould
Scott Hamilton
Alfred Hitchcock
Chris Isaak
Michio Kaku
Jurgen Klinsmann
Ross MacDonald
D.G. Rossetti
Johann Strauss
Edgar Winter

The interpretation for this parallel aspect for males is a synthesis of what is in these famous men's biographies and the distribution of aspect search results. Here is the interpretation:

You could be born with a limitation that you must overcome. Chiron has to do with overcoming all kinds of limitations, which can include health problems, weakness, social prejudice, insecurity, and fears. This aspect endows you with compassion and hope. You could work on behalf of a children's charity. You can work to heal sick people. Your energy level, your passion for life, and your performance tend to be at a high level. You can be very disciplined. The discipline required in the field of science should come easily to you. Chiron orbits in between Saturn and Uranus, so Chiron has something of the natures of both of those planets.

Moon Contraparallel Chiron—the Psychologist

The occupation of Psychologist/Psychiatrist was the most popular occupation relative to all 22 occupations when looking for charts with Moon contraparallel Chiron. Here are the search results for that aspect:

Moon contraparallel Chiron using an orb of 1°	16	374	0.0428	Psychol
Moon contraparallel Chiron using an orb of 1°	83	2026	0.0410	Writers
Moon contraparallel Chiron using an orb of 1°	41	1002	0.0409	Politico
Moon contraparallel Chiron using an orb of 1°	60	1472	0.0408	Painter
Moon contraparallel Chiron using an orb of 1°	25	622	0.0402	Murder
Moon contraparallel Chiron using an orb of 1°	100	2604	0.0384	Businessmale
Moon contraparallel Chiron using an orb of 1°	102	2723	0.0375	Life-80s
Moon contraparallel Chiron using an orb of 1°	45	1206	0.0373	Astrologers
Moon contraparallel Chiron using an orb of 1°	52	1408	0.0369	Actor
Moon contraparallel Chiron using an orb of 1°	12	326	0.0368	Computer
Moon contraparallel Chiron using an orb of 1°	15	418	0.0359	Pilots
Moon contraparallel Chiron using an orb of 1°	18	509	0.0354	Businessfemale
Moon contraparallel Chiron using an orb of 1°	127	3646	0.0348	Science
Moon contraparallel Chiron using an orb of 1°	30	876	0.0342	Deranged
Moon contraparallel Chiron using an orb of 1°	116	3438	0.0337	Military
Moon contraparallel Chiron using an orb of 1°	59	1793	0.0329	Alcohol
Moon contraparallel Chiron using an orb of 1°	20	619	0.0323	Engimech
Moon contraparallel Chiron using an orb of 1°	23	726	0.0317	Lawyers
Moon contraparallel Chiron using an orb of 1°	142	4839	0.0293	Athletes
Moon contraparallel Chiron using an orb of 1°	61	2171	0.0281	Teacher
Moon contraparallel Chiron using an orb of 1°	34	1248	0.0272	Musician
Moon contraparallel Chiron using an orb of 1°	13	555	0.0234	Healers

Famous men born with this aspect within an orb of 12 minutes include:
Garth Allen
William Bligh
James Caan
John Dee
Mark Hatfield
Vojislav Kostunica
Bruce Lee
Robert S. McNamara
Jay North
George S. Patton
Linus C. Pauling
Kyle Petty
Mark Phillips
James Earl Ray
Martin Scorsese

Few psychologists have made it into the Famous Charts, but by comparing these men who have the contra-parallel aspect to the earlier men who have the parallel aspect, you can see that the parallel aspect tends to be more peace-loving while the contraparallel is more confrontational.

The interpretation for this contraparallel aspect for males is a synthesis of what is in these famous men's biographies and the distribution of aspect search results. Here is the interpretation:

You can see things differently from the other people in your group. You can get into conflict. You can develop your fighting skills. You can be athletic. There is no pretense to you. You are as direct with others as you try to be with yourself. You can be reacting against the painful actions of cold-hearted people. You could feel locked in, like you are stuck in a limiting situation that is out of your control. This aspect energizes you to look for solutions to problematic situations. Your experiences could lead you to the field of psychology, in which you could make a career of helping other people to heal, recover, and let go of abuse and fear.

So these are three samples from a research project that is expected to yield a total of 480 interpretations, 240 interpretations for males and 240 interpretations for females.

The most surprising finding of this research project is that I found strong common themes for declination aspects to the East Point, also known as the Equatorial Ascendant, which is the point in the chart where the Ascendant would be if the person were born on the equator. What causes this to make sense is how astrologers ignore celestial latitude and are comfortable reducing the planets to their longitudinal positions on the ecliptic. If the ecliptic plane is so astrologically special, why shouldn't the equatorial plane be special?

A Geocentric Review of John H. Nelson's Work: Planetary Position Effect on Short-Wave Signal Quality

By John Stephen DeLapp

ABSTRACT: Many of us who learned astrology in the 1960s and '70s will remember legendary John H. Nelson, an employee of the Radio Corporation of America whose job was to find a way around geomagnetic disturbances in the earth's ionosphere that interfered with worldwide short-wave radio communications. Nelson succeeded in his job for 25 years by computing certain geometric angles between the planets of the solar system. Despite numerous papers and lectures explaining his methods, even before prestigious organizations such as NATO and NASA, no one has ever repeated his degree of success. The hypothesis of this paper is that there was more to Nelson's methods than he publicly acknowledged.

The Story of John Nelson

In March 1951, John H. Nelson rocked the world of astronomers and astrologers alike when he began publishing papers describing a method of forecasting disturbances in Earth's ionosphere, which in turn enhanced or diminished short-wave radio transmission between North America and Europe, by observing sunspots and angular planetary positions relative to the sun.

In those days, short-wave radio was the Radio Corporation of America's means of providing communication service for ships at sea and a worldwide wireless communication system in competition with underseas cables. The fly in the ointment, however, was that, while short wave signals could travel great distances (much beyond "line of sight"), good reception was dependent upon a stable ionosphere which, periodically and unexpectedly, it was not.

It was radio propagation analyst J.H. Nelson who was tasked to test the theory that sunspots and the consequent space weather were the cause, and in 1946, RCA set him up with an observatory and a good telescope atop their office building in New York City, supported his years-long study and observations, and then eventually reaped the benefits of his accurate forecasting service.

Now the short of it is that Nelson began to forecast radio disturbances with sunspot observations alone, making note that "The type of the sunspots, their age and activity, together with their position on the face of the sun, were declared to be the determining factors of disruptive bombardment."[1] However, "After about two years of careful research with both sunspots and magnetic storms Mr. Nelson concluded that sunspots were only a small part of the answer. It was evident to him that some natural force besides sunspots were in some way involved in the phenomena that he was studying."[2]

Continuing his research, Nelson began to include the planets and their heliocentric angular (0, 90, 180, 270 degree) relationships to one another.[3] Nelson also considered other points of interest: The nodal points of the planetary orbits, their perihelion and aphelion positions and, later in his work, added divisions of 45, 15, or 7.5 degrees of longitude his basic "hard" angles and named them "harmonics."

Including the planetary positions with his sunspot observations significantly improved forecasts, ranging from a few days and weeks to years in advance. Nelson developed a reliable forecasting service that was accurate 85 per cent of the time according press accounts from RCA. *John Nelson enjoyed nearly two decades of providing practical, usable information to an American for-profit corporation whose business it was to provide a reliable worldwide service. Nelson enjoyed invitations to speak before organizations such as NATO*[4] and was encouraged by NASA to detail his methods in formal papers, which he did in his work *Cosmic Patterns.*[5]

The novelty of Nelson's work waned with the passage of time, however, as the advance of technology and satellites in space took up the earthly communications work load, relegating the prominence of short-wave signals to ham radio enthusiasts. And in the academic community, there was no excitement for replicating Nelson's work. The astrologers had long seized on Nelson's findings as proof of their belief system, and the academics (I presume) had no desire to add fuel to that fire.

As for me, the area of my greatest astrological interest has been severe weather analysis, tropical cyclones in particular. I had been aware of Nelson's work, but when I finally found his papers online and gave them a good read, I was heartened to learn that his methods were very similar to my own.

That was more than 15 years ago. Recently I have had occasion to refamiliarize myself with Nelson's work in preparation for experimental forecasting of hurricanes during this 2018 season. Since I had always been puzzled by Nelson's use of *heliocentric aspects* to forecast events on Earth, I decided to check his examples against my *geocentric* ephemeris.

What immediately became apparent stunned me and I was chagrined that I hadn't seen it earlier.

As I began thumbing through my ephemeris to compare the disturbance periods with the Planets and Signs, it was the Eclipse information that stood out right away and when I began tabulating the data, I was amazed to see how many of the disturbance periods had occurred during eclipse cycles so that even the quarter Moons and inconjuncts in the data were applying to or separating from a solar or lunar eclipse. And then there were the Full Moons, the New Moons, and the actual solar and lunar eclipses.

An Organized Look at Nelson's Examples

From the three publications cited[6], there can be found 26 qualitatively ranked examples of exceptional geomagnetic disturbances and radio blackouts that John Nelson used to illustrate the technique of his method.

The following Table 1 details each example's source, the time period of geomagnetic disturbance, Nelson's descriptive rank of the disturbance, the nearest lunar aspect and taking note if it was on an eclipse cycle. In two cases I included a quarter Moon that was approaching or departing an eclipse because of the Sun's proximity to the lunar nodes.

Table 1 Nelson's Disturbance Examples and Lunation Data					
Data Source	Disturbance Period	Days	Rank of Disturbance	Lunar Aspect	Saros Cycle
1 (b)	6/19-22 1948	4	Slight	Full Moon	
2 (b)	8/19-21 1948	3	Slight	Full Moon	
3 (c)	4/24-30 1960	7	Moderate	New Moon	
4 (c)	4/10-17 1961 Peak 4/15	8	Moderate	New Moon	
5 (c)	8/4-5 1941	2	Severe	Inconjunct	
6 (ac)	9/18-21 1941	4	Severe	New Moon	Eclipse
7 (c)	10/2-5 1942	4	Severe	Quarter	
8 (A)	1/3 1946	1	Severe	New Moon	Eclipse
9 (a)	7/27 1946	1	Severe	New Moon	
10 (a)	1/23-25 1947	3	Severe	New Moon	
11 (a)	5/13-17 1947	5	Severe	Quarter	Eclipse
12 (ab)	2/23-25 1948	3	Severe	Full Moon	
13 (ab)	4/19-23 1948	5	Severe	Full Moon	Eclipse
14 (a)	4/11-13 1949	3	Severe	Full Moon	Eclipse
15 (c)	7/15-17 1960	3	Severe	Quarter	
16 (ac)	3/23-27 1940	5	Very Severe	Full Moon	Eclipse
17 (a)	2/7-10 1944	4	Very Severe	Full Moon	Eclipse
18 (c)	3/26-30 1945	5	Extr Severe	Full Moon	
19 (b)	10/14-15 1948	2	Very Severe	Inconjunct	Eclipse
20 (b)	10/7-8 1949	2	Very Severe	Full Moon	Eclipse
21 (b)	4/1-6 1950	6	Very Severe	Full Moon	Eclipse
22 (b)	9/30-10/4 1950	5	Very Severe	Quarter	Eclipse
23 (b)	9/20-26 1951	7	Very Severe	Quarter	Eclipse
24 (c)	9/22-23 1957	2	Very Severe	New Moon	
25 (c)	8/30-31 1960	2	Extr Severe	Quarter	Eclipse
26 (c)	11/12 1960	1	Extr Severe	Quarter	
Totals	26 Time Periods	97 Days		8 Sol/Lun Eclipses	13 Eclipse Cycles

What the heck is going on here? You don't need to be a professional statistician to see the overwhelming number of Full Moons and eclipse cycles in this list of Nelson's examples of his technique. The Full Moon and eclipse cycle associations with disturbance periods are extremely obvious.

Nelson was very straightforward as to his method. I don't think he described it particularly well, but he did write, repeatedly, it was just sunspot observations and *heliocentric* planetary angles that he considered, and when the sunspot activity diminished by 1954[7], it became just the heliocentric aspects, perihelion, aphelion and nodal positions that he used to forecast geomagnetic disturbances on our planet.

Is it possible that after all of Nelson's detailed astronomical and radio signal observations that he could have been oblivious as to what was going on with our Moon, the closest astronomical object to that which he was studying so intently, the earth's ionosphere?

This seems very odd to me and I think it is worth having a close look at Nelson's data to see if these apparent associations with lunar activity are something that could have happened merely by chance. So, what I have done is create a control group of 26 randomly generated[8] time periods (see Table 2 to compare with the Nelson sample.

	Random Dates		Days	Lunar Aspect	Saros Cycle
Table 2 Randonly Generated Time Periods and Lunation Data					
1	3/24 -27	1947	4	Semi-sextile	
2	3/28-30	1940	3	Trine	Eclipse
3	7/10-16	1940	7	Quarter	
4	1/17-24	1956	8	Quarter	
5	4/11-12	1958	2	Quarter	Eclipse
6	7/6-9	1957	4	Trine	
7	6/17-20	1953	4	Quarter	
8	12/18	1951	1	Trine	
9	7/19	1943	1	Inconjunct	Eclipse
10	3/19-21	1943	3	Full Moon	
11	11/23-27	1953	5	Trine	
12	12/18-20	1956	3	Inconjunct	
13	11/11-15	1960	5	Sextile	
14	1/25-27	1961	3	Trine	
15	10/28-11/1	1946	5	Sextile	
16	4/15-18	1950	4	New Moon	
17	2/28-3/4	1958	5	Inconjunct	
18	10/19-20	1951	2	Trine	
19	2/26-28	1956	3	Full Moon	
20	4/23-24	1944	2	New Moon	
21	7/21-26	1940	6	Inconjunct	
22	4/25-29	1940	5	Trine	Eclipse
23	9/14-20	1958	7	Sextile	
24	12/21-22	1943	2	Sextile	
25	2/20-21	1955	2	Semi-sextile	
26	3/23	1952	1	Semi-sextile	
Totals	26 Time Periods		97 Days	0 Sol/Lun Eclp	4 Eclipse Cycles

Obviously, the random samples in Table 2 are quite different than the (not random) handpicked data from Nelson's sample.

What I propose to do is apply a basic statistical analysis of the data to determine what the probability is that the apparent Lunar associations could have occurred (*or were selected*) simply by chance.

Armed with data from the Nelson examples and the comparable random dates control group, we can run some experiments, but first, a word about my plan for testing.

Hypotheses Testing with Chi-Square "Goodness of Fit"

A really good statistical tool for astrological work is the Chi-square (kee-square) Test which can be found at numerous places online and also is included in the Microsoft Excel Spreadsheet program.

There are a number of reasons why Chi-square is well suited to astrological work, but we don't need a stats lesson right now. Suffice to say that Chi-square works great for categorical type variables, like planets, signs, aspects, new moons, eclipses, etc. For any numbers' junkies in the audience, I'll include the Chi-square details in a table with each example.

There is one caveat: Nelson's examples are a small data set. I am using Chi-square even though I am pushing the limits on the "Expected" values, which most textbooks suggest a minimum of 5. However, it is acceptable to combine categories to increase the Expected count, which I did and the difference was negligible. Also, I double checked my results with a different test, the Binomial distribution, and came to the same conclusions. I choose to demonstrate with Chi-square on account of its simplicity and applicability to astrological research.

First, we begin with a theory. My theory, my research hypothesis, is that Nelson either knowingly picked these examples because of their lunar activity, but did not want to reveal it, or, he didn't know, and lunar activity is so closely correlated to geomagnetic disturbance that any period of disturbance must reveal a correspondence to some emphasized lunar event.

The bad news is that there isn't enough of Nelson's work available to test the research hypothesis. We only have a 97-day window into Nelson's 25-year research and forecasting career. The good news is there is enough of Nelson's work to test the opposite of the research hypothesis which is the null hypothesis of no difference.

Testing the null hypothesis of no difference is standard statistical practice and simply means that you compare your results against what is normal or expected, and if a difference does exist an assessment can be made to see if that difference could have occurred merely by chance, or if it is so significant as to suggest a factor of association, or of correlation, or even the possibility of causation.

To bring an experiment to a proper conclusion, one must have a point of decision as to whether the test was a success or a failure. In statistical testing, Significance Levels are the deciding 'cut off' points at which the researcher may confidently support or reject the 'null hypothesis', and Significance Levels are expressed as a probability (p), in decimal form, from 0.0 to 1.0, which is the possibility that an event occurred by mere accident, sampling variation, or 'random chance'.

Significance levels are pretty standard, but they do vary quite a bit, the most common being:

- (p) = .10 which is 10 percent or 1 chance in 10 (moderate significance)

- (p) = .05 which is 5 percent or 1 chance in 20 (most commonly accepted level)

- (p) = .01 which is 1 percent or 1 chance in 100 (very high significance level)

Three Experiments

Specifically, I would like to test three phenomena:

- The coincidence of disturbances occurring during a 29.5-day eclipse cycle

- The coincidence of disturbances occurring on the day of a solar or lunar eclipse

- The distribution of regular monthly lunar aspects occurring during disturbances

I will lay out the pertinent variables for each test, including the control group, illustrate the data graphically, then detail a Chi-square analysis and determine if any differences are significant.

Experiment One: The Coincidence of Disturbances Occurring During a 29.5-day Eclipse Cycle

There seem to be a lot of eclipse cycles in Nelson's examples, so the question naturally arises: how many 29.5-day eclipse cycles would you expect to occurr during 26 independent time periods, cumulatively totaling 97 days, over a span of 21.3 years?

Looks complicated, but it really isn't.

The series of Nelson's examples range from January 1940 through April 1961.

This is what I will call the "population space."

In that space, from my ephemeris[9], I count the following: Full Moons, 260; New Moons, 264; Lunar Eclipses, 48; Solar Eclipses, 48. Averaging the New and Full Moons gives us a total of 262 lunation cycles. Doing the same for lunar and solar eclipses gives us a total of 48 eclipse cycles.

So the frequency of an eclipse cycle coinciding with any one lunation cycle is

48 eclipse cycles ÷ 262 lunation cycles = .183 or 18.3 percent.

Therefore, the expectation that any portion of an eclipse cycle would be occurring during any of the 26 disturbance periods in Nelson's sample, and also in the 26 random sample control group, is:

26-time periods x .183 = 4.8 (5) eclipse cycles expected

And that means that we should expect about five eclipse cycles to be in effect in both the Nelson and random sample data sets.

And that also means our null hypothesis has as its baseline expectation a score of 4.8 eclipse cycles from which to measure any differences.

So then what does our data tell us?

Chart 1 visually illustrates the number of eclipse cycles in Nelson's sample (13), the expected average (4.8) and in the random dates control group (4).

Chart 1

What is immediately obvious is that there are more than three times as many eclipse cycles in Nelson's sample of disturbances as in the control group of exactly the same size, 26 time periods, totaling 97 days.

A Chi-square test will quickly determine what is the likelihood of so many eclipse cycles occurring during geomagnetic disturbances merely by chance:

Nelson Sample	observed	expected	difference	diff^2	(diff^2)÷expected
Eclipse Cycles	13	4.8	8.2	67.24	14
Reg-Lunation Cycles	13	21.2	-8.2	67.24	3.17
Totals	26	26		Chi^2	17.17
			degree of freedom =		1
			per Excel	(p)=	0.00003

This test yields a significance level of (p) 0.00003

The bottom line is that there is only 1 possibility out of 300,000 that this result could occur merely by chance or normal sample variation.

Therefore, the null hypothesis that there are no significant differences in these samples is *rejected*, and the 'alternative hypothesis' that Lunar Activity may be associated with geomagnetic disturbances is *supported*.

Experiment 2: Frequency of Disturbances occurring on the day of a Solar or Lunar Eclipse

As is the case of the month-long eclipse cycles that permeate Nelson's examples, so also do the actual solar and lunar eclipses appear very often to coincide with geomagnetic disturbance periods. In fact, looking again at Table 1, it seems that as the severity of disturbance increases, so do the number of eclipses.

How can we go about analyzing this phenomenon?

First, we return to our ppopulation space: January 1940 thru April 1961 contains 7,790 days.

Again, from our ephemeris we find 48 solar + 48 lunar = 96 total eclipses in that space.

So then the frequency of a solar or lunar eclipse occurring on any one day in the population space is 96 solar/

lunar eclipses ÷7,790 Days = 0.0123.

The series of Nelson's examples within that population space is 26 time periods comprising a cumulative total of 97 days.

How many eclipses, either solar or lunar, may we expect in a 97-day period of time?

Simple: 0.0123 x 97 days = 1.2 eclipses should be expected in both Nelson's samples and the random 97-day control group detailed in Table 2.

And similar to the previous experiment, we may use the expected average of 1.2 eclipses as a baseline score from which to measure any differences in the data.

Chart 2 graphically demonstrates the rather extreme difference in the number of solar/lunar eclipses in the random dates control group and Nelson's sample: 0 versus 8.

Chart 2

So what can Chi-square tell us about these differences?

Nelson Sample	observed	expected	difference	diff^2	(diff^)÷expected
Solar or Lunar Eclipse	8	1.2	6.8	46.24	38.53
Other Lunar Aspect	18	24.8	-6.8	46.24	1.86
Totals	26	26		Chi^2 =	40.39
				degree of freedom =	1
				(p) =	0.0000000002

The significance level is (p) 0.0000000002. That's huge. In more familiar terms, the likelihood of this result occurring by chance is 1 in 20,000,000,000, or oOne chance in 20 billion!

This result is so extreme that it has to be suspicious, so let's check it another way. Let's do the Chi-square test on the random sample result of 0 eclipses in the control group.

Random Sample	observed	expected	difference	diff^2	(diff^2)÷expected
Solar or Lunar Eclipse	0	1.2	-1.2	1.44	1.2
Other Lunar Aspect	26	24.8	1.2	1.44	0.058
Totals	26	26		Chi^2 =	1.258
				degree of freedom	1
				(p)=	0.2620177695

This result tells us that the likelihood of no eclipses occurring in any 97-day period of time is (p)=0.262 or 26 percent. This makes sense as 97 days is 26 percent of a full calendar year, a little over 3 months, and Eclipses occur in approximate six-month intervals.

There is no choice here: the null hypothesis of no difference must be *rejected* (again) and the alternative hypothesis that Nelson either picked these examples because of the lunar associations, or perhaps lunar activity may actually cause disturbances in the ionosphere.

As amazing as these results are, I've saved the most extreme for last: geomagnetic disturbances coinciding with any of the 12 aspects the Moon makes to the Sun every 29.5 days.

Experiment 3: Distribution of regular monthly Lunar Aspects Occurring during Disturbances

Referring again to Table 1, there seems to be an emphasis on certain lunar lspects in the examples Nelson has provided. My method of determining which Ptolemaic aspect to choose to represent each of Nelson's examples was to ascertain which aspect was in effect closest to either the start of, or the center of, each of Nelson's disturbance periods, depending on the length of each time period considered. Of course, this method is arbitrary but seems to be the simplest and most logical. The lunar aspects for the random sample control group were chosen in the same manner.

Our research question has to be: How significant are the numbers of the New, Quarter, and Full Moon aspects that coincide with the periods of geomagnetic disturbances in Nelson's data?

The period of time from one New Moon to the next is 29.5 days, and along the way Luna makes successive 30 degrees angles that we like to call aspects: a conjunction (0°), a waxing semi-sextile (30°), waxing sextile (60°), and so on to the opposition (180°) and then a repeat as Luna wanes to her next conjunction.

The number of the seven different types of Ptolemaic Moon to Sun aspects in any one lunar cycle is a total of 12, and the number of each is: New Moon (1); Sextile (2); Inconjunct (2); Semi-sextile (2); Quarter (2); Full Moon (1); Trine 2.

What we need to know is when the relative frequency of any one of these aspects occurring during any one particlar time period that we may be interested in? Very simply, we divide one aspect by the total of 12 aspects (1 ÷ 12), to get a basic frequency of .083 for a Full or New Moon and twice that for the other aspects, 2 ÷ 12 = .166.

Applying this formula to a sample size of 26 time periods would give an expected average of the following:

Table 3		
Lunar Aspects	*Frequency x Sample Size (26)*	*Expected Number of Each Aspect*
NewMoon	.083x26 =	2.17 ExpectedAverage
Semi-sextiles	.166 x 26 =	4.33 Expected Average
Sextiles	.166 x 26 =	4.33 Expected Average
Quarters	.166 x 26 =	4.34 Expected Average
Trines	.166 x 26 =	4.33 Expected Average
Inconjuncts	.166 x 26 =	4.33 Expected Average
Full Moon	.083 x 26 =	2.17 Expected Average
12 Aspects		26 Total

These are the numbers of each lunar aspect we should expect, on average, in either the Nelson data set or the random sample control group and also we may use these averages to compute the significance of any differences that exist. Next, we need a summary of the lunar aspects found in each of the Nelson and control group data sets from Tables 1 and 2:

Table 4		
Lunar Aspects	*Random Dates Control Group*	*Nelson's Disturbances Examples*
New Moon	2	7
Semi-sextile	3	0
Sextile	4	0
Quarter	4	7
Trine	7	0
Inconjunct	4	2
Full Moon	2	10
Totals	26	26

With these data now in hand we can proceed with our analysis.

Chart 3 displays the distribution of lunar aspects occurring during the 26 dates of the random control group from Table 2 compared to the expected average:

Chart 3 graphically illustrates both a similarity and a difference between the expected average and the control group, the largest difference being the 7 trines in the control group versus 4.33 expected. How the two graphs are similar is in the general pyramid-like shape of each, giving the impression of a normal curve.

However, even though that one difference sticks out like a sore thumb, the reality is that the random sample control group distribution is well within the bounds of normal sample variation.

Here is the Chi-square test of the random sample control group versus expected average:

Random Sample		Chi-square Goodness of Fit			
	Observed	Expcted	Difference	Diff^2	Diff^2 ÷ Expected
New Moon	2	2.17	-0.17	0.029	0.013
Semi-sextile	3	4.33	-1.33	1.769	0.409
Sextile	4	4.33	-0.33	0.109	0.025
Quarter	4	4.34	-0.34	0.116	0.027
Trine	7	4.33	2.67	7.129	1.646
Inconjunct	4	4.33	-0.33	0.109	0.025
Full Moon	2	2.17	-0.17	0.029	0.013
	26	26		Chi-sqr =	2.158
Totals			Degrees of Freedom =		6
			Chi^2 per Excel	(P) =	0.905

The result is that the likelihood of this distribution of lunar aspects in the random dates control group occurring by normal sample variation is 90.5 percent, or more than 9 chances out of 10.

Our conclusion must be that there is no significant difference between the random sample control group and the expected average. So, in this case of control group v. expected, the null hypothesis *cannot* be rejected.

On the other hand, we have this:

Chart 4 compares the expected average to the periods of geomagnetic disturbances. Please recall that the original planetary hard angles Nelson used to predict disturbances were 0, 90, 180, and 270 degrees, which is exactly what these lunar aspects are: New Moons, Quarter Moons, and Full Moons.

Chart 4

These differences are extreme. The fact is, Excel's Chi-square test puts the probability of this sample occurring by random chance at an infinitesimally low of (p) = 0.0000000005. That's 1 chance in 50 Billion.

Nelson Sample		Chi-Square Goodness of Fit			
	Actual	Expected	Difference	Diff^2	Diff^2 ÷ Expected
New Moon	7	2.17	4.83	23.33	10.75
Semi-sextile	0	4.33	-4.33	18.75	4.33
Sextile	0	4.33	-4.33	18.75	4.33
Quarter	7	4.34	2.66	7.08	1.63
Trine	0	4.33	-4.33	18.75	4.33
Inconjunct	2	4.33	-2.33	5.43	1.25
Full Moon	10	2.17	7.83	61.31	28.25
Totals	26	26		Chi-Sqr =	54.88
			Degrees of Freedom =		6
			Chi ^2 per Excel	(P) =	0.0000000005

Again, as is the case in the first two experiments, this evidence is more than enough to *reject* the null hypothesis of no difference and *supports* the alternative hypothesis that Nelson either picked these examples knowing of the lunar associations, or lunar activity is closely correlated with, and may actually cause, geomagnetic disturbances on planet Earth.

Conclusion

Keeping in mind that the most commonly accepted significance level for a wide variety of statistical tests is (p) .05, or just 1 chance in 20, compare that to the results of our three experiments.

Probability of Nelson's Geomagnetic Disturbance Periods coinciding with:

- Month long Eclipse Cycles (p) 0.00003 (1 chance in 300,000)
- Solar and Lunar Eclipses (p) 0.0000000002 (1 in 20 Billion)
- New, Quarter and Full Moons (p) 0.0000000005 (1 in 50 Billion)

A simpler way of describing these results: There is a 99.999+ percent certainty that these results are not due to chance.

Even more succinct: *It is certain these results are not due to chance.*

I think that it is a very curious fact to point out and remember that while no one ever refuted the accuracy of Nelson's forecasts, beginning around 1946 through about 1970, for RCA (and for other organizations such NATO and NASA no less), no one has ever been able to replicate his method either.

How can that be?

For me, the answer is crystal clear. Nelson (and maybe RCA, too) was very aware of the influence of the Moon on the geomagnetic disturbances affecting short-wave radio signals, but rather than announce that to the world, he camouflaged his method in a haystack of thousands of heliocentric aspects. I think he (and RCA) chose to solve the physics and business problems of radio transmission without causing other sociological/religious problems. Think about it. We're talking 1940s, 1950s and early 1960s. Nelson was already experiencing heated criticisms from astronomers. Can you imagine the outcry from the pulpits and universities if he was forecasting by the Moon? Heresy! Sorcerer! There would be cartoons lampooning Nelson in a pointed hat and wizard's robes prognosticating from atop the RCA building.

Still, Nelson's solution to a difficult problem and his resulting forecasting success generated a lot of curiosity and many invitations to speak. It's just my opinion, but I believe he had to explain in some way that wouldn't rock the boat but not be totally untruthful either.

The reason no one has repeated his success is that no one has ever considered the Moon as a factor. More than that, I suspect that Nelson was really using geocentric planetary positions (a.k.a. astrology) as well. In the 7,790 day population space we have examined, there are 12,239 heliocentric aspects to consider, an average of 1.57 a day. That's so many, something is bound to coincide with a geomagnetic disturbance. In contrast, there are only 5,916 geocentric aspects in the same period of time, (0.76 a day) less than half, and my first glance at those data give me the impression that the geocentric aspects have a lot more directness and potency.

I believe that this information opens the door to a new line research. If Nelson's method could be replicated geocentrically and a forecasting service developed for today's short-wave ham radio enthusiasts, it would be the first scientific, repeatable, and practically applicable method to which classical astrology may be applied.

Endnotes

[1]Nelson, J. H. *Radio Forecasting Techniques*. Text of presentation at June 1953 symposium of the Professional Group on Communications Systems, pp. 19-20.

[2]Nelson, J. H. *Shortwave Radio Propagation Correlation with Planetary Positions*. 1951, RCA Communications, Inc., New York, p. 33. Nelson, J. H. *Cosmic Patterns*. 1961, American Federation of Astrologers, Tempe, Arizona, p. 2.

[3]Nelson, J. H. Shortwave Radio Propagation Correlation with Planetary Positions. 1951, RCA Communications, Inc., New York, p. 27.

[4]Nelson, J. H. *Cosmic Patterns*. 1961, American Federation of Astrologers, Tempe, Arizona, p. 3.

[5]Nelson, J. H. *Cosmic Patterns*. 1961, American Federation of Astrologers, Tempe, Arizona, p. 4.

[6]Nelson, J. H. *Shortwave Radio Propagation Correlation with Planetary Positions*. 1951, RCA Communications, Inc., New York. Nelson, J. H. *Planetary Position Effect on Short-Wave Signal Quality*. January 21-15, 1952, paper presentd at the AIEE Winter General Meeting, New York. Nelson, J. H. *Cosmic Patterns*. 1961, American Federation of Astrologers, Tempe, Arizona.

[7]Nelson, J. H. *Radio Forecasting Techniques*. Text of presentation at June 1953 symposium of the Professional Group on Communications Systems, p. 22.

[8]www.browserling.com/tools/random-date

[9]Michelsen, The American Ephemeris for the 20th Century.

[10]Nelson, J. H. *Cosmic Patterns*. 1961, American Federation of Astrologers, Tempe, Arizona, p. 61.

Moon's Mathematical Nodes

By Rui Fernandes

ABSTRACT: As we all know, the Moon's nodes are the intersection of our satellite's orbit with the ecliptic plane and although they have been used primarily by Hindu astrologers in the traditional Jyotisha, they became, with time, an integrating part of the western astrological thinking as well, specially linked to the karmic background study and interpretation analysis. Although Western astrologers were focused mainly in the interpretation and relationship between the planets, signs, houses, and aspects, the lunar nodes—with the Vedic names Rahu (ascending node) and Ketu (descending node)—are currently, if not above, at the level of the black moon Lilith, or the Arabic parts, like the significant Pars Fortunae used by most astrologers—important immaterial points taken into account in the delineation and study of a natal chart and subsequent transits study. The current essay allows—that is the primary objective and goal—more precision, maneuver, latitude and mainly simplicity in their calculation on the absence of a computer, when using the traditional calculation model—still widely used—based on tabular printed ephemeris data with steps of one day. Also, the article shows a glance of a current study almost completed, which will launch a mathematical way of calculus of the planetary orbital elements outside the known usual parameters, which, with some work, might result in a new approach for the calculation of precise ephemeris.

Method

Astrology, in its computational model, had always a solid mathematical and geometry background. In this article, I am going to show how relatively easy it can be to compute an approximate value for the ascending Moon node, knowing just two spherical coordinates of our major and natural satellite.

It's common knowledge that the Moon's nodes are the intersection of our satellite's orbit with the ecliptic plane and although it has been used primarily by the Hindu astrology *Jyotisha*, it has become an integrating part of the western astrological thinking as well, specially linked to the karmic background study and interpretation analysis.

Suppose then that we don't know either the velocity or the accurate Cartesian positions of the orbiting body—just its spherical positions in space, the ecliptic longitude (λ) and latitude (β). We don't know, obviously, its distance either, as it's shown in the ephemeris books for manual use.

I have been developing an approximate mathematical method for calculating the respective osculating elements of a body, namely the ascending node, with these knowledge restrictions, or better, taking into account the possible lack of information. The principle is to use a set of two different and sequential positions of the body in space referenced to the main body. We'll also assume that for a period of two times Δt (our time step) the elements won't change significantly which in fact occurs; the true osculating nodes are always in motion (mainly retrograde).

We wish to calculate this particular set of elements for the orbiting body at time *t*. So, we'll establish the following three position points and their distances calculated for the time *t – Δt* and *t + Δt*:

$$A = \left[A_x, A_y, A_z\right], for\ (t - dt)$$
$$B = \left[B_x, B_y, B_z\right], for\ (t)$$
$$C = \left[C_x, C_y, C_z\right], for\ (t + dt)$$
$$A_r = \sqrt{A_x^2 + A_y^2 + A_z^2}$$
$$B_r = \sqrt{B_x^2 + B_y^2 + B_z^2}$$
$$C_r = \sqrt{C_x^2 + C_y^2 + C_z^2}$$

We're going to calculate the corresponding nodes for point **B** at time **t**.

The rectangular coordinates of any of these points, are easily calculated with a tabulated ephemeris. If a body **P** has an ecliptic longitude λ and a latitude of β then its Cartesian coordinates become:

$$P_x = r . cos(\beta) . cos(\lambda)$$
$$P_y = r . cos(\beta) . sin(\lambda)$$
$$P_z = r . sin(\beta)$$

Since distance is not important here (and in fact unknown) **r** is equal to 1 (so A_r, B_r and C_r will be also equal to 1—a unit measure).

It's not necessary to calculate **B**. This point is the mid value. From **A** and **C**, we can quantify its cross product:

$$H_x = A_y . C_z - A_z . C_y$$
$$H_y = A_z . C_x - A_x . C_z$$
$$H_z = A_x . C_y - A_y . C_x$$

This vector is perpendicular to the orbit and will give us the directions of its intersection to the ecliptic plane.

So, at this point, we can actually calculate an approximate value of the Ω (ascending node) parameter for the time **t**:

$$\Omega = atan2\ (H_x, -H_y)$$

Note that this vector does not have the same magnitude as the one calculated if we were starting from the correct positions and velocities of our body. The descending node will be logically equal to this value plus 180 degrees.

The **ATAN2** function is a safe precaution to obtain real results in geometry calculations. Let's look at this example: usually it appears in the manuals that the *medium coeli* can be achieved from the following formula:

$$MC = tan^{-1}(tan(LST).cos(\varepsilon))$$

where **LST** is the Local Sidereal Time and ε the obliquity of the ecliptic, which is almost correct. But let's suppose that our local sidereal time is of 90 degrees; we get an error for **tan (90°)**—which is infinite. The same happens for a 270° **LST** value. And we must be cautious in the quadrant we are working. A body can be in the third quadrant, but the **tan⁻¹** (arctangent) calculation result will be as if it was in the fourth, because the **tan⁻¹** function only give us results between -π and π through zero (in the first and fourth quadrants).

If we define, however, the **MC** with the correct Cartesian coordinates the **ATAN2** function will never give an error except if incorrect values are used, like x and y being equal to zero (undefined).

$$\begin{cases} x = cos(LST).cos(\varepsilon) \\ y = sin(LST) \end{cases}$$
$$so\ MC = atan2(y,x)$$

For future reference, here are the guidelines of the function **ATAN2**:

$$f(x) = atan2(y,x)$$
$$x = 0, y > 0 \xrightarrow{then} 90°$$
$$x = 0, y < 0 \xrightarrow{then} 270°$$
$$x > 0, y > 0 \xrightarrow{then} tan^{-1}(y,x)$$
$$x < 0, y < 0 \xrightarrow{then} tan^{-1}(y,x) + 180°$$
$$x > 0, y < 0 \xrightarrow{then} tan^{-1}(y,x) + 360°$$
$$x < 0, y > 0 \xrightarrow{then} tan^{-1}(y,x) + 180°$$

Nevertheless, a small test with the Moon's orbit—the most complicated of the solar system—with the previous simple algorithm showed that for the time span from JD2396759.0 (January 1, 1850, at 12h) to JD2816788.0 (January 1, 3000, at 12h), for a **Δt** = 0.13 days (3.12 hours), the maximum error of our calculated Ω in arc seconds is *less than one second of arc (0.9)*.

For a step of one day, it's about *58 seconds—less than one minute—with an average modulus error of 21.5 seconds*. Half of that step (12 hours), gives a maximum error of *14.1 seconds, and an average error of 5.2 seconds of arc*.

These tests showed that a specific best fitted **Δt** must be used in order to the result won't be less accurate. But why?

It's logical that since the Moon moves so fast (about 12 to 14 degrees per day), the greater the value of **Δt**, the greater the error in our value. Another important fact to add, is that if the values in the z-axis are too close to zero (very near the nodes) the error increases (in those cases either we increase the **Δt** or choose other reference dates). So the results can be, actually, improved in its error by choosing, for instance, the appropriate **A** and **C** points. This is just a premier presentation. We made our tests against the true osculating ascending node of date using apparent positions.

If we are using a tabulated printed ephemeris (great for manual quick calculations), we'll be stuck (pass the expression) with a **Δt** equal to one day. But our error will still not exceed one minute of degree at most, and will round the 21.5 average seconds of error (about ½ of minute).

If we use for comparison the formula for the mean ascending node of Chapront[1], for instance, for the same time period of 1,150 years, we get a maximum error of almost two degrees toward the true values—near 125 times worse than our own results. Even if it's the mean node, the difference is substantial.

For extensible demonstration purposes, analyzing further, we could also extract from this plain vector the value of the Moon's orbit inclination, from:

$$i = atan2(\sqrt{h_x^2 + h_y^2}, h_z)$$

And so on.

Let's try a practical example, for the moon on January 1, 2000, at 12h.

The spherical Moon coordinates around that date, one day before (December 31, 1999, 12h) and one day after (January 2, 2000, 12h), are:

$$A = \begin{cases} \lambda_{dt-1} = 211.20888615231° \\ \beta_{dt-1} = 5.23381090468° \end{cases}$$

$$C = \begin{cases} \lambda_{dt+1} = 235.27209991595° \\ \beta_{dt+1} = 4.88294678314° \end{cases}$$

From here we calculate the rectangular coordinates for both reference points:

$$A_x = cos(5.23381090468) \times cos(211.20888615231) = -0.8517180083$$
$$A_y = cos(5.23381090468) \times sin(211.20888615231) = -0.51599932243$$
$$A_z = sin(5.23381090468) = 0.091220247328$$
$$C_x = cos(4.88294678314) \times cos(235.27209991595) = -0.56761224451$$
$$C_y = cos(4.88294678314) \times sin(235.27209991595) = -0.81888391246$$
$$C_z = sin(4.88294678314) = 0.085120372343$$

Now for our vector:

$$H_x = -0.51599932243 \times 0.085120372343 - 0.091220247328 \times (-0.81888391246)$$
$$H_x = 0.030776738573$$
$$H_y = 0.091220247328 \times (-0.56761224451) - (-0.8517180083) \times 0.085120372343$$
$$H_y = 0.020720824669$$
$$H_z = -0.8517180083 \times -0.81888391246 - (-0.51599932243) \times (-0.56761224451)$$
$$H_z = 0.40457064139$$

Finally, we calculate our node and the difference against the true one:

$$\Omega_{true} = 123.95406594733°$$
$$\Omega_{calculated} = atan2(0.030776738573, -0.020720824669) = 123.95090495072°$$
$$\Delta = (123.95406594733 - 123.95090495072)$$
$$\Delta = 0.00316099661° = 11.3 \text{ seconds}$$

We reached a value with an error of just 11.3 seconds of arc degree—acceptable, in my opinion. If the step was the previous mentioned 3.12 hours, the margin error would be less than one second—almost neglegible.

Conclusion

This small article is only a preview draft of the algorithms being implemented mathematically by me to calculate other important astrological quantities. The mechanical foundations of astrology are indeed mathematical.

Through mathematics and applied geometry calculus, we can actually achieve very accurate astrological values and quantities making the whole celestial mechanism a little more understandable in the paper. Not to mention their explicit and implicit relationships. This modest essay is just an example of what might be achieved disregarding the lack of precise—or better complete—information with a use of a simple pencil, a common calculator and a piece of paper.

Endnote

[1] Chapront-Touzé, M.; Chapront, J., *Lunar tables and programs from 4000 B.C. to A.D. 8000*, 1991.

The Study of Leukemia Through Medical Astrology

Abdol-Hussein Heidari

ABSTRACT: In this research article, leukemia (a type of blood cancer) is studied in 15 AA rated charts. The method that is used here is testing the rules of medical astrology related to leukemia using the tropical western system. The aim is to see which effective factors of leukemia are repeatedly seen and also to find new astrological combinations that indicate this disease. At first the medical definition along with the astrological rules for leukemia is given and then those rules are tested on AA rated charts. It was observed that the factors that have been considered for leukemia seem to have an effective role in determining this illness. It was seen that any close connection with the North Node (Rahu) or nodal axis includes conjunction, square, opposition, and trine can afflict a planet and has an important role in leukemia. The effects of the sixth, eighth, and twelfth houses are studied and the role of the sixth house was very prominent.

Introduction

Medical astrology is one the important branches of astrology that still needs many researches to understand the kind of disease, its acuteness or timing of that. Also the similarities in the signs of diseases make it difficult to exactly distinguish them or pin point the illness. One of the best ways to do so is to collect reliable nativities (AA rated charts) and then test the astrological rules on them and observe which of them repeats in most of the cases. Here, considering leukemia as a special kind of blood cancer, the astrological rules of that is given and then are tested on 15 AA rated charts. Generally, astrological combinations for a disease contain the house(s) related to it and also the significators which are planets signifying the parts of the body are involved. An important factor to be considered in all sicknesses is the power of the chart of the native that can show the strength or weakness of them by checking the Ascendant, Sun (as significator for body), Moon (as significator of mind) and positive and negative aspects,conjunctions,placements of them The second thing is understanding the potential and intensity of the disease's acuteness that can be seen through the astrological combinations of that special disease and finding the amount of the afflictions (effects of malefic planets in conjunction or aspect or the bad placement of a planet) on significators and houses related to the illness. Another essential determinant in medical astrology is longevity of the native. If the chart shows a good longevity but there are combinations of disease too, there are two possibilities: The native will get sick at the last years of life when potential transits and/or progressions arrive or if he gets sick earlier he will be resisting the disease and may overcome that or may have to fight till the end of the life. Then the astrologer should have some methods for recognizing the longevity of the native. Here the concentration is on checking the combinations that show the possibility of leukemia in the charts.

Medical Definition of Leukemia

There are different kinds of leukemia and even they can be categorized and distinguished astrologically. Here the term leukemia is applied for each type and they are not separated and the general shape of disease is considered.

The Centers for Disease Control and Prevention defines leukemia as a cancer of the bone marrow (the soft, sponge-like tissue in the center of most bones that makes blood cells) and blood. The two main kinds of leukemia are

- Lymphocytic leukemia (also known as lymphoblastic leukemia), when the body makes too many of a certain kind of white blood cells, called lymphocytes.

- Myelogenous leukemia (also known as myeloid or myelocytic leukemia), when the body makes too many of a certain kind of white blood cells, called granulocytes.

Leukemia can be acute or chronic. Acute types of leukemia progress quickly, while chronic types of leukemia progress slowly, leading to different treatments.[1]

Astrological Rules for Blood Cancer that Can be Used for Leukemia

1. Serious afflictions to the Ascendant /Ascendant lord (planet that governs the Ascendant) as a general sign for the weakness of the body;[2]

2. Saturn and Sun represent Bones;[2, 3]

3. Mars is related to the blood, marrow, red coloring matter in blood;[2]

4. Moon signifies all kinds of the fluids in the body;[3]

5. Neptune can also be checked for bone diseases;[2]

6. Tenth house signifies bone;[4]

7. Eleventh house signifies bone marrow.[7]

8. Sixth, eighth and twelfth houses are negative houses that their lords (from the lord, I mean the owner of the sign).[8]

Method of Analysis Using the Western System

Western charts are studied this way:

The condition of the Ascendant of the chart is studied, as per conjunctions, aspects on the Ascendant, the placement of Ascendant lord, the position of the Ascendant lord is checked as per the placement, aspects, conjunctions and also Ascendant lord's dispositor (lord of the sign in which the Ascendant lord is placed). Here the effects of nodes on the Ascendant lord or on its dispositor is also checked.

The condition of the Moon is checked as per the placement, aspects, conjunctions and also the Moon's dispositor (lord of the sign in which the Moon is placed). Here the effects of the nodes on the Moon or on its dispositor are also checked.

The condition of Mars is checked as per the placement, aspects, conjunctions, and also Mars' dispositor (lord of the sign that Mars is placed). Here the effects of nodes on the Mars or on its dispositor is also checked.

The condition of the tenth house of the chart is studied, as per conjunctions, aspects, on the tenth house cusp, the placement of the lord of the sign of the tenth cusp). The position of the tenth lord is checked as per the placement, aspects, conjunctions, and also the tenth lord's dispositor (lord of the sign in which the tenth lord is placed). Here the effects of nodes on the tenth lord or on its dispositer is also checked.

The condition of the eleventh house is studied, as per conjunctions, aspects on the eleventh house (eleventh house cusp), the placement of the lord of the sign in which the eleventh cusp is placed). The position of the eleventh lord is checked as per the placement, aspects, conjunctions and also eleventh lord's dispositor (the lord of the sign in which the eleventh lord is placed). Here the effects of nodes on the eleventh lord or on its dispositer are also checked.

The condition of the Sun and Saturn (significators of bone) is checked as per the placement, aspects, conjunctions, and also their dispositor (lord of the sign in which they are placed). Here the effects of nodes on these two or on their dispositor is also checked.

All of the above factors should be considered and the negative effects on them should be observed accurately to see which of these are repeated in most of the cases and if they are important factors in leukemia at all.

Notes: The orb for conjunctions, aspects, etc. are considered five degrees. The lord of a house is the lord of the sign on the cusp. Comprehensive research in leukemia is also done on 20 AA rated charts by applying Vedic and Western systems simultaneously, but because of space considerations it will be presented later as other research.

Case Studies

15 AA rated charts of leukemia cases were selected from astrodatabank website [8]. In general they are in two categories: leukemia at early ages of life and those with leukemia at old age. Here just static analysis (analysis of the potential strength and weakness of the chart without checking the timing and the onset of disease) is done for diagnostic purposes with timing given in a separate research article.

Note: 15 case studies are referenced by [c1], [c2]... [c15] in the reference page under the title Case Studies.' And the pictures of the charts are given the end of this article.

In the Western system, the lord of a house means the lord of the sign of the relevant house's cusp.

Case 1

This is a case of a child diagnosed with leukemia in March 2006. Birth data: July 22, 2005, 1:34 p.m., Concord, Massachusetts (see chart below).

1. Ascendant: Ascendant lord Mars placed in the sixth house of disease. Mars square Saturn.

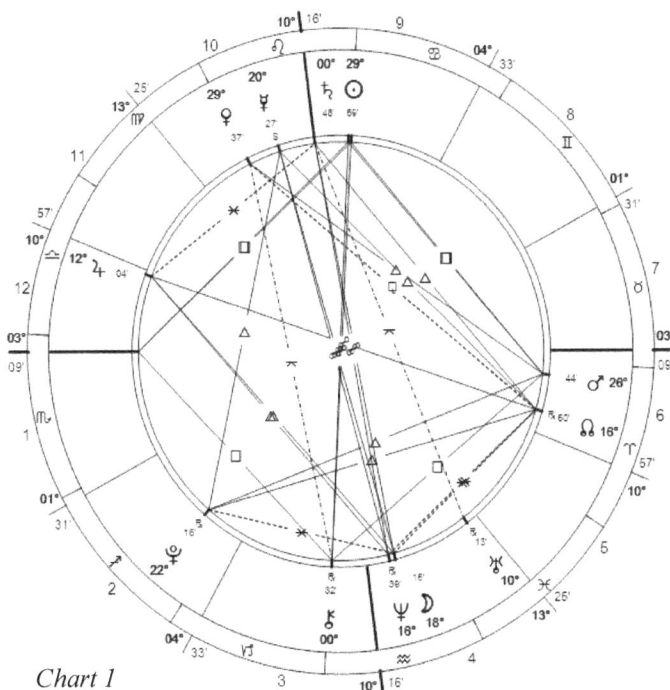

Chart 1

2. Moon: Close conjunction with Neptune, opposition Mercury (eighth lord) in the tenth house, Moon's dispositor (Moon's sign lord) Saturn is combust.

3. Tenth House: Tenth lord (Sun) square Mars in the sixth house.

4. Eleventh House: Eleventh lord (Mercury, also the eighth lord) opposition Moon and Neptune.

5. The Sun and Saturn (significators of bones). Both Sun and Saturn square Mars in the sixth house.

6.Summary: Ascendant, Moon, Mars tenth house, eleventh house, Sun and Saturn are negative for health.

Case 2

This native was diagnosed with acute myelogenous leukemia and died of the disease at age 36 years old. Birth data: August 30, 1974, 11:07 p.m., Boston, Massachusetts.

1. Ascendant: Ascendant cusp is closely opposition Neptune in the sixth house of disease. Ascendant lord, Mercury, is in close conjunction with twelfth lord, the Mars. Mercury is square North Node.

2. Moon: Moon opposite Venus, the sixth lord. Moon's dispositor Saturn is placed in Cancer, its detrimental sign and Saturn also is in close square with Uranus in the sixth house of disease.

3. Mars: An opposition with Jupiter but well placed.

4. Tenth House: Tenth lord (Saturn) is in its detrimental sign of Cancer and is in a very close square with Uranus in the sixth house of disease. Saturn's dispositor (sign lord) is Moon that is opposition Venus, the sixth lord.

5. Eleventh House: Eleventh lord (Jupiter) placed in its own sign of Pisces but opposition Mars (twelfth lord) and Mercury. It is also closely square the North Node (Rahu).

6. The Sun and Saturn (significators of bones): Sun is in a close square with Neptune in the sixth house. Sun's dispositor, Mercury, is in close conjunction with Mars (twelfth lord). Saturn has been checked above.

Summary: Except Mars, all factors are weak for health because of the connections they have with negative houses (6, 8, and 12), combustion, being in a detrimental sign, bad position of dispositor, and square the North Node.

Case 3

This native died of leukemia at age of 51. Birth Data: December 26, 1954, 7:20 p.m., Boston, Massachusetts.

1. Ascendant: Ascendant lord, the Sun, is in close conjunction with the North Node (Rahu). Sun's dispositor is Saturn and the dispositor of Saturn, Mars, is in the eighth house of disease.

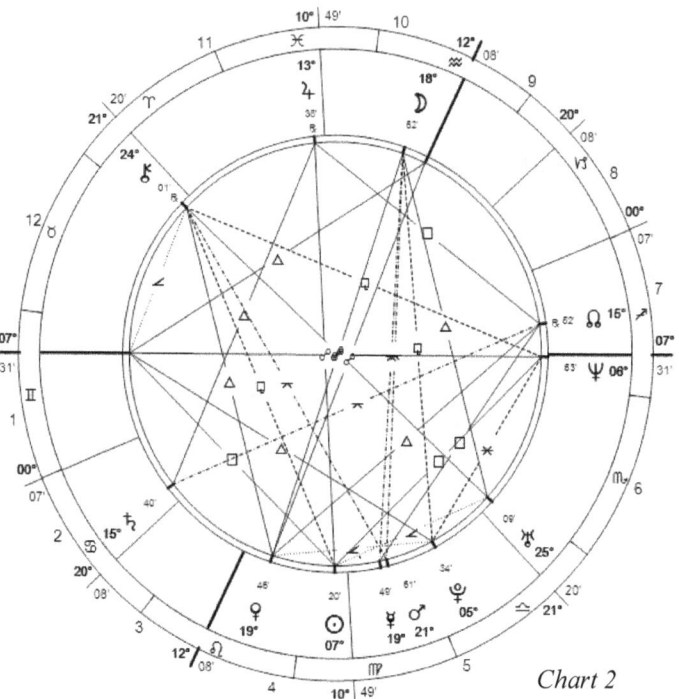

Chart 2

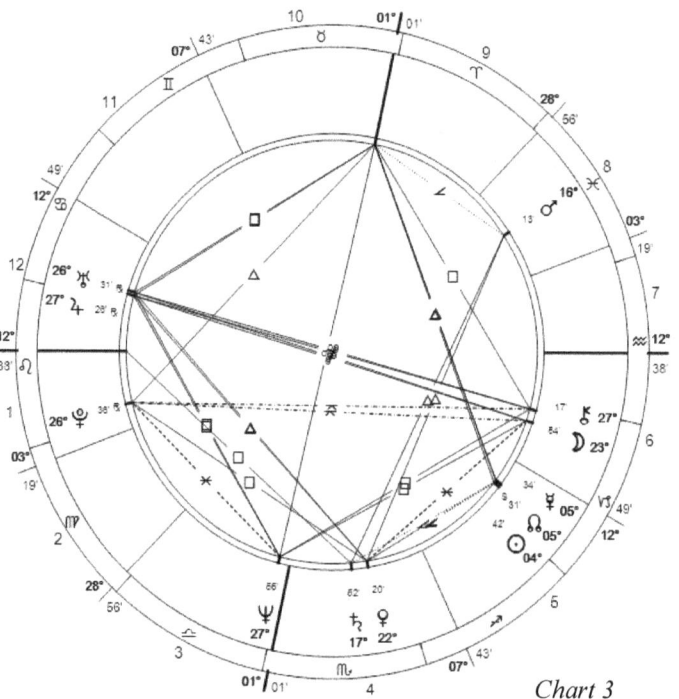

Chart 3

2. Moon: Moon has occupied the sixth house, the main house of disease, and Capricorn, its detrimental sign. Moon is opposition Uranus and Jupiter in the twelfth house, another house of disease. Also, Jupiter is the eighth lord. Moon's dispositor is Saturn and the dispositor of Saturn, Mars, is placed in the eighth house of disease.

3. Mars: Mars is in the eighth house. Its dispositor Jupiter is in the twelfth house.

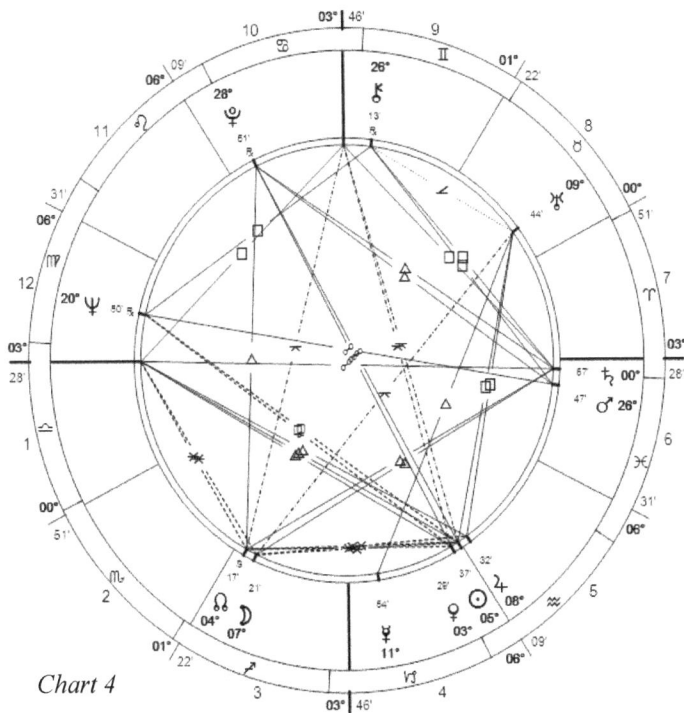
Chart 4

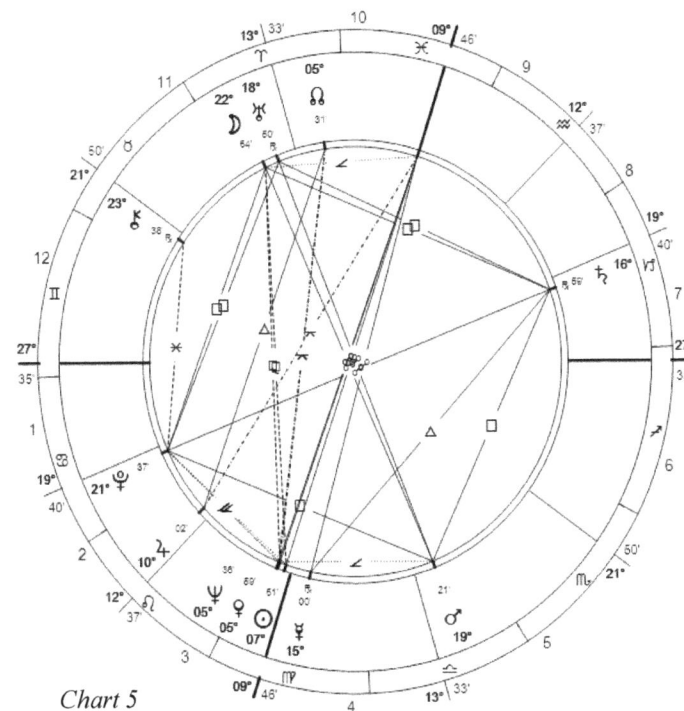
Chart 5

4. Tenth House: Tenth lord, Venus, is in Scorpio conjunction Saturn, the sixth lord of the chart. Venus' dispositor, Mars, is in the eighth house.

5. Eleventh House: Its lord Mercury is in close conjunction with the North Node. Also, it is combust.

6. The Sun and Saturn (significators of bone) are weak and afflicted.

7. Summary: All factors are negative for health because of the connection with 6, 8, 12 houses of disease, conjunction with North Node, bad position of dispositor, in detrimental sign, and combust.

Case 4

Native died of leukemia at age 73. Birth data: January 25, 1938, 9:50 p.m., Los Angeles, California.

1. Ascendant: Ascendant lord Venus is combust and its dispositor Saturn is in the sixth house of disease and conjunct Mars, the sixth and twelfth lord of the chart.

2. Moon: The Moon is conjunct the North Node (Rahu). Its dispositor Jupiter is combust. Jupiter's dispositor, Saturn, is in the sixth house of disease in Aries, its debilitation sign.

3. Mars: Mars is in the sixth house of disease. Its dispositor is Jupiter and we have already seen its condition.

4. Tenth House: Tenth lord is Moon and we saw the condition of the Moon.

5. Eleventh House: The eleventh lord is the Sun in close conjunction with the eighth lord, Venus. Sun's dispositor is Jupiter and we have seen its condition before.

6. The Sun and Saturn (significators of bone): Both have been discussed before.

7. Summary: All factors are negative because of their connection with the sixth, eighth, and twelfth houses of disease, conjunction the North Node, and in debilitation sign, weakness of dispositor and combustion.

Case 5

The native's death at age 67 was the result of leukemia. Birth data: September 1, 1931, 12:35 a.m., Ovilla,

Texas.

1. Ascendant: Ascendant lord Mercury is in its own house. It is well placed and not afflicted.

2. Moon: It is in eleventh house with Uranus. Its dispositor Mars is placed in Libra, its detrimental sign. The Moon is also opposition Mars, the sixth lord.

3. Mars: Mars is in Libra, its sign of detriment. Its dispositor Venus is combust. Mars is also square Saturn (eighth lord) and Pluto.

4. Tenth House: Venus, the twelfth lord is close to the tenth cusp. The tenth's lord, Jupiter, is well placed with no afflictions.

5. Eleventh House: Mars is in its detrimental sign and its dispositor Venus is combust.

6. The Sun and Saturn (significators of bone): Sun is with Venus, the fifth and twelfth lord. The Sun's dispositor, Mercury, is well placed and not afflicted. Saturn is in its own house and thus well placed, but square Uranus and opposition Pluto.

7. Summary: Moon, Mars, and the eleventh houses are afflicted but other factors are good. Maybe in such cases we can distinguish leukemia at old age from leukemia at early ages. It needs to be combined with the astrological rules of estimating longevity to foretell this with more confidence.

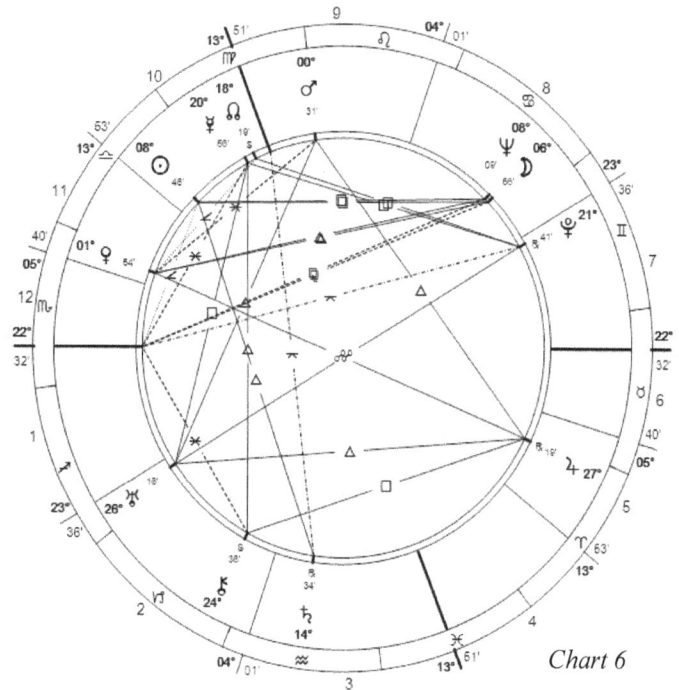

Chart 6

Case 6

The native's death occurred as a result of leukemia at age 86. Birth data: October 2, 1904, 10:20 a.m., Berkhamsted, England.

1. Ascendant: Mars, its lord, is in Virgo and its dispositor Mercury is well placed in Virgo but conjunction North Node and square Pluto and Uranus.

2. Moon: The Moon is in the eighth house in Cancer conjunction Neptune.

3. Already discussed.

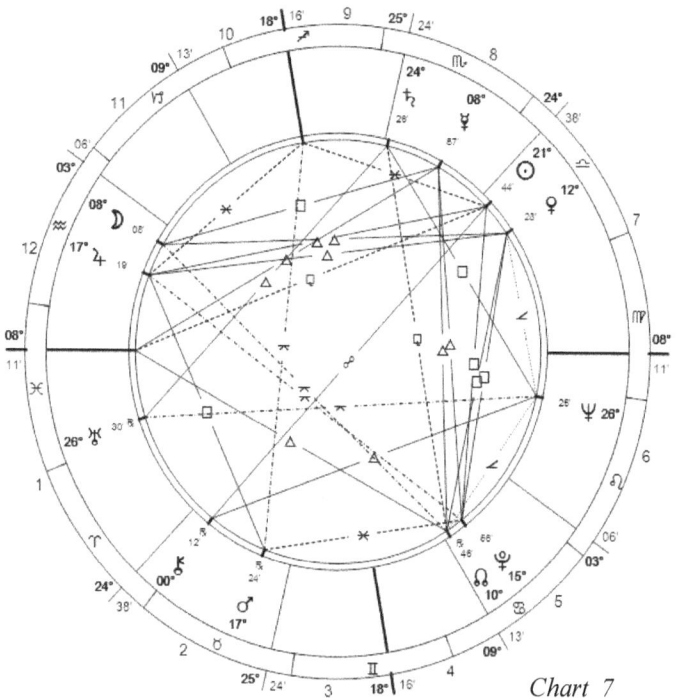

Chart 7

4. Tenth House: North Node is close to the tenth cusp. Tenth lord Mercury is well placed in Virgo but conjunction North Node and square Pluto and Uranus.

5. Eleventh House: Eleventh lord Venus is in Scorpio and its dispositor Mars has already been discussed.

6. The Sun and Saturn (significators of bone): The Sun is debilitated in Libra. Saturn is in its own house of Aquarius.

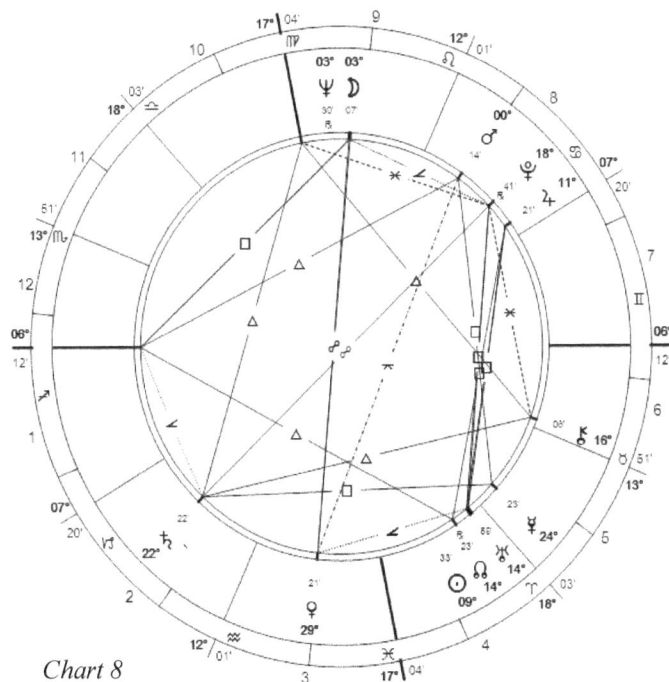

Chart 8

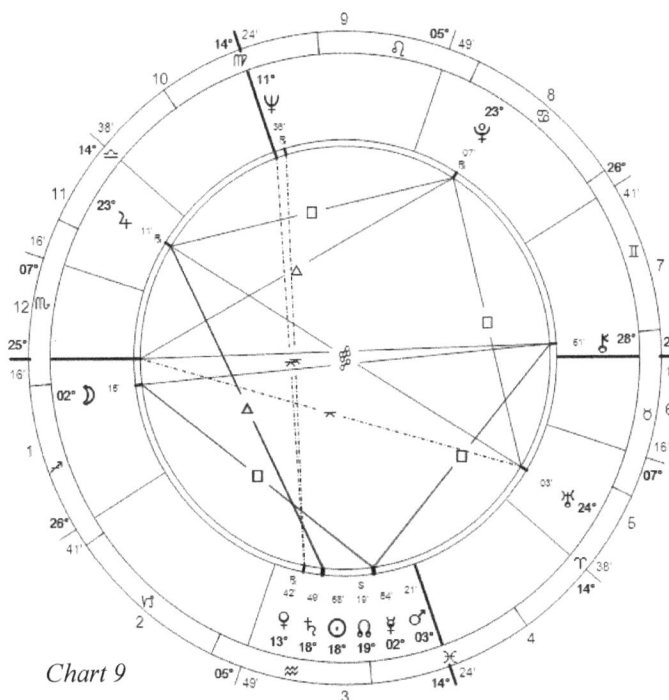

Chart 9

7. Summary: Recovery and protection factors, including good position of dispositor and being well placed in their own sign, are clearly seen in addition to some negative factors, including the debilitation of the Sun and some connections with the eighth house and North Node.

Case 7

This native died of Leukemia at age 73. Birth data: October 15, 1926, 4:00 p.m., Canton, Ohio,

1. Ascendant: Ascendant lord Jupiter is in the twelfth house and opposition Neptune in the sixth house. Jupiter's dispositer, Saturn, is in the eighth house.

2. Moon: The Moon is in the twelfth house, and its dispositer, Saturn, is in the eighth house.

3. Mars: Mars is square Jupiter in the twelfth house. Mars' dispositer, Venus, is well placed in Libra, but to some extent combust. It is square Pluto and North Node.

4. Tenth House: Tenth lord Jupiter is in twelfth house, and Jupiter's dispositer, Saturn, is in the eighth house.

5. Eleventh House: Saturn, the eleventh house lord, is in the eighth house.

6. The Sun and Saturn (significators of bone): Both have been discussed.

7. Summary: Factors are negative for health because of the weakness of dispositors, connections to the sixth, eighth, and twelfth houses of disease, combustion, square the North Node.

Case 8

Native died of leukemia at age 62. Birth data: March 30, 1931, 11:00 p.m., Douglas, Arizona.

1. Ascendant: Ascendant Lord Jupiter is in the eighth house and exalted. Jupiter is square Uranus and North Node. Jupiter's dispositor Moon conjunction Neptune and opposition Venus, the sixth lord.

2. Moon: Conjunction Neptune and opposition Venus, the sixth lord. Its dispositor, Mercury, is in Aries square Saturn.

3. Mars: Mars is in the eighth house. Its dispositor, Sun, is exalted.

4. Tenth House: Tenth lord Mercury is in Aries square Saturn. Its dispositor Mars is in the eighth house.

5. Eleventh House: North Node and Uranus are close to the eleventh cusp. Eleventh lord Venus is in Aquar-

ius opposition Uranus.

6. The Sun and Saturn (significators of bone): The Sun, although square Jupiter in the eighth house, is exalted in Aries. Saturn is in its own sign of Capricorn and opposition Pluto in the eighth house.

7. Summary: Along with some negative factors like connections with the sixth and eighth houses and weakness of dispositor, recovery factors, including exaltation, strong dispositor and being well placed in their own house are also seen.

Case 9

Death occurred from leukemia at age 6. Birth data: February 8, 1934, 2:05 a.m., Port Angeles, Washington.

1. Ascendant: Ascendant lord Mars is closely conjunct debilitated Mercury that is also the eighth lord. Mars' dispositor, Jupiter, is in Libra in a close square with Pluto in the eighth house.

2. Moon: The Moon in close square with Mars (twelfth lord) and Mercury (eighth lord). Its dispositor, Jupiter, is square Pluto in the eighth house.

3. Mars: Already discussed.

4. Tenth House: Neptune is close to the tenth cusp. Tenth lord Mercury is debilitated and conjunction the twelfth lord Mars.

5. Eleventh House: Eleventh lord Venus is combust in Aquarius. Venus' dispositor, Saturn, is in its own sign of Aquarius but also combust.

6. The Sun and Saturn (significators of bone): Conjunction Venus (sixth lord), and North Node. Saturn is totally combust and close to the North Node.

7. Summary: Negative features like connections with the sixth, eighth, and twelfth houses, weakness of dispositor, debilitation, conjunction with the North Node, and combustion are greater than the positive factors, such as Saturn well placed in its own sign .

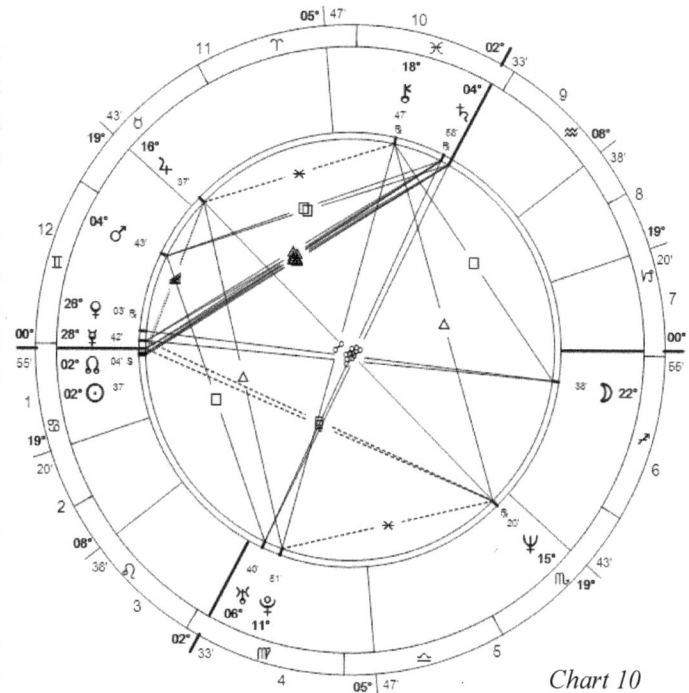

Chart 10

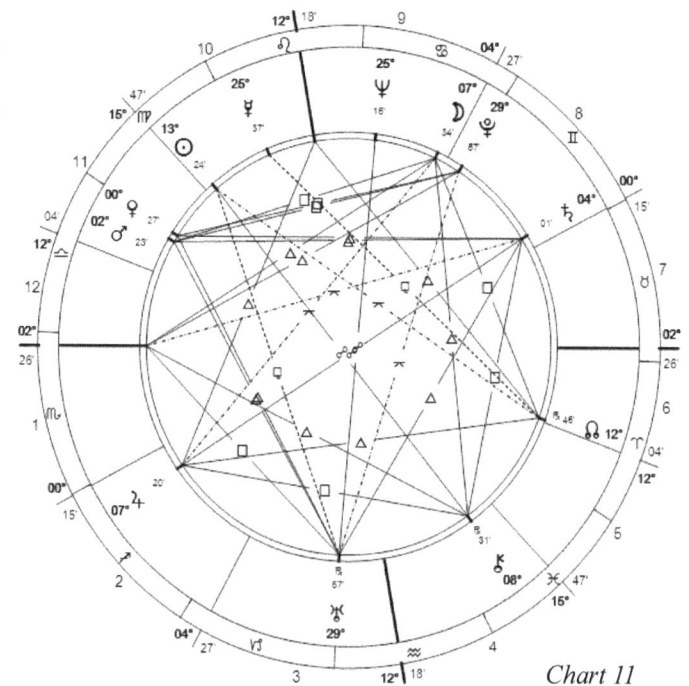

Chart 11

Case 10

Death by leukemia at age 33. Birth data: June 24, 1964, 4:05 a.m., Zagreb, Croatia

1. Ascendant: North Node is very close to the first cusp. Also Venus, the twelfth lord is close to the Ascen-

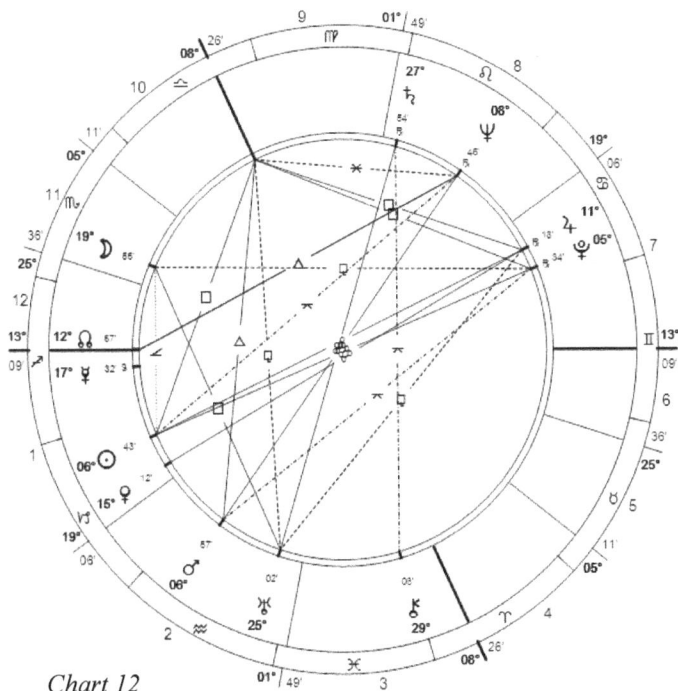

Chart 12

dant cusp. Ascendant lord, the Moon, is in the sixth house opposition Venus, the sixth lord. Its dispositor, Jupiter, is opposition Neptune.

2. Moon: The Moon is in the sixth house opposition Venus, the sixth lord. Its dispositor, Jupiter, is opposition Neptune.

3. Mars: It is placed in the twelfth house square the eighth lord Saturn and Uranus. Its dispositor, Mercury, is combust and close to the North Node and also Venus, the sixth lord.

4. Tenth House: Saturn, the eighth lord, is close to the tenth cusp. The tenth lord, Jupiter, is opposition Neptune and its dispositor Venus is in the twelfth house and debilitated and combust.

5. Eleventh House: Its lord is Mars, as already discussed.

6. The Sun and Saturn (significators of bone): The Sun is close to the North Node and its dispositor, Moon, is placed in the sixth house. Saturn is opposition Neptune and its dispositor is Jupiter in the sign of Venus, the sixth lord and debilitated and placed in the twelfth house.

Summary: All factors are negative because of their connection with the sixth, eighth, and twelfth houses, combustion, closeness (conjunction) to the North Node, debilitation and weakness of the dispositor.

Case 11

This individual died of leukemia at age 42. Birth data: September 6, 1912, 9:50 a.m., Maisons Laffitte, France.

1. Ascendant: Its lord, Mars, conjunction twelfth lord Venus. Mars is in its detrimental sign square Moon and also Pluto in the eighth house. Mars' dispositor, Venus, is well placed in its own sign but afflicted by its close conjunction with the sixth lord Mars.

2. Moon: The Moon is well placed in its own sign, Cancer, and square Mars, the sixth lord.

3. Mars: Already discussed.

4. Tenth House: Tenth lord Sun is well placed and not afflicted.

5. Eleventh House: Its lord, Mercury, is well placed.

6. The Sun and Saturn (significators of bone): Sun has been discussed. Saturn is in the eighth house square Sun and opposition Jupiter.

7. Summary: There are both positive factors—Venus and the Sun well placed in their own signs—and negative factors—connections to the sixth, eighth, and twelfth houses.

Case 12

This individual died of leukemia at age 42. Birth data: December 29, 1918, 6:00 a.m., Yzeures-sur-Creuse, France

1. Ascendant: Nodal axis is close to the first cusp. Mars, Ascendant lord, is opposition Neptune in the eighth house. Mars' dispositor, Saturn, is in the eighth house opposition Uranus.

2. Moon: It is debilitated in Scorpio. Its dispositor is Mars, previously discussed.

3. Mars: See above.

4. Tenth House: Tenth lord Venus is combust. Its dispositor Saturn is in the eighth house opposition Uranus.

5. Eleventh House: Previously discussed.

6. The Sun and Saturn (significators of bone): Well placed but opposition Jupiter and Pluto. Sun's dispositor Saturn, previously discussed, is in the eighth house.

7. Summary: Negative features like closeness to the North Node, weakness of dispositors, combustion, and connections to the eighth house are clearly seen.

Case 13

The native is still alive. At age 15 she was diagnosed with leukemia.[9]

1. Ascendant: Its lord, Mars, is well placed but the dispositor of Mars, Mercury, is in the twelfth house.

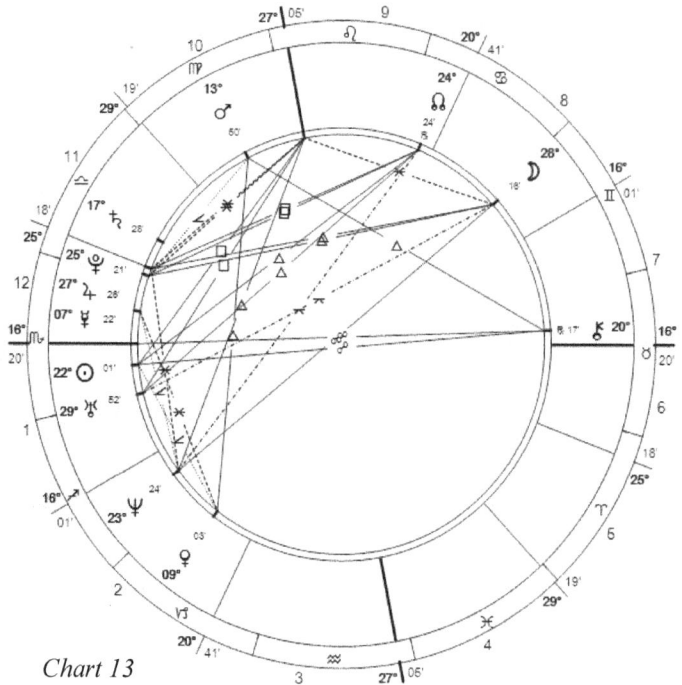

Chart 13

2. Moon: It is placed in the eighth house opposition Neptune. Its dispositor, Mercury, is in the twelfth house.

3. Mars: Already discussed.

4. Tenth House: Tenth lord Sun is well placed. Even a trine with the North Node can afflict a planet and here the Sun is in a close trine with the North Node. Its dispositor Mars has already been discussed.

5. Eleventh House: Its lord Mercury is in the twelfth house.

6. The Sun and Saturn (significators of bone): Sun has been discussed. Saturn is exalted in Libra.

7. Summary: Both positive factors including Sun and Mars are well placed and Saturn is exalted Saturn. There are negatives like Saturn trine the North Node and connections to the eighth and twelfth houses; negatives seem stronger.

Case 14

Died of Leukemia at age 48. Birth data: January 14, 1937, 10:30 a.m., Naples, Italy.

1. Ascendant: Its lord Mars is well placed in Scorpio.

2. Moon: In a square with Uranus, its dispositor Saturn is in the twelfth house and opposition Neptune in the sixth house.

3. Mars: Well placed.

4. Tenth House: Tenth lord Saturn in twelfth house opposition Neptune.

5. Eleventh House: Eleventh lord Saturn previously studied.

6. The Sun and Saturn (significators of bone): Sun opposition Pluto. Sun's dispositor Saturn was previously discussed.

7. Summary: There are positive factors like Mars being well placed in its own sign, and negative factors like the weakness of dispositor and connections to the twelfth house.

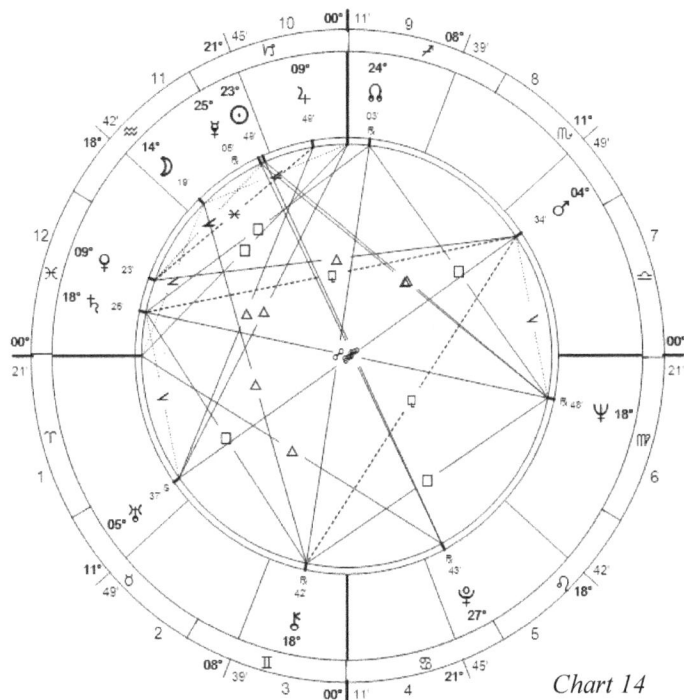

Chart 14

Case 15

This individual died of leukemia at age 32. Birth data: April 12, 1926, 2:50 a.m., Dawn, Texas,

1. Ascendant: Its lord Saturn is in Scorpio in the tenth house square Neptune. Saturn is in a trine with the North Node (Rahu) . It was previously mentioned that a trine with the North Node is an affliction.

2. Moon: The Moon is in a close square with the North Node in the sixth house.

3. Mars: Well placed.

4. Tenth House: Twelfth lord Saturn is close to the tenth cusp but the tenth lord Mars is well placed.

5. Eleventh House: The eleventh lord is in a square with Saturn, the twelfth lord.

6. The Sun and Saturn (significators of bone): Sun is in Aries very close to the sixth lord, the Moon. The Sun is in a close square with the North Node. Saturn is trine North Node.

7. Summary: There are positive factors, including Mars well placed in its own sign, and negative factors like a trine with the North Node and connections to the sixth and twelfth houses. But negative ones are seen more often.

Conclusions

1. The factors that have been considered for leukemia seem to have an effective role in determining this illness. But the affliction of these factors may not show leukemia for all the natives because of the similarities among symptoms of different diseases.

2. The affliction of one or more leukemia astrological factors by the North-South Nodes can show this disease. When effective planets for leukemia (Moon, Mars, Sun, Saturn, or lords of the tenth or eleventh) are in square, conjunction, opposition, or trine one of the nodes, the afflicted significator can show leukemia if other factors are also weak.

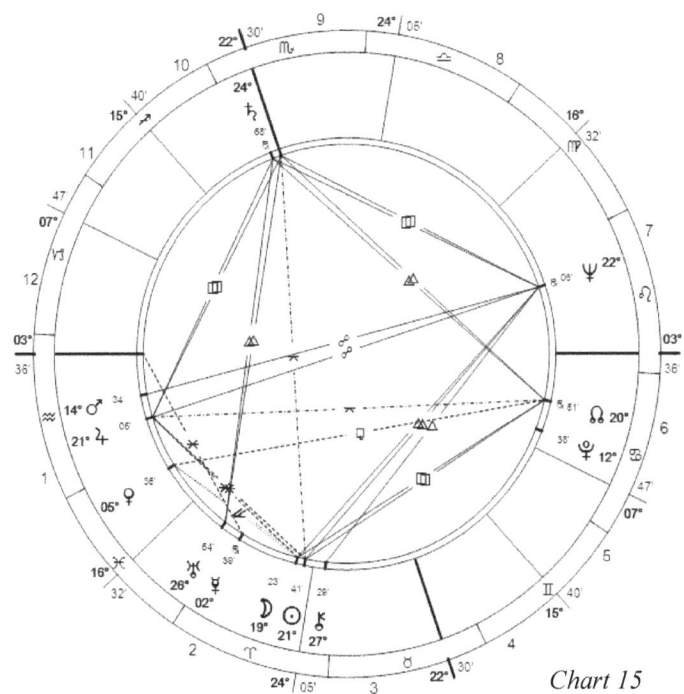

Chart 15

3. Here just the static analysis of the disease is considered, meaning progressions and transits for timing of the disease are not considered.

4. Longevity is a determinant factor that can show if the disease can kill the native or not. Sometimes disease is not acute but the complications of a disease's treatment kills the native if longevity shows the end of the na-

tive's life. The matter of longevity in medical astrology can also be researched.

5. The dispositor of the planets or lords of relative houses of leukemia have an important role in understanding the negative or positive effects.

6. The dispositor of a planet has an important role in determining the weakness or strength of that planet in the case of leukemia.

7. Combustion of planets is another negative factor that can totally destroy the significations of the planet and it was clearly observed about leukemia.

8. An aspect means a connection that can happen through conjunction, square opposition etc. When a planet is in such connection with another planet in the sixth, eighth, or twelfth house, that planet has potential to make health issues.

9. Exaltation, free from negative aspects, being well placed (not being in the sixth, eighth, or twelfth houses or debilitation, etc.) are compensation factors that can mitigate the disease or if there are more can totally compensate the negative effects.

References
1. https://www.cdc.gov/cancer/leukemia/index.htm
2. Diane L. Cramer. Dictionary of Medical Astrology, 1st ed., AFA,2003,p.10
3. Umang Taneja. Nadi Astrology, 6th ed., 2009, reprint 2016.
4. B. V. Raman. Hindu Predictive Astrology, 8th ed. Raman Publications, 1963, p.355.
5. V. K. Choudhry. How To Study Divisional Charts, 1st ed, Sagar Publications,1990.
6. V. Goel. Predict Comprehensively through Divisional Charts,1st ed,Vani Publications, 2010.
7. M. S. Mehta. Analyzing Horoscope Through Modern Techniques,3rd ed., Sagar Publications, 2007.
8. www.astro.com
9. https://en.wikipedia.org/wiki/Vanessa_Bayer
10. https://en.wikipedia.org/wiki/Stefano_Satta_Flores

Case Studies
1. https://www.astro.com/astro-databank/Research:Medical:_Leukemia_50171
2. https://www.astro.com/astro-databank/Cronin,_Rich
3. https://www.astro.com/astro-databank/Butcher,_Susan
4. https://www.astro.com/astro-databank/James,_Etta
5. https://www.astro.com/astro-databank/Boxcar_Willie_(Singer)
6. https://www.astro.com/astro-databank/Greene,_Graham
7. https://www.astro.com/astro-databank/Peters,_Jean
8. https://www.astro.com/astro-databank/Richey,_Joe
9. https://www.astro.com/astro-databank/Research:Medical:_Cancer_7378
10. https://www.astro.com/astro-databank/Research:Engineer_44552
11. https://www.astro.com/astro-databank/Fath,_Jacques
12. https://www.astro.com/astro-databank/Robin,_Mado
13. https://www.astro.com/astro-databank/Bayer,_Vanessa
14. https://www.astro.com/astro-databank/Satta_Flores,_Stefano
15. https://www.astro.com/astro-databank/Mayfield,_Thomas_Edd

About the Contributors

Alan Annand

Alan Annand (BA-Literature, BSc-Physics) is a graduate of both the British Faculty of Astrological Studies (1980) and the American College of Vedic Astrology (2003). A past President of the Astrological Society of Montreal, and formerly the North American tutor for the FAS correspondence courses, he now conducts an international practice from Toronto. He has written several astrology books (*Mutual Reception*, *Parivartana Yoga*, *Stellar Astrology: Volumes 1 & 2*) and is the author of the *New Age Noir* crime novels featuring an astrologer whom one reviewer has called "Sherlock Holmes with a horoscope." www.navamsa.com

José Luis Belmonte

International lecturer, author of four books and several research articles, José Luis Belmonte is finishing his dissertation for a master's degree on anthropology (cultural astrology and astronomy) at Wales University; and is currently studying classical philology at the University of Barcelona. He studied at Kepler College from 2007 until 2011, and has an engineering degree in telecomunications from Ramon Llull University. A private astrologer, teacher of astrology, and researcher on the history of Babylonian and Hellenistic astrology, business astrology, and archetypes, he lives in Barcelona, Spain with his wife and daughter.

Ancuta Catrinoiu

Ancuta Catrinoiu has been a passionate about astrology since she was 11 years old when she discovered the Chinese zodiac. From then on, she has read and continues to read any book that helps her understand the mechanisms of astrology and give her much-sought answers to the value of self and life. In August 2013, she established the Facebook page Stiinţa Stelelor (The Science of the Stars), where he regularly writes about the most important astrological events of the time. She started giving astrological consultations after graduating from the Fidelia School of Astrology in December 2013, initially to her friends and now to an extensive category of clients. Also, she is a member of Romanian Astrologers Association. Her intention is to translate the symbolism of astrology to everyone and to provide astrological advice to all those interested in discovering their true meaning and purpose of life. At present, while working within a multinational company, she works on her own Web site, stiintastelelor.ro, which she plans to launch next year. She can be reached at cuti_r@yahoo.com.

Steve DeLapp

Self-employed entrepreneur since high school, business owner of several transportation related businesses as well as automotive diagnosis and repair. Learned basic astrology through the Rosicrucian Fellowship correspondence course in the mid 1970s, have been an observer and researcher of mundane astrology ever since with particular interest in Tropical Cyclones and Severe storms. Was an active member of NCGR in the 1990's and have given lectures at the Baltimore, Annapolis and Richmond chapters on the subject of the wealth of astrological information in the Judeo-Christian scriptures and also Dane Rudyhar's theory of Geodetic Equivalents. Have recently retired from business to devote full time to observing/forecasting Hurricanes and Severe Weather on my website, Astroweather.com, and to also publish the research. sjdelapp@gmail.com

Rui Fernandes

Rui Fernandes, born in May 1967, is a self-taught student and researcher since childhood on several and completely distinct areas. From the plain logic of the fields of astronomy and math (achieved a bachelor's degree at the University of Porto in astronomy) to the mystic, mythological, religious, archeological, and spiritual, the author always tried to achieve an equilibrium point of understanding and balance between these sub-realities which form a whole. The gathered knowledge was employed in a professional Web site of astronomy and celestial mechanics research program, and in a journal dedicated to all the subjects of interest mentioned that at first sight would collide. Currently, several astrology research projects are being implemented in practice. All his life has been dedicated to scientific and occult studies, with the simple and plain philosophy that "there is no religion superior to the truth."

John Halloran

Starting with a public domain astrology program in 1985, John Halloran has been creating software tools for astrologers for 33 years. Halloran Software's AstrolDeluxe for Windows included a research module. Its Famous Charts collection has grown to include 5500 of the most famous people. AstrolDeluxe Platinum does 26 types of searches. John has researched biographies to write aspect pattern interpretations and male and female interpretations for Chiron, the Moon's Nodes, the Black Moon Lilith, and the 45-degree and 135-degree aspects. He recently finished researching 480 male/female declination parallel/contraparallel interpretations for sale to his software customers. He created an 1100-page aspect frequency reference table for 22 categories of people to supplement the process of synthesizing personal details from biographies into his interpretations.

Cornelia Hansen

Since receiving her master's degree in early childhood development at the California State University at Northridge, Cornelia Hansen has been a pre-school director and Los Angeles Children's Center teacher. In 1982 she received a second master's degree from Antioch University in Clinical Psychology. She was on staff of the Hollywood Counseling Center for four years while working toward her license as a marriage, family and child therapist. While there, she taught "Mommy & Me" and parenting skills classes. She was in private practice with Encino Psychological Associates for 17 years. She studied astrology with Joan McEvers and Marion March through Aquarius Workshops and wrote a column for their magazine, *Aspects*, for several years. Her forthcoming book, *Kidwheels: Understanding the Child in the Chart* will be published in 2018 by Wessex Astrologer, Ltd.

Abdol-Hussein Heidari

I am Abdol-Hussein Heidari and I was born in Iran on 1982 .I graduated in Mechanical Engineering from Persian Gulf University and at the same time started practicing different branches of Classical Vedic Astrology. After some years practicing classics, then I became familiar with the founder of the "Modern Theory of KP, 4 step theory, Mr.Gondhalekar and directly learned stellar Astrology from him and practiced that along with classical Vedic system to advanced level for 12 years and have researched on many case studies and gave predictions as per stellar Astrology or classical Vedic Astrology principles. I have done some researches in Medical astrology using a systematic, scientific and formulated analysis applying different systems of Astrology.

Nick Kollerstrom

I've been on the advisory board of the UK's astro-research journal *Correlation* since its foundation, thirty-five years ago. Also I've brought out the British Moon-gardening calendar *Planting by the Moon* for about the same length of time. That came from my studies within the Rudolf Steiner and Bio-Dynamic movement. I have academic history of astronomy articles up online from years gone by. I personally knew most of the people referred to in this article: the Gauquelins, John Addey, Neil Michelson etc. Somes published are posted here: www.astrozero.co.uk/astroscience/koll2indx.htm . Last year I received a grant from the Urania Trust for re-examining the Gauquelin databases.

Alphee Lavoie

Kyösti Tarvainen is a retired mathematics researcher and teacher. He earned an M.Sc. in technical mathematics from Helsinki Technical University, 1974 and a Ph.D. in systems engineering from Case Western Reserve University, USA, 1981. He is an emeritus docent in systems analysis at the Systems Analysis Laboratory, Helsinki Technical University. While studying in the U.S., he listened to radio programs hosted by John Manolesco, who sometimes answered questions based on the astrological chart of the listener. This aroused an interest in studying astrology. Kyösti joined the Finnish Astrological Society and later served as its president for seven years. Due to his mathematical expertise, it was natural that statistical studies became his special area in astrology.

Jagdish Maheshri

Jagdish Maheshri is a contemporary Vedic astrologer. He has published and presented research papers at Baltimore and Philadelphia NCGR conferences. In 2012 he spoke at the UAC. Recently he spoke at the conference in New Delhi and won the outstanding global astrologer award. He is a recipient of Catherine & Ernest 2016 research grant. He served as a NCGR Research Director 2010-2017. He holds a PhD, teaches (online) Vedic astrology, authored several articles, appeared on radio shows, and hosts website www.astroinsight.com. In 1995, he discovered a unique Ninefold Progression technique and explains in his book, "It's All in Timing." He can be reached at jmaheshri@astroinsight.com

Marilyn Muir

Marilyn Muir, LPMAFA, professional astrologer and instructor for over 40 years, has had her own radio and television shows with a variety of astrological columns. She has been a speaker at several national conferences and astrological groups and a writer for both online and print periodicals and research journals. She is a Past President of the South Florida Astrological Association and founder of Mission: Aquarius, Inc., a metaphysical church and school founded in 1978. Her books in print or e-book are *Astrology: The Symbolic Language* and *Presidents of Hope and Change*. Several more books are scheduled for publication in 2018 including *The Astrology of Coma, Tarot: The Symbolic Language, Numberology: The Symbolic Language, Astrological Choices* and *The Family* (astrological relationships). Marilyn lives in central Florida and can be reached at mmuir@cfl.rr.com

Glenn Mitchell

Glenn Mitchell, who prefers to be called Mitch, is an astrologer with 30+ years experience. He is a student of Noel Tyl and of David Cochrane. His primary occupation is research methodologist and faculty member at a prestigious college of medicine in the United States.

Michael Munkasey

Michael Munkasey has received professional-level accreditations from every major US Astrological Organization. He has lectured world-wide on different astrological subjects. He received the UAC 2008 Award for Discovery, Innovation and Research. A Vietnam veteran, he has college degrees in both engineering and management. His public sector work background for various industries was in the information technology areas of user support and education, data collection, data arrangement, and data evaluation. At UAC 2018, he received the James H. Holden Book Award for *House Keywords . . . and More.*

Pamela Rowe

Pamela Rowe, LPMAFA, FMFAA, Diploma Cosmobiology (Hons) is one of the most highly qualified astrology teachers in Australia She holds Professional certification from the American Federation of Astrologers, where she served on the AFA Board of Directors for more than 18 years and received the Catherine T. Grant Award for Outstanding Education/Research Achievements in Astrology. She is also a Fellow Member of the Federation of Australian Astrologers and served as FAA Victorian Branch President, National Secretary and National Vice-President. Pamela began studying astrology in 1971, has practiced professionally since 1977 and lectured throughout Australia, U.S. and New Zealand, including the astrology component for the International Yoga Teachers Association. Her involvement in popular astrology includes extended periods at television and radio stations plus four years scripting and recording Dial-a-Horoscope for Telecom Australia, broadcast nationwide. She was also the astrological columnist for the widely distributed Australian *Sunday Herald-Sun* newspaper. Her articles on astrology have been published in Australia, U.S. and Germany and her research interest is health. She is the author of *The Health Zodiac* and *Practical Guide to Astrology*. Since 2001 she has run a highly successful astrology correspondence course in Australia and is dedicated to astrological research.

Kyösti Tarvainen

Kyösti Tarvainen is a retired mathematics researcher and teacher. He earned an M.Sc. in technical mathematics from Helsinki Technical University, 1974 and a Ph.D. in systems engineering from Case Western Reserve University, 1981. He is an emeritus docent in systems analysis at the Systems Analysis Laboratory, Helsinki Technical University. While studying in the U.S. he listened to radio programs hosted by John Manolesco, who sometimes answered questions based on the astrological chart of the listener. This aroused an interest in studying astrology. Kyösti joined the Finnish Astrological Society and later served as its president for seven years. Due to his mathematical expertise, it was natural that statistical studies became his special area in astrology.

www.ingramcontent.com/pod-product-compliance
Lightning Source LLC
Chambersburg PA
CBHW080615270326
41928CB00016B/3073